Separation of Powers and Legislative Organization

This book examines how the constitutional requirements of the lawmaking process, together with factional divisions within the parties, affect the distribution of power within the House. Gisela Sin's consideration of constitutional actors and intraparty factions in the analysis of House rule making marks a significant departure from previous theories, which postulate the House as an institution that sets its rules in isolation. Sin argues that, by constitutional design, the success of the House in passing laws is contingent on the preferences of the Senate and the president; House members thus anticipate these preferences as they make strategic decisions about rules. Through an examination of major rule changes from 1879 to 2013, the author analyzes how changes in the preferences of constitutional actors outside the House, as well as their political alignments vis-à-vis House factions, predict the timing of rule changes and the type of rules adopted.

Gisela Sin is Assistant Professor of Political Science at the University of Illinois at Urbana-Champaign. She studies political institutions with an emphasis on the strategic elements of separation of powers and is currently working on a book on presidential veto politics in Latin America. She is coauthor of a book on Argentinean institutions, *Congreso, Presidencia, y Justicia en Argentina*, and her research has been published in *Comparative Political Studies*, the *Journal of Law, Economics, and Organization*, *Studies in American Political Development*, the *Journal of Politics in Latin America*, *Perspective on Politics*, and *Public Choice*. Sin has presented her work at universities throughout Latin America and Europe and was a scholar in residence at Universidad de Salamanca and a Fulbright Scholar in the United States. She holds a Ph.D. in political science from the University of Michigan and a B.A. from Universidad del Salvador in Argentina.

"While most congressional scholars (myself included) generally don't look to the Constitution to explain chamber rules, after reading Professor Sin's groundbreaking work, I am convinced. The amazing thing about her argument is that it is on the one hand obvious, but on the other almost completely overlooked by a generation of congressional scholars. This book will drive significant revisions to both theories of Congress and theories of legislative design more generally."

– William Bianco, Indiana University

"In this highly original book, Gisela Sin argues that considerations of bargaining influence vis-à-vis the Senate and Executive shape rules choices within the House of Representatives. It is an important departure from existing chamber-centric accounts of historical procedural developments, and a much needed foray into the strategic implications of bicameralism."

– John D. Wilkerson, University of Washington

Separation of Powers and Legislative Organization

The President, the Senate, and Political Parties in the Making of House Rules

GISELA SIN
University of Illinois, Urbana-Champaign

CAMBRIDGE
UNIVERSITY PRESS

CAMBRIDGE
UNIVERSITY PRESS

32 Avenue of the Americas, New York, NY 10013-2473, USA

Cambridge University Press is part of the University of Cambridge.

It furthers the University's mission by disseminating knowledge in the pursuit of education, learning, and research at the highest international levels of excellence.

www.cambridge.org
Information on this title: www.cambridge.org/9781107048799

© Gisela Sin 2015

First published 2015

Printed in the United States of America

A catalog record for this publication is available from the British Library.

Library of Congress Cataloging in Publication data
Sin, Gisela, author.
Separation of powers and legislative organization : the President, the Senate, and political parties in the making of House rules / Gisela Sin.
    pages   cm
Includes bibliographical references and index.
ISBN 978-1-107-04879-9 (hardback)
1. United States. Congress. House.   2. Legislation – United States.   3. Separation of powers – United States.   4. United States. Congress. House. – Rules and practice.   I. Title.
KF4990.S57   2015
328.73'07653–dc23   2014009944

ISBN 978-1-107-04879-9 Hardback

To Nate, Sophia, and Tobias

Contents

Figures and Tables

FIGURES

TABLES

Acknowledgments

This book started as my dissertation at the University of Michigan. I was fortunate to be surrounded by extraordinary faculty in a remarkable academic environment. I am especially indebted to my dissertation committee members, who patiently took the time and helped guide the project that ultimately evolved into this book: Skip Lupia, who served as chair; Ken Kollman, Jake Bowers, and Liz Gerber. Each of them offered valuable advice, careful criticism, and constant enthusiasm. In Michigan, it was Jenna Bednar, Dan Carpenter, and Rick Hall who first sparked my interest in U.S. politics. Countless talks with them, as well as their classes, were essential to broadening my understanding of how American political institutions interact with each other. Scott James at UCLA was also important in the origins of this book. During a year-long stay in Ann Arbor, Scott generously met with me for hours every week for a directed reading in which he shared his vast knowledge of U.S. history and politics.

Many other people have helped to bring this book to fruition. Without a doubt, I owe my greatest professional debt to Skip Lupia. As my mentor and teacher, he has been both my toughest critic and my strongest booster. Skip was the first person to share my enthusiasm about the core idea of this book and encouraged me from the beginning to refine and further strengthen the social science that supports it. I have benefited tremendously from his insight, patience, and willingness to talk with me about anything related to this book. His intellect, craftsmanship, and pure love of learning have been a constant source of inspiration to me.

After arriving at the University of Illinois, I was privileged to receive the helpful advice and support of my colleagues in the Department of Political Science. They generate a stimulating intellectual environment conducive to scholarly work that influenced the development of this book in myriad ways. My deepest gratitude goes to my friends and colleagues Scott Althaus, Jake Bowers, Damarys Canache, Xinyuan Dai, Samantha Frost, Craig Koslofsky,

Jeff Mondak, Bob Pahre, Milan Svolik, Wendy Tam Cho, Bonnie Weir, Matt Winters, and Cara Wong. These scholars provided multiple rounds of feedback, were sounding boards and thoughtful contributors at various stages, and never ceased to encourage me to push this project forward. I have also benefited from constructive feedback from Bill Bernhard, Laura Hastings, Pete Nardulli, Tom Rudolph, Tracy Sulkin, and John Vasquez. Some of my colleagues may not even be aware of the major effect that a casual conversation had on my thinking. Throughout this project I was also privileged to interact with a number of very bright graduate students: Chase Boren, Jillian Evans, Chris Grady, Katie Graham, David Hendry, Gina Reynolds, Jamie Scalera, and Carly Schmitt. They provided excellent research assistance and listened patiently as I developed many of the ideas for this book.

I am especially grateful to my friend and mentor, Jim Kuklinski, for his profound understanding of what I seek to accomplish in this book. The insights he provided helped make it approximate the vision originally set for it. He read countless drafts of the manuscript and was always willing to provide the tough but necessary feedback that often led to long discussions and even longer revisions. Jim's intellectual worldview has also shaped my own.

Jose Cheibub stands for genuine friendship and professionalism. I am grateful to him for reading many drafts, and even though its subject is somewhat removed from his principal academic interests, Ze did so with the utmost seriousness and constantly pushed me to improve the manuscript. He has been a wonderful mentor since we both arrived at Illinois, and I am grateful for his kindness and constant enthusiasm for new ideas.

Brian Gaines has also been a wonderful colleague and took large chunks of time to discuss my argument in great detail. This book has benefited tremendously from Brian's unique exactitude with the subject matter as well as his mastery of the English language.

Many other scholars outside Michigan and Illinois contributed to this book. John Aldrich read various portions of it throughout the years, and he has my deep gratitude for his excitement about the project, as well as his insightful comments. I thank Chris Achen, Scott Adler, Bill Bianco, Chuck Cameron, Dan Carpenter, Gary Cox, Larry Evans, Will Howell, Jeff Jenkins, Orit Kedar, Yanna Krupnikov, Glen Krutz, Adam Levine, David Rohde, Richard Valelly, John Wilkerson, and Alan Wiseman, who offered constructive feedback at different stages and made valuable contributions to the completion of this book.

Both the University of Michigan and University of Illinois provided generous grants and leaves that were essential to this book's completion. I appreciate the financial help from the Gerald Ford Fellowship at the University of Michigan, the Political Science Department at the University of Illinois, and the University of Illinois Research Board. The NSF funded the EITM program, which put me into contact with a tight and vibrant community of scholars. For data I thank Sarah Binder, Keith Poole, Eric Schickler, and Gary Young.

I also extend my gratitude to Jesse Menning, who provided programming assistance at the very beginning of this project and made exceptionally valuable comments on some of the early chapters. I have benefited greatly from seminar participants at Florida State, Pittsburgh, Universidad Catolica de Chile, Universidad Torcuato Di Tella, University of Illinois, University of Virginia, and Instituto de Iberoamerica at Universidad de Salamanca.

It was also a genuine pleasure to work with Cambridge University Press to bring this book to print. I thank the team of Lew Bateman, Shaun Vigil, Mark Fox, and Bhavani for providing support and amazing attention to detail and for making the final steps of completing this book a smooth process. I am also grateful to the two anonymous reviewers for their enormous contributions to this book.

My longtime friends, colleagues, and hotel-sharing group deserve special recognition: Rosario Aguilar, Carolina De Miguel, Damarys Canache, Mariely Lopez-Santana, and Valeria Palanza. All the people in this group took the time to help each other with our various projects while forming wonderful personal relationships. Conversations with these beloved friends continue to shape my work and the contours of my life.

Bonnie Weir helped me stay focused on what is important in academia and life, even during hard times. She has been an amazing friend, always ready to lend a hand with anything I need. Bonnie and her husband, Milan, have also played a unique role in my family's life in Urbana. Both have created countless special memories for my children and me. I don't think any of us can imagine celebrating Valentine's Day, Easter, or Halloween without their presence.

Numerous friends from Argentina, some dating back to my childhood, also deserve my gratitude. I am confident that without them none of this would have been possible. Analia Bejar, Lili Caivano, Gabi Catterberg, Brad Gorbet, Marina Hondeville, Leo Nusblat, Valeria Palanza, Evange Petrizza, and Juan Carlos Ughetti were there by my side, to support the effort of going through grad school and writing this book. Clarisa Bejar shared my whole academic life, from elementary school in La Pampa, through college in Buenos Aires, and finally grad school in Michigan. I deeply cherish her patience, love, and good humor throughout the years. Clarisa is literally "one phone call away" from being by my side for any reason. No matter where or how far our paths have gone, all these "amigos" are dear to me.

I also want to extend my appreciation to the friends I made in Urbana: Traci and Jonathan Pines, Janet Morford, Brianna Lawrence, Carmen and Juan Loor, Ivana and Pega Hrnjak, Carmen Ugarte, Marlah and Erik McDuffie, Kathy Anthony, Christy Lleras, Andy Gewirth, Jenn Kirwan, and Amy and Matt Rosenstein. From play dates to dinner parties to school functions, I have enjoyed watching our children grow up together in Urbana.

One friend deserves special recognition for carrying me through the process of researching and writing this book: Nancy Abelmann. I can't even begin to imagine where I would be without her professional support and personal friendship. Nancy's "first book" group was a remarkable sounding board, and I was extremely fortunate to be a participant. She has been an important source of encouragement, advice, and common sense. Nancy shaped the work in innumerable ways: She read draft chapters, proofread, and suggested more succinct ways to communicate my ideas. I am also thankful to her for introducing me to an amazing editor, Maria Gillombardo. Maria read the manuscript many times and helped polish and refine its prose. Working with her has been amazing.

My family provides the unconditional loving environment crucial to my professional and personal well-being. My parents, Tati Silva and Noty Sin, have been a constant source of reassurance and love. They have done more than any child could ask for, including making enormous sacrifices to ensure that I could pursue a career in academia. My mother's triumphs in her life continuously inspire me in the conduct of my own. She is my definition of motivation. Her core values as a mother who recognizes what I want out of life and relentless encouragement to achieve my goals are the same values I hope to instill in my children. I am extraordinarily fortunate to have her unwavering support to achieve my dreams, no matter how far from home they took me.

My in-laws, Carol and Michael Schmitz, also "lived" this project and infused it with their enthusiasm and constant affection. Their warmth and caring nature always made me feel at home and one of the family. They were essential in keeping me on track with the manuscript by reading it and providing valuable feedback from outside the box. I also appreciate having been able to spend many wonderful summer and winter holidays with Ted, Erica, Adam, and Susan Schmitz and my nieces, Alexandra, Olivia, Addison, and Caroline.

My grandparents, Lola, Maneco, Mame, and Nona, were also a source of continuous inspiration. My brother Sebastian always took the time to be there for my family and me when we were in Argentina. I am also thankful to my stepmother, Liliana; my sister Valeria; and my brothers Maxi and Poqui. All of them were constantly cheering me on. Finally, I owe special gratitude to my sister Luciana. Her willingness to come to Urbana and endure one of the harshest winters on record to help take care of my family at the end of this process made all the difference.

My extended "familia" is too large to name, but Tia Gladys, Kitty, Pochi, Sonia as well as Tio Chino, Pity, Antonio, and Jorge provided me with support through phone calls, e-mails, Skype, and WhatsApp. Their love, together with the constant anecdotes, jokes, and messages from my cousins Christian, Benchy, Bebo, Rafa, Juan, Jose, Joaquina, Lichy, and Facu, provided me with much-needed relief and connection to Corrientes. I am also extremely touched by my family, who eagerly received with open hearts the presence of my children, Sophia and Tobias, every summer during these last seven years.

One of the largest debts is to my husband, Nate Schmitz. Nate's support since my years as an undergraduate has been unconditional. His faith in the merits of my project's goals has made the experience of being an assistant professor far better than it would otherwise have been. His cooking improved quite a bit over that time to the benefit of the whole family. Finally, I wish to thank my daughter, Sophia, and my son, Tobias. They are constant reminders of the importance of enjoying life to the fullest, especially outside academia. I hope I make them proud, and I look forward to celebrating this accomplishment with them. Nate, Popa, y Toto, los quiero mucho!

I

A Constitutional Perspective on House Organization

In January of every odd year, following the November congressional elections, the U.S. House of Representatives organizes itself anew by adopting its formal rules of procedure. First, a House majority decides whether to change the rules at all; if it chooses to do so, it then decides what the new rules will be. To the casual observer of national politics, these decisions might seem mundane, but they are in fact crucially important. And this is why countless scholars and political pundits have paid considerable attention to House rules.

Often, the decisions are puzzling. Consider two recent examples. At the beginning of the 110th Congress, in January 2007, the newly elected Democratic majority in the House adopted a package of rules and procedures stipulating that any mandatory spending increases or tax cuts must be offset with respective tax increases or spending cuts elsewhere. This "pay-as-you-go" (or simply, "pay-go") rule was the most visible commitment of the new House Democratic majority to reduce the budget deficit and national debt, which, it argued, had swollen as a consequence of Republican tax cuts and military spending. Two years later, in January 2009, the same Democratic majority reversed those rules and procedures. Under the new rules, almost any bill could easily be exempted from pay-go requirements by giving it an emergency designation as a response to an act of war, terrorism, natural disaster, or prolonged period of slow economic growth.

A second puzzling occurrence followed the November 2010 congressional elections, when Republicans gained a majority of the seats in the U.S. House of Representatives. When House Republicans met in January of 2011, they adopted a rule change that abolished the so-called Gephardt rule, which automatically increased the debt ceiling upon passage of a budget resolution. First adopted in 1979, the Gephardt rule had provided political cover for Democrats and Republicans alike, by exempting House members from having to cast a politically unpalatable vote on raising the debt ceiling. With the rule's elimination, the House now *had* to hold a separate vote on the debt, which most Republicans did not want to raise. The vote requirement on the debt ceiling immersed the country in an acrimonious debate during the summer of 2011. The policy paralysis also drove the country close to defaulting on its debt obligations, an event that contributed to Standard and Poor's decision to downgrade the U.S. credit rating for the first time in history.

Why, in January 2009, did the Democratic majority reverse the pay-go requirements that, in the name of fiscal discipline, it had adopted only two years earlier? Why, in January 2011, did the newly elected Republican House majority decide to eliminate a rule that had long helped House members avoid lengthy and detrimental debates over increasing the federal debt limit?[1] Had the Democrats, in the first case, and the Republicans, in the second, lost all semblance of rationality?

Given the considerable attention that political scientists have given to understanding House-rule changes, one might expect existing research to offer ready answers to these questions. Surprisingly, it is hard to find explanations of the seemingly puzzling behavior of House Democrats in 2009 and House Republicans in 2011. This state of affairs arises in good part because extant theories of House rule making share an implicit assumption: The House makes and changes rules largely for purposes of internal management. This assumption has led scholars to look inward rather than outward, thus limiting their analyses only to changes in the preferences of House members and not to changes in the larger political environment within which House members function.

Yet, I argue, the two rule changes noted previously, as well as many others, can be understood only by accounting for the encompassing separation of powers bargaining structure, of which the House is only one part. Most fundamentally, decisions about House rules are made not in isolation, but within the constitutionally established separation-of-powers bargaining structure. Representatives recognize that they achieve policy goals by passing new laws; and Article I, Section 7 of the Constitution states that bills become laws only if a House majority, a Senate majority, and the president agree on wording or

---

[1] Not only did Republicans rescind the Gephardt rule in 2011, they also chose Representative Ron Paul (R-TX) to be chairman of the House Financial Services' Subcommittee on Domestic Monetary Policy and Technology, which controls the Federal Reserve. Paul, one of the most conservative members of the Republican delegation, had consistently supported the elimination of most federal agencies, including the Federal Reserve, while advocating fiscal and monetary policies that included the abolishment of the individual income tax and a return to a fixed exchange rate based on the gold standard. Princeton economist Paul Krugman expressed his surprise at this apparent paradox in a *New York Times* opinion piece where he wrote, "How, after runaway banks brought the economy to its knees, did we end up with Ron Paul, who says 'I don't think we need regulators,' about to take over a key House panel overseeing the Fed?" (Krugman 2010). Why did the Republican majority give Paul substantial control over the main institution capable of affecting monetary policy, and especially so when the country was facing the greatest economic crises since the Great Depression?

if two-thirds of the Senate and the House approve. If members of the House want to make laws, they need to bargain – implicitly or explicitly, publicly or privately – beyond the House itself. Therefore, long before a Congress's first bill reaches the president's desk, House members have a strong incentive to anticipate the dynamics of the impending congressional session. By constitutional design, the success of the House is highly contingent on the actions of the Senate and president; and by constitutional design, therefore, House members must anticipate those actions at the very time they revise (or not) their rules.

In addition, the House majority party itself often consists of distinct groups holding differing views on specific policies. Indeed, an extensive literature has shown that intraparty groups are an enduring and critically important feature of U.S. political parties, both inside and outside of formal governmental institutions (e.g., DiSalvo 2012; Key 1949; Reiter 2004; Schousen 1994). The presence of at least two factions within the major parties, a phenomenon that has existed throughout the country's history, motivates members of each group to anticipate how the preferences of the Senate and president will affect the dynamics of policy making with respect to their own particular interests. In turn, when the House majority party considers rule changes, it contemplates how it should distribute power between the two groups, given a particular Senate-president configuration. A prominent theme throughout the remainder of this book is that the preference alignment of the House majority intraparty groups vis-à-vis the Senate and president holds the key to understanding rule choice.[2]

I follow previous theories of House organization in portraying House members as rational, strategic, and policy-oriented. Like these earlier theories, my work emphasizes the importance of political parties in House organization (Aldrich and Rohde 2000; Aldrich and Rohde 2001; Binder 1997; Cox and McCubbins 1993; Cox and McCubbins 2005; Rohde 1991). It adds a focus on intraparty politics; specifically, on the different ideological factions within the House majority party and their relationships with the Senate and president. I also borrow from theories that center on the ideological balance of power on the House floor (Schickler 2000; Schickler 2001) and expand those perspectives by taking into account the balance of power among all three constitutional actors needed to enact laws. In a word, mine is a model in which legislative rules depend on the game being played among the Senate, president, and House majority party factions.

---

[2] The focus on the majority party follows the lead of Cox and McCubbins (2005), who convincingly document that, since 1880, power in the House has been in the hands of the majority party, and rule changes are intended to redistribute power within it, not between the majority and minority parties. This is not to suggest that the minority party has become irrelevant, as I show later. However, debates over House rule changes center on how those changes will affect the balance of power between the majority party groups in the policy-making process.

Does viewing House-rule changes as a game of strategic politics driven by a broader bargaining environment help us to understand the puzzling rule changes described earlier? In a word, yes. Observing only House membership would not have generated a prediction that House Democrats would reverse the pay-as-you-go rule they had adopted two years before. Indeed, the new 2009 House Democratic majority was actually more conservative than the 2007 majority it replaced. Most of the newly elected Democrats replaced Republicans, and the number of moderately conservative "Blue Dog" representatives reached fifty-five, the highest number since the group's emergence in 1994. The *New York Times* characterized the 2008 freshman class as serving "to broaden a moderate coalition" that was "more conservative on social issues" (Phillips 2009). In the same article, the *Times* quoted political scientist Gary Jacobson as saying that the cumulative effect of the 2006 and 2008 congressional elections was "to move the Democratic caucus somewhat to the right.... You're not going to get the Berkeley wish-list out of this crowd" (Phillips 2009). He might have added, "Neither should the new Democratic House membership, on its face, be inclined to reverse 'pay-as-you-go.'"

Consider, however, the changed policy-making environment that the House Democratic majority faced at the beginning of 2009. A new Democratic president, Barack Obama, had just been elected to replace Republican president George W. Bush. The strict pay-go rules that the House had adopted in 2007 were designed to enhance the bargaining power of the House Democrats vis-à-vis a Republican president; these same rules were no longer optimal now that a Democrat had been elected to the White House. With Obama in the presidency, the Democratic agenda, which presupposed increased spending in areas like energy, health care, and education, had a realistic chance of becoming law. The 2007 pay-go rules were too rigid for the House Democratic leadership, and the party as a whole, which now needed greater flexibility to advance its legislative agenda.[3] Why would conservative Democrats allow for this change? The more conservative 2009 Democrats agreed to abandon pay-go because they knew that the supermajoritarian requirements in the Senate would constrain policy from moving too far toward the liberal side.[4]

---

[3] The new rules package also severely restricted the minority party's right to offer a motion to recommit, requiring that any vote to recommit an amended bill should include instructions that it be returned to the floor "forthwith" (i.e., the House must vote on the amended bill within minutes). The goal of this rule change was to curb the minority's ability to put Democrats in politically awkward positions. During the 110th Congress Republicans often proposed amendments that forced Democrats to vote on controversial issues and sometimes even to shelve bills (e.g., in the first five months of 2007 the Republican minority party used the motion to recommit successfully ten times; only two of those involved the pay-go provision (*Roll Call*, May 17, 2007)).

[4] For example, these constraints were visible in the total price of the 2009 stimulus package, which was significantly lower than the House's initial proposal, reflecting the need to overcome a filibuster in the Senate and gain three Republican votes.

To understand the House Republicans' seemingly inexplicable decision in January 2011 to abolish the Gephardt rule similarly requires consideration of the bargaining context in which Republican House members found themselves. The Republican Party had made strong pledges both to avoid a tax increase and to reduce government spending. At the beginning of the 112th Congress, however, the Republican House majority faced a Democrat-controlled Senate and a Democratic president, and thus recognized that major bills could die in the Senate or be vetoed by the president.[5] Moreover, an influx of Tea Party candidates into the House meant that opposition to a tax increase and support for reducing government spending would be even more formidable than they had been in the preceding congressional session.

In abolishing the Gephardt rule, Republicans gave outlier members within their delegation, most notably those elected with Tea Party support, the power to block any attempt to increase government borrowing. As majority whip Kevin McCarthy (R-CA) put it, "The freshmen made our hand so much stronger" (Dennis, MacGillis, and Montgomery 2011).

The requirement of a separate, public vote on the debt ceiling also helped Republicans to condition their votes on policy concessions from the White House (Mann and Ornstein 2012). Indeed, from the very opening of the 111th Congress, both Speaker Boehner (R-OH) and House budget chairman Paul Ryan (R-WI) signaled Obama that their price for supporting a higher debt ceiling was broad spending cuts (*CQ*, January 6, 2011). In a closed-door caucus meeting on January 2011, majority leader Eric Cantor (R-VA) stated to his delegation: "I'm asking you to look at a potential increase in the debt limit as a leverage moment when the White House and President Obama will have to deal with us" (Dennis, MacGillis, and Montgomery 2011).

Did the rule change have the impact the Republicans expected? Apparently it did. Abolishment of the Gephardt rule gave Speaker Boehner (R-OH) greater bargaining power to negotiate with the Senate majority leader and the president. It enabled him to work toward a significant deficit reduction without increasing taxes, by arguing that no debt limit increase would even be considered by a substantial portion of his conference unless it was predicated on budget cuts. As the authors of a *Washington Post* article put it,

> In the end, the White House backed off its demand for new tax revenue and agreed to a multi-phase deal that may produce only spending cuts. In return, Congress gave the Treasury sufficient borrowing power to pay the government's bills through the 2012 election. (Dennis, MacGillis, and Montgomery 2011)

As part of the agreement to raise the debt ceiling, moreover, the House created a Joint Select Committee on Deficit Reduction, which was tasked with proposing

---

[5] The new rules also substituted the previous "pay-go" rule established by the Democrats in 2007 with a new "cut-go" rule so that any new spending programs could only be supported by equal spending cuts elsewhere, and not through tax increases. In contrast, under the Democrats' pay-go rules, tax increases were allowed as a mechanism to enact deficit-neutral laws.

at least a $1.2 trillion deficit reduction by November 23, 2011. If the committee did not reach an agreement that the House and the Senate approved, then a "sequestration" budget process would be automatically triggered to recover the money for deficit reduction equally from defense and nondefense accounts in 2013.[6] Republicans and Democrats reached the agreement hours before the United States was about to default on its debt obligations.

Would the same Democratic majority have rescinded "pay-go" in 2009 had a Republican president still been in office? Would the Republican majority have abolished the Gephardt rule had Republicans controlled the presidency and Senate? I believe not. Although both rule changes appear puzzling when viewing the House in isolation, the strategies behind them are not at all mysterious from a broader institutional perspective. Nor are these changes anomalies. Rather, they are only two examples of a long history of seemingly puzzling House-rule decisions that other theories seem not to explain. Recognizing that the House majority party takes the preferences of other constitutional actors into account when deciding on rules and procedures transforms the inexplicable into the obvious. Strategic political calculation about the broader bargaining environment motivates many House-rule decisions.

This book aims to demonstrate, theoretically and empirically, that the preferences of the Senate and the president, as well as the configuration of the House majority party factions, are paramount in the adoption of House rules. In Chapter 2, I make a case for incorporating both features of the American political system into the study of House rule making. One feature, rooted in the Constitution, gives the Senate and president crucial roles in policy making. The other, the existence of factions in the House majority party, captures the challenges its leaders face when adopting rules that set the agenda, control scheduling, and allocate power.[7]

That other constitutional actors enter into House members' calculations might seem obvious. However, it marks a significant departure from existing theories of House organization, which implicitly view the House as an organization unto itself. In Chapter 3, I develop a Constitutional Theory of Legislative Organization that shows how the constitutional requirements of lawmaking demand a more expansive coalition than just a House majority; it must include a Senate majority and possibly the president. I show how House members' knowledge that the Senate and president can effectively influence the final form of all legislation shapes the rules they adopt.

If legislators and many others think in terms of the constitutional separation of powers, then why have not students of Congress also done so? In part, the

---

[6] The process is similar to the one enacted as part of the 1985 Gramm-Rudman-Hollings antideficit law and the 1997 balanced budget law, although it differed in terms of timing. This time, the automatic budget cuts would not occur immediately, but rather in 2013.

[7] I do not consider factions within the Senate. Instead I represent the Senate very simply, as a unitary actor. For an excellent account of the workings within the Senate see Lee (2009).

answer lies with scholarly specialization. Research has become so narrowly focused that political scientists increasingly claim expertise in the presidency, or in one or the other chamber of Congress. It is a natural step, then, to focus on how a particular institution manages itself internally, without regard for context. Furthermore, House members themselves sometimes speak as though House rules are designed primarily for internal management. One would not expect the Speaker or other House members to announce that House-rule changes are intended to counter a partisan change in the Senate and/or president, let alone to rein in a faction within the majority party. Yet, remembering that legislators are foresighted beings who anticipate the legislative process and policy outcomes leads directly to consideration of how they might use rules to strengthen their bargaining power vis-à-vis the Senate and president. Indeed, the Constitution renders it impossible for House members to ignore these other actors, at least as long as they care about policy outcomes. And thus political scientists should not ignore them, either.

In Chapters 4 and 5, I show how changes in partisan control of the Senate and presidency, combined with House intraparty groups' dynamics, affect the timing and directionality of rule adoption in the House. I generate two key predictions: First, a House majority adopts new rules and procedures when changes in the preferences of constitutional actors alter the set of bills that could become law; and, second, the alignment among the preferences of five key actors – the two majority intraparty groups, minority party, Senate, and president – strongly influences whether new rules centralize power in the Speaker or decentralize it across the majority intraparty groups.

I test these implications about timing and directionality of rule changes by analyzing House rule adoptions from 1879 through 2013. First, I examine the timing of rule changes in the House, identifying the factors that influence House members to change power-sharing arrangements in some Congresses and not others. Second, I consider how changes in the alignment between the House majority intraparty groups and minority party, on the one hand, and the Senate and president, on the other, influence whether new rules centralize power in the hands of the Speaker and his faction or decentralize it across the majority party factions. The analyses show that majority intraparty groups choose rules so as to maximize their gains, given the configuration of preferences among all the constitutional actors.

Finally, Chapter 7 revisits the iconic revolt against Speaker Cannon in 1910, during which a group of progressive Republicans and Democrats stripped Cannon of his powers on the Rules Committee. I show that all constitutional actors must be taken into account to understand the revolt, and that policy outcomes serve as the mechanism that connects constitutional actors' preferences with rule changes. My explanation of the revolt challenges the currently prominent view.

2

Constitutional Actors and Intraparty Groups

Two important features of American politics profoundly influence House bargaining over power-sharing agreements. One is the constitutionally stipulated separation of powers structure; the other, the presence of distinct ideological groups within the House majority party. These two features of U.S. national policy making serve as my point of departure for understanding House-rule changes. I devote more space to the latter because intraparty groups are less familiar to political scientists than the constitutional framework.

CONSTITUTIONAL ACTORS

In arguably one of the greatest political experiments of all time, the Founding Fathers established a separation of powers system for the United States, built on the idea that no single branch – presidency, legislature, or courts – or legislative chamber – House or Senate – should be able to run roughshod over the others and thus over the American people. This system of checks and balances has served as the bedrock of American governance for more than two centuries.

This constitutional framework, within which House rules and procedures are adopted, establishes minimum requirements for bills to become laws. Any bill needs the support of both House and Senate majorities, as well as the signature of the president; or, alternatively, supermajorities from both the House and the Senate. Perhaps precisely because these constitutional requirements are so ingrained in the fabric of American politics and policy making, scholars have largely overlooked them in their analysis of rule making in the House.

Article I, Section 7 of the Constitution states that bills become laws only if a House majority, a Senate majority, and the president agree on wording; or if two-thirds of both the Senate and House approve. If House members want to make laws, they need to bargain beyond the House itself. Figure 2.1 depicts the

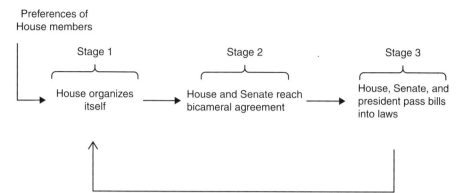

FIGURE 2.1. House organizational decisions within a constitutional framework.

legislative process as consisting of three stages, and underlines the simple fact that the Constitution requires House members seeking to achieve legislative objectives to prevail in all three stages, not just the first.

Stage 1 consists of House members deciding on a power-sharing arrangement. Every two years, at the beginning of each Congress, the House of Representatives chooses the rules that will govern its collective behavior. Although political scientists (Binder 1997; Schickler 2001) have documented that House rules limit the influence of some legislators while expanding that of others, Article I, Section 5 of the Constitution states only the following: "Each House may determine the rules of its proceedings, punish its members for disorderly behavior, and, with the concurrence of two thirds, expel a member." In other words, Section 5 offers no guidance about how the House should organize itself.

The Constitution mandates that the House and Senate approve identical bills. Stage 2 dynamics thus entail the House and Senate seeking agreement on a bill that can be sent to the president. If the House and Senate pass different versions of a bill, then the two chambers must eliminate all differences before seeking presidential approval.[1] An outcome can emerge from informal back-and-forth bargaining or by formally shuttling the bill between the chambers. Most commonly, for important legislation, a conference committee produces a bill. Whichever process the chambers pursue, neither chamber can impose its will; each needs the consent of the other.[2]

---

[1] An important feature of the U.S. Constitution is that the House and Senate share equal power to determine legislative outcomes (Longley and Oleszek 1989). This is not true for many countries, in which one of the two chambers has the last word to decide on the legislation sent to the president.

[2] Even though an extensive literature has focused on "who wins, the House or the Senate," there is no consensus on whether one chamber gets its way more often than the other. Some scholars have found that the House is advantaged in negotiations due to the chamber's superior ability to develop policy specific expertise (Steiner 1951; Strom and Rundquist 1977). Others contend

Only when majorities in both chambers agree on a joint outcome does the bill reach stage 3. At this stage, the bill is subject to an "up or down" vote in the House and the Senate, with no possibility of amendments.[3] At this point, legislators must decide between no bill at all and the bill generated by the bargaining process between the two chambers. If the House and Senate agree on a bill, it is sent to the president, who can either veto or sign it into law. If he vetoes it, then two-thirds of the House and Senate need to approve the bill for it to become a law. The preferred outcome of a House majority materializes only when the Senate and president, or a substantial proportion of the Senate and the House, prefer the House-Senate agreement to no bill at all.

By constitutional design, the passage of bills entails complex dynamics among president, Senate, and House, all of whom are driven by partisan-based preferences. A Democratic House majority might need to negotiate with a Democratic Senate and president; or with a Republican Senate and president; or with some combination of the two. Equivalent situations occur when there is a Republican House majority. When choosing rules for the upcoming Congress, House members will naturally take into account their expectations about the challenges and opportunities that lie before them, challenges and opportunities that are defined by the partisan configuration of the other constitutional actors. Appendix A shows, by Congress, how the configurations of preferences among House majority, Senate majority, and president have varied since 1879.

Because House members achieve policy objectives in large part by passing laws, the separation of powers framework established by the Constitution compels House members to consider the Senate and the president when making laws. Since the bulk of politics and policy making is partisan in nature, the partisanships of the Senate and president shape the strategies House members use to optimize their leverage in the policy process.

INTRAPARTY GROUPS

The existence of ideologically distinct House intraparty groups that seek to achieve their particular policy goals also shapes the House's rule making decisions, since the rules typically codify the majority intraparty groups' relative

---

that the Senate is advantaged. Arguments vary, and include the following: (1) The Senate committees and conferees draw more directly and more completely upon the support of their parent chamber than do House committees and their conferees (R. F. Fenno 1973; Vogler 1970); (2) the Senate's political decisions are more in line with the demands of interest groups and constituents (Manley 1973); and (3) the Senate usually acts on legislation after it has already been passed by the House, and thus it can make adjustments that the House will accept (Strom and Rundquist 1977).

[3] There are some internal rules by which the House can deal with nongermane amendments inserted by the Senate and agreed upon by the conferees. However, the rules only delay the process of approving the bill, and do not give the House a "line item veto" over conference reports (Bach 2001).

power within the governing coalition. Pundits and members of the media routinely refer to intraparty groups when describing congressional support for bills or ongoing negotiations within the parties to choose their leaders. To take one example, the media depicted the election of the only contested GOP leadership slot in November 2012 as a race between the moderate and conservative wings of the Republican Party. The *Washington Post* stated that the race was seen as "a test for conservatives pushing for greater roles in House leadership" (*Washington Post,* November 14, 2012), while *Roll Call* stated that "the battle has been described by aides as one between mainstream and leadership-friendly Republicans … and more hard-line conservatives" (*Roll Call*, November 13, 2012). Kathy McMorris Rodgers (R-WA), a supporter of the party leadership's priorities, and Tom Price (R-GA), former chairman of the conservative Republican Study Committee and member of the Tea Party Caucus, battled to become chair of the House Republican Conference. Indeed, most leadership battles can be characterized as disputes between factions of the majority party to control power within the governing coalition.

Intraparty groups consist of clusters of individuals within a party who share an ideology and a set of core policy preferences (Rae 1994; Reiter 1980; Sartori 1976). Differing most commonly in their claims regarding the purpose and ideal size of the federal government, the groups have tended to overlap with distinct geographical regions.

The differences between the Republican majority factions during the first ten years of the twentieth century exemplify this ideology-geography overlap. Conservative Republicans defended the interests of the industrial core and advocated minimal federal involvement in the economy, favoring the intervention of the federal government only to impose high tariffs that would protect industrial goods from external competition. They overwhelmingly represented states east of the Mississippi River, where most of the industrial activities took place and where the financial centers were located (Gould 2003; Gwinn 1957; Hasbrouck 1927; Nye 1951). Progressive Republicans stressed the interests of farmers and advocated greater involvement of the federal government in the regulation of businesses, especially railroads and big corporations. Most of the progressive Republicans were from Wisconsin and rural states west of the Mississippi River (Chiu 1928; Gould 2003; Gwinn 1957; Nye 1951; Reiter 1998; Schousen 1994), where issues such as the regulation of railroads, whose services were routinely used by farmers, were of the utmost importance.[4]

Intraparty groups are an enduring and all-pervasive feature of U.S. political parties. Historians and political scientists have documented their presence throughout the Republic's existence, and in a variety of settings (Brennan 1995; Dobson 1972; Gerring 1998; Goldman 1979; Gould 1974; 1978; 2001;

---

[4] For accounts in other historical periods see, for example, Barfield 1970; Bensel 1984; Burns 1963; DiSalvo 2012; Galloway 1969; Gould 2003; Hasbrouck 1927; Manley 1973; Patterson 1966; Reinhard 1983; Schousen 1994; Sinclair 1982; Wiseman 1988.

2003; Kent 1928; Key 1949; Morgan 1969; Patterson 1966; 1967; Peskin 1984; Polsby 1981; Reinhard 1983). Negotiations between intraparty groups play a crucial role in primary campaigns and during the presidential nomination process, including the parties' national conventions.[5] For example, Reiter (1996; 1998; 2001; 2004) studied the "bifactional structure" of American parties by examining roll calls at national conventions, and found factionalism to be a persistent feature of the Democratic and Republican Parties since 1830. Other scholars have portrayed the policy making process within Congress as a constant negotiation between intraparty groups (Bensel 1984; Poole and Rosenthal 1997; Schousen 1994; Sinclair 1982). Bensel (1984) focused on "sections" in the United States (i.e., core and periphery) to argue that they have always been a feature of the American political system. He states that "the sectional alignment of political conflict has been extraordinarily stable ... sectionalism operating through the two major parties came to dominate the institutional structure of Congress" (Bensel 1984, 6). Remarkably stable, intraparty groups tend to endure across decades, often by associating themselves with a particular caucus or similar kind of organization.[6]

My analysis begins with the 46th Congress (1879–1881). During the 1879–94 period, the House majority enacted a series of rules to empower themselves so that they could determine business in the chamber. As Cox and McCubbins (2005) posit:

> The rules of the legislative game have been heavily stacked in the majority party's favor since the readoption of Reed's rules.... Reed set out at the beginning of the 1880s to change the House's rules, to enable the majority party to enact its agenda.... Rules since then have not returned the House to anything like the playing field it had prior to Reed's reforms.... Some changes had important political effects, but they did not restore to the minority any abilities that it had enjoyed prior to the Reed revolution. (Cox and McCubbins 2005, 55)

If, as Cox and McCubbins convincingly argue, the majority party controls the House agenda and the redistributions of power, then rather than evaluate rules in terms of redistribution of power between the majority and minority parties, as Schickler (2000; 2001) and Binder (1997) have effectively done, one should instead view rules in terms of reallocating power between the groups within the majority party.

For this reason, I place ideological divisions within the majority party front and center, right alongside the Senate and president. Majority intraparty groups

---

[5] For accounts of intraparty group bargaining in primaries and conventions see, for example, Black and Black 2002; Brennan 1995; Cohen et al. 2008; Gerring 1998; Herrera 1993; Kent 1928, Key 1949; Patterson 1966; Rae 1989; 1994; 1998; Reiter 1980; 1996; 1998; 2001; 2004; and Shafer 1988.

[6] I regard parties as coalitions that articulate and aggregate the preferences of groups that have different ideas over which means are more appropriate for achieving their goals (Aldrich 1995; Eldersveld 1964; 1982; Key 1964).

are important because when the House considers whether to change its rules, and, if so, precisely how to change them, it is essentially determining how it should distribute power among the groups that compose the majority party. As I show in later chapters, taking intraparty groups into account revises prevailing conclusions about why the House majority adopts a particular set of rules at a particular time, and how those rules affect the House's bargaining strategies vis-à-vis other constitutional actors.[7]

Given the importance of intraparty factions throughout U.S. history and to this study, the following discussion summarizes the ideological divisions that have existed within the parties over the past one hundred and thirty years. To complete the task, I followed a substantive and labor-intensive path to identify factions. It relies heavily on leading sources on parties and party factions in history and political science.

Identifying Intraparty Groups

To identify intraparty groups, political scientists commonly use DW-NOMINATE scores. NOMINATE is a statistical model that translates roll call votes into one or two factors commonly regarded as measures of "ideology." DW-NOMINATE scores are calibrated to permit comparisons across time on a common metric or scale. They are readily available and their widespread use affords them legitimacy. However, for two reasons I decided not to employ them. First, when scholars use the scores, they must choose cut points in the ideological continuum defined by these scores. Typically, researchers do not justify these choices on the basis of in-depth substantive knowledge. For instance, McCarty, Poole, and Rosenthal (2006) define "moderate" House members of both parties as those falling in the −0.25 to 0.25 range, and classify those between −1 and −0.25 and between 0.25 and 1 as (relatively) "extreme." Fleisher and Bond (2004) define the moderate zone differently, as +/−0.2. Neither set of researchers offers a strong justification of its choice. Second, and more importantly, the DW-NOMINATE scores are based on bills that made it to the floor and received a roll call, a basis that is not appropriate for my endeavor, because the very thing I want to study, the distribution of power in the House, determines the fate of bills. Bills considered on the floor are endogenous to the distribution of agenda-setting power.

To identify the key House majority intraparty groups and the periods during which they existed, I examined works on intraparty groups in Congress and supplemented that information with scholarly analyses of intraparty group activities in presidential primaries and in state and national politics. On the basis of intensive reading of the relevant literature, I distinguished the factions in terms of two factors: their ideologies, defined as their preferences about the

---

[7] As I show in later chapters, including intraparty groups in the analyses also has important implications for how to code rule changes.

role and scope of the government in the economy and society, and the geographical areas they represented.[8] I identified factions and members therein for every Congress between the 46th and the 112th. At a minimum, three sources had to converge on their identifications of factions. I also used DiSalvo's 2012 book, which was published after I had initially identified the factions, to assess the reliability of my own coding. He conducts a systematic study of party factions between 1868 and 2010, documenting the importance of factions to party politics, presidential nomination battles, and the president's agenda between 1868 and 2010. Following Mayhew, he created a checklist of criteria that had to be met before a faction could be classified. They include "ideological distinctiveness, temporal durability, and organizational capacity" (2012, 1).[9] The intercoder reliability between his categorizations and mine is 0.87.[10]

During most periods, each party had at least two identifiable intraparty groups, which I describe in detail in the next section. In the instances when parties had more than two intraparty groups, I generally was able to reduce them to two groups. Ever since the late 1990s, for instance, the Democratic Party has been divided among the New Left, the New Democrats, and the Blue Dogs. I combined the New Democrats and Blue Dogs into a single intraparty group, given their similar views regarding fiscal discipline and levels of spending.

Table 2.1 summarizes the House intraparty groups in the Democratic and Republican Parties for the 1879–2013 period, as well as the state and regional affiliations of their legislators. In naming the intraparty groups, I employed labels that others have commonly used. Since many of the characteristics of intraparty groups overlap during the years close to the beginning of one period and the end of another, the periods do not represent clear-cut demarcations. Rather, I use them broadly to organize the discussion.

---

[8] Aldrich 1995; Barfield 1965; Bensel 1984; Berdahl 1951; Brady and Bullock 1980; Burns 1963; Champagne 2009; Cohen et al. 2008; Gerring 1998; Gould 2003; Gould 1974; Harris 1976; Hofstadter 1963; James 2000; Katznelson, Geiger, and Kryder 1993; Kent 1928; Key 1949; Mayer 1967; Poole and Rosenthal 2011; Milkis 1993; Polsby 1981; Rae 1989; 1994; 1998; Reiter 2004; 2001; 1980; 1998; Sanders 1999; Schousen 1994; Shafer 1988; 2003.

[9] DiSalvo made multiple sweeps using different sources: (i) works by historians (general period political histories, general histories of the major parties, histories of specific factions, and biographies of factional leaders); (ii) primary party documents (platforms, speeches, congressional votes); and (iii) newspapers and magazines.

[10] There are two factions that DiSalvo does not distinguish: conservative and agrarian Democrats between 1879 and 1897. In this regard, I followed leading scholars, who argue that issues like monetary policy and tariffs deeply divided the Democratic Party during this period (e.g., Clanton 1998; Goldman 1966; Grantham 1983; Harris 1976; Hollingsworth 1963; James 2000; Morgan 1969). The next section provides more information on this faction. We also have some other minor differences. For instance, he argues that the northern/liberal/labor Democratic faction only formally organized in the late 1950s, although he recognizes that the group had informally operated since the 1930s, especially in opposition to the southern Democratic faction, which he claims existed as an informal group since the 1930s. I classified the Democratic Party as divided between southern/conservatives and northern/liberals since the 1930s.

TABLE 2.1. *Intraparty groups in the Democratic and Republican parties,*
1879–2013

Period	Groups within the Democratic Party	Groups within the Republican Party
46th–54th (1879–1897)	Conservative Democrats[a] Agrarian Democrats[b]	Stalwart Republicans[i] Half-breed Republicans[j]
55th–72nd (1897–1933)	Conservative Democrats[c] Reform agrarian Democrats[d]	Conservative Republicans[k] Progressive Republicans[l]
73rd–91st (1933–1971)	Conservative/southern Democrats[e] Liberal Democrats[f]	Conservative Republicans/ New Right[m] Liberal Republicans[n]
92nd–112th (1971–2013)	New Democrats/Blue Dogs[g] New Left Democrats[h]	Moderate Republicans[o] New Right[p]

[a] Representatives from the Northeast – Connecticut, Delaware, Maine, Massachusetts, New Hampshire, New Jersey, New York, Pennsylvania, Rhode Island, and Vermont.

[b] Representatives from the South (e.g., eleven states from the Confederacy plus Maryland, West Virginia, and Kentucky) and the West.

[c] Representatives from the eleven states from the Confederacy (e.g., South Carolina, Mississippi, Florida, Alabama, Georgia, Louisiana, Texas, Virginia, Arkansas, North Carolina, Tennessee) plus Delaware, Maryland, West Virginia, Missouri, Kentucky, New York, Pennsylvania, and Illinois.

[d] Rest of the states.

[e] Legislators from the urban East: Connecticut, Delaware, Maine, New Hampshire, New Jersey, New York, Pennsylvania, Massachusetts, Rhode Island, and Vermont.

[f] Legislators from the rural West, agricultural Midwest, and South.

[g] Representatives from all states east of the Mississippi with the exception of Wisconsin.

[h] Representatives from states west of the Mississippi, plus Wisconsin.

[i] The conservative Democrats include the southern Democrats that emerged in the 1930s. These are legislators from the eleven states from the Confederacy (South Carolina, Mississippi, Florida, Alabama, Georgia, Louisiana, Texas, Virginia, Arkansas, North Carolina, Tennessee) plus Oklahoma and Kentucky.

[j] Liberal Democrats include the traditional liberal-labor Democrats and the New Left Democrats that emerged in the 1970s, with representatives from the Northeast, Midwest, and West.

[k] Conservative Republicans include the traditional conservatives from the 1930s–1960s (like Taft) and the members of what became the New Right. Representatives from the South, Midwest, and West became the conservative Republican faction.

[l] Representatives from Connecticut, Delaware, Maine, Massachusetts, New Hampshire, New Jersey, New York, Pennsylvania, Rhode Island, and Vermont.

[m] I put together New Democrats and Blue Dogs because their preferences are closer to each other than to those of the New Left. New Democrats are from the suburban West and South. To classify Blue Dogs I simply used their membership lists for every Congress starting in the 104th.

[n] New Left Democrats that emerged in the 1970s, with representatives from the Northeast, Midwest, and urban West.

[o] Representatives from Connecticut, Delaware, Maine, Massachusetts, New Hampshire, New Jersey, New York, Pennsylvania, Rhode Island, and Vermont.

[p] Conservative Republicans include the traditional conservatives from the 1930s–1960s (like Taft) and the members of what became the New Right. Representatives from the South, Midwest, and West became the conservative Republican faction.

The relationships between the House majority intraparty groups and the Speaker of the House are especially significant, since the intraparty group closer to the Speaker's preferences presumably has a better chance, all else equal, of incorporating its preferences into bills that the House passes. Throughout the book, I refer to the faction with preferences closer to the Speaker as the Speaker group and the faction with preferences further from the Speaker as the non-Speaker group. The Speaker group holds most of the agenda-setting powers and can propose a distribution of power to other factions at the beginning of a congressional term.

I used leading sources on House Speakers to classify their positions within their own parties, focusing on how these sources characterized the Speaker before he was elected, including his/her policy preferences and support within the party in his quest to become Speaker.[11] The support within the party became especially clear when identifying how the Speaker won his or her way to the party leadership. If at least three sources suggested the Speaker emerged from a certain faction, or had been a member of it, I coded that faction as the Speaker's faction. For instance, I classified Speaker Henry Rainey (D-IL) during the 73rd Congress (1933–1934) as closer to the northern/liberal faction within the Democratic Party because scholarly work characterizes his previous thirty years as legislator as "maverick progressive" (Champagne 2009; Davidson, Hammond, and Smock 1998), and often refers to him as the "Illinois LaFollette" (Peters 1990). Rainey supported low tariffs and progressive taxes and made his way to the leadership over the opposition of the House's mostly conservatives majority party establishment (Davidson, Hammond, and Smock 1998). Column 6 of Appendix A identifies the Speaker's faction by Congress beginning in 1879; I also provide more detail on each Speaker in the next section.

I also documented the intraparty groups' positions with respect to presidents. If the president's party was the same as the minority party in the House, I coded them as similar. If the president belonged to the same party as the House majority, I used the American presidency series published by the University of Kansas as well as leading studies of each president to classify whether the president was closer to the Speaker or non-Speaker group. To make this determination, at least two sources had to agree. I focused on the political career of the president, the policies he supported prior to rising to the presidency, and the factions that supported him during the party's nominating convention and primary campaign.[12] The sources I used documented the trajectories of the many

[11] Beth and Saturno 2001; Bolling 1968; Champagne 2009; Chiu 1928; Davidson, Hammond, and Smock 1998; Evans and Oleszek 1997; Galloway 1969; Green 2010; Goldman 1990; Jenkins and Stewart 2012; Jones 1970; Kornacki 1990; Malone 1962; Martin 1954; Mooney 1964; Offenburg 1963; Peabody 1976; Peters 1990; Polsby and Rosenthal 2019; Rae 1994; 1989; Reinhard 1983; Ripley 1967; Robinson 1930; Rohde 1991; Shelley 1977; Sinclair 1995; Swenson 1982; Truman 1959.
[12] Baer 2000; Binkley 1962; Blumenthal 1986; Bornet 1983; Brennan 1995; Brodsky 2000; Chamberlain 1946; Cherny 1985; Clancy 1958; Clements 1992; Coletta 1973; Doenecke 1981;

candidates, as well as the factional battles fought on the convention floor (for earlier presidential candidates) or during the primary season (for contemporaneous candidates).

I followed this route instead of using DW-NOMINATE or Common Space scores for presidents because these scores are based on the public positions of presidents on selected votes during their presidential terms.[13] Votes on which the president assumes a public position are not a random selection, but instead a product of careful calculation (Clinton, Jackman, and Jackman 2013). Presidents are strategic on whether they "go public" in their support of certain measures (Canes-Wrone 2006), given that they sometimes want to shape public debate or influence legislators' votes in Congress. Furthermore, these scores reflect strategic positions over the whole presidency, while the ideological position of the president with respect to majority party factions as the House adopted new rules is what matters in my theory. Column 7 of Appendix A reports the position of each president since 1879 with respect to the House factions.

In what follows, I describe the House intraparty groups in more detail. The discussion is organized chronologically. Within each period, I characterize factions within House Democrats and House Republicans. The goals are to distinguish the House intraparty groups' positions, and to locate their policy preferences vis-à-vis those of the Speaker and president. Appendix A shows, by Congress, the configurations of preferences among House majority, Senate majority, and president since 1879.

Majority Intraparty Groups within the Democratic and Republican Parties

1. 46th–54th Congresses (1879–1897)

<u>Conservative Democrats and agrarian Democrats</u>
<u>Stalwart Republicans and half-breed Republicans</u>

The persistent division within each of the parties during the last quarter of the nineteenth century personified the tension between the demands of eastern

---

Ekirch 1974; Fausold 1985; Ferrell 1998; Giglio 2006; Goldman 1990; Gould 1991; 2003; 2009; Graff 2002; Greene 1995; 2000; Greenstein 2003; Hirsch 1973; Hollingsworth 1963; Hoogenboom 1988; James 2000; Jones 1993; Kaufman and Kaufman 2006; Kazin 2006; Link 1954, 1956; McCoy 1984; McJimsey 2000; Milkis 1993; Milkis and Nelson 1998; Morgan 1969; Mowry 1958; Neal 1984; Nye 1951; Pach, Richardson, and Richardson 1991; Parmet 1976; Polsby and Wildavsky 1976; Reichard 1975; Reiter 1998, 2001; Shafer 1988, 2000; Shlaes 2013; Skowronek 1993; Small 1999; Socolofsky and Spetter 1987; Soule and Clarke 1970; Spielman 1954; Sundquist 1968; Trani and Wilson 1977; Welch 1988; Zelizer 2010. When the American presidency series and one more source coincided, I coded the president as being closer to that faction.

[13] The scores for presidents after Eisenhower are based on data gathered by *Congressional Quarterly*, which identifies the president's public positions on bills that made it to the floor and were voted on.

industrialists, on one hand, and those of western, midwestern, and southern agriculturalists, on the other.

Within the Democratic Party, conservative Democrats and agrarian Democrats sharply diverged on the issues of tariffs, monetary policy, and the role of the government in regulating the economy. Agrarian Democrats consisted primarily of representatives from the agrarian Midwest, South, and West (Gerring 1998; Goldman 1979; Goodwyn 1978; Sanders 1999) and constituted the majority of the Democratic delegation in the House during this period. Conservative Democrats consisted primarily of legislators from the Northeast (Gerring 1998; Goldman 1979; Morgan 1969; Sanders 1999; Woodward 1951).[14] As Woodward (1951) notes, the "conservative, Eastern wing of the [Democratic] party [was] a wing that was devoted to the defense of the new economic order."

Agrarian Democrats favored bimetallic currency (so that the unit of currency would be backed by a fixed rate of exchange between gold and silver), strong railroad regulations, and low tariff rates, whereas conservative Democrats defended the newly emerging economic power of the growing industrial Northeast, opposed any type of income tax, and favored the gold standard and weak regulation of the economy.

Currency was a highly contentious issue. Agrarian Democrats supported the maintenance of bimetallic currency (Goldman 1966) and expansion of the banking system (Hollingsworth 1963), which ensured access to easy credit and cheap money, both of which benefited farmers. They advocated silver coinage and expansion of the money supply ("soft money"). Analyzing roll call data, Harris (1976) finds that "each monetary roll call had a clear-cut inflationary-deflationary dimension, and southern and western Democrats voted persistently for inflation" (Harris 1976, 485). In contrast, conservative Democrats generally favored the gold standard, which meant monetary stability, high interest rates, and a restricted volume of currency. The only Democratic president in the 1879–1896 period, Grover Cleveland, also favored the gold standard (Clanton 1998; Hollingsworth 1963; Morgan 1969).[15] His preferences regarding monetary policy became a highly contested issue that strongly divided conservative from agrarian Democrats.

With respect to tariffs, agrarian Democrats endorsed the traditional Democratic position of low tariffs. High tariffs increased prices for

[14] Connecticut, Delaware, Maine, Massachusetts, New Hampshire, New Jersey, New York, Pennsylvania, Rhode Island, and Vermont.
[15] For instance, in his first annual message to Congress in 1885 Cleveland advocated the abolishment of the Bland-Allison Law, which required the government to buy a certain amount of silver every month at the market price and to put it into circulation as standard silver dollars. Furthermore, during his second presidency, he strongly supported the repeal of the Sherman Silver Purchase Act, by which the Treasury had to buy each month an amount of silver equal to the domestic production of silver. The Sherman Act was enacted in 1890, with the objective of raising the price of silver and increasing the amount of money in circulation.

consumers and protected the eastern monopolies, favoring industrial districts over agricultural ones. For agrarian Democrats, "the tariff was a sectional tax on agricultural producers for the benefit of monopolistic eastern industrialists" (Harris 1976). Conservative Democrats were more divided regarding the tariff issue, although a substantial portion of this faction favored protectionism. President Cleveland backed the reduction of tariffs, as evidenced by his support of the House version of 1888 Mill's Tariff Reduction bill.

Railroad regulation was another important matter. Railroads expanded the market for goods and influenced the development of the iron and steel industry, agriculture, big business, and finance. However, farmers complained about the exorbitant rates charged for freight, a hallmark of unregulated and discriminatory practices. Railroads discriminated in rates and services among different shippers, localities, and articles; created "pools" among different lines that fixed prices and divided the profits; and lowered the rates at competitive points but then increased them to make up for the losses at noncompetitive points. James (2000) notes that "what enraged [farmers] the most was the arbitrary power the railroads seemed to exercise in their daily lives" (57). Agrarian Democrats demanded unambiguous legislation that would correct the abuses of railroads and prohibit discrimination between short and long haul so that rates that were established would only depend on the distance traveled (James 2000). They opposed the creation of a national railroad commission, alleging that railroad interests would commandeer it, as had been the case for many of the state railroad commissions (Grantham 1983). In contrast, conservative Democrats backed the creation of a federal railroad commission and a mild regulatory law with provisions limited in scope and flexible in application (James 2000). Thus, all the regionally influenced ideological differences between agrarian and conservative Democrats centered on three issues: currency, railroad regulation, and tariff rates (Gerring 1998; Morgan 1969; Sanders 1999).

These issues also marked the differences within the Republican Party, which was deeply divided between the stalwarts and the half-breeds (Dobson 1972; Foner 1988; Goldman 1990; Gould 2003; Morgan 1973; Poole and Rosenthal 1997; Schousen 1994).[16] As Rae summarizes:

> The tension between the requirements of eastern industry [stalwarts] and western agriculture [half-breeds] was a constant feature of Republican politics. The high protective tariffs sought by industry were a perennial item in Republican platforms, but the party also needed the support of the small farmers of the Midwest and West, who sold on a world market, were dependent on eastern credit for their mortgages and machinery, and who relied upon eastern-controlled railroads to transport their produce. (Rae 1989, 13)

The stalwarts, also called the "Old Guard," comprised most of the legislators from the Confederacy, the border states, and three large, urbanized northern

---

[16] A less-influential group within the party was the liberal Republicans, composed of intellectuals from the Northeast; after 1884, they were known as the Mugwumps.

states – New York, Pennsylvania, and Illinois, the latter represented, respectively, by the three most prominent Republican machine politicians, Roscoe Conkling, James Cameron, and John Logan (Goldman 1990; Gould 2003; Jordan 1971; Morgan 1973; Schousen 1994). Because the stalwarts' power was based on patronage, they opposed civil service reform efforts. They supported President Grant after 1872 and intensely resisted the end of Reconstruction in the South (Morgan 1969; Wang 1997).

The half-breeds represented the moderate wing of the Republican Party, especially in their position on terminating Reconstruction (Dobson 1972; Goldman 1966; Jordan 1971; Morgan 1969). This group was primarily composed of representatives from "safe" seats in the Midwest and New England (Gould 2003; Hirsch 1973; Peskin 1984). The half-breeds advocated fiscal protectionism and high tariffs to consolidate their alliance with industrialists (Berdahl 1949; Morgan 1969; Doenecke 1981; Peskin 1984; Ross 1910).[17]

In terms of House control, Democrats were the House majority during two-thirds of the period (twelve years in total), while Republicans controlled the House for only three Congresses. Specifically, Democrats controlled the House majority in the 46th Congress (1879–1881), 48th–50th Congresses (1883–1889), and 52nd–53rd Congresses (1891–1895), while Republicans held the House during the 47th (1881–1883), 51st (1889–1891), and 54th (1895–1897) Congresses.

The three Democratic Speakers in this period – Samuel J. Randall (D-PA) during the 46th Congress; John Carlisle (D-KY) during the 48th, 49th, and 50th Congresses (1883–1889); and Charles Crisp (D-GA) during the 52nd and 53rd Congresses (1891–1895) – were closer to conservative Democrats. Thus, agrarian Democrats represented the non-Speaker group, although they had a somewhat favorable position regarding Speakers Carlisle and Crisp. Carlisle was antiprotectionist, an issue that resonated with agrarian Democrats. However, he opposed agrarian Democrats when defending the gold standard and supporting a weak railroad commission, positions that were advocated by conservative Democrats. For instance, James (2000) documents the various instances in which Carlisle's manipulation of committee assignments (especially the Commerce and Coinage Committee) in favor of northeastern Democrats was crucial for the adverse report of monetary and railroad legislation. Overall, then, Carlisle aligned more closely with conservative Democrats. Agrarians supported Speaker Crisp at the beginning of his term because he favored free silver. However, Crisp's prominent role in the repeal of the Sherman Silver Purchase Act of 1890, and his support for President Cleveland, motivated agrarian Democrats to desert him (Malone 1962; Martin 1954). Therefore,

---

[17] Skowronek argues that half-breeds needed to *"consolidate a lucrative alliance with industrial capital, and build a centralized and independent party organ that could coordinate and direct political activity at the national level"* (1982, 60).

conservative Democrats held the Speaker position during these Congresses (46th, 48th, 49th, 50th, 52nd, and 53rd), although their power within the party would begin to wane with the emergence of William Jennings Bryan in national politics.

On the Republican side, J. W. Keifer (R-OH) held the Speakership during the 47th Congress (1881–1883), while Thomas B. Reed (R-ME) held it during the 51st and 54th Congresses (1889–1891, 1895–1897). Keifer belonged to the half-breed intraparty group, although stalwarts also backed his election for Speaker in the 47th Congress because they believed he was the more acceptable option.[18] Speaker Reed was supported primarily by stalwarts in the 51st and 54th Congresses; in the 51st Congress, he succeeded over William McKinley (R-OH), who was supported by Republican president Benjamin Harrison.[19]

With regard to presidents, stalwart Republicans supported Chester A. Arthur, who became president after Garfield was assassinated, and served from 1881 to 1885 (Clancy 1958; Hofstadter 1955; Gould 2003; Morgan 1969). In 1885, Grover Cleveland, the only Democratic president in the period, won the presidential election against Republican half-breed James Blaine. Grover Cleveland, who governed for two nonconsecutive terms (1885– 1889, 1893–1897), was supported by conservative Democrats. In 1888, Grover Cleveland was defeated by Republican Benjamin Harrison. Given the divergences between the preferences of Speaker Reed and President Harrison, I placed President Harrison closer to the non-Speaker group during the 51st Congress, when Reed was Speaker of the House. In 1896, William McKinley successfully won the presidency with strong support from the half-breeds, who had also favored him in their opposition to the presidential nomination of stalwart Thomas B. Reed.

By the last quarter of the nineteenth century the intraparty groups within each party were regionally divided on economic issues.

2. 55th–72nd Congresses (1897–1933)

Conservative Democrats and reform agrarian Democrats

Conservative Republicans and progressive Republicans

The central policy issue dividing the intraparty groups within the Democratic and Republican Parties during the first three decades of the twentieth century

---

[18] Jenkins and Stewart (2012) explain that "his [Keifer] sudden rise was connected to a deal struck between two stalwarts leaders, former-Senator Roscoe Conkling, the New York Party boss, and Senator Donald Cameron, the Pennsylvania party boss.... [However] Conkling did not view Keifer as a "prime stalwart", as Keifer had supported John Sherman (OH) and then James Garfield, rather than backing Grant, in the Republican National Convention of 1880. Still, Keifer ... in Conkling's mind, was the best option among the 'eligible' candidates" (Jenkins and Stewart 2012: 261).

[19] The political relationship between Speaker Reed and President Harrison was very tense. In his study of Speaker Reed, Robinson mentions that "when in 1889 Harrison was nominated for president by the Republicans ... [reporters asked Reed] if he would mount the Harrison bandwagon, Reed remarked, 'I refuse to ride on the ice wagon'" (Robinson 1930, 283).

was the proper response of government to industrialization – how quickly, and by what measures, the federal government should take action (Aldrich 1989; Barfield 1970; Berdahl 1951; Galloway 1969; Harbaugh 1973; Hofstadter 1963; Mayer 1967; Shepsle 1978; Wilensky 1965). Although both conservative Republicans and conservative Democrats believed that the responsibilities of the government should be minimal, progressive Republicans and reform agrarian Democrats endorsed a stronger role of the federal government in regulating the economy. In general, Republicans controlled Congress and the presidency during the 1900s and 1920s, while Democrats controlled it during the 1910s.

Within the Democratic Party, tariffs, monetary policy, and the role of the federal government continued to be the main issues of disagreement (Gerring 1998). Until Wilson's election in 1912, the Democratic Party was marked by the emergence of William Jennings Bryan, who unsuccessfully campaigned for the presidency in 1896, 1900, and 1908 (Cherny 1985; Kazin 2006).[20] The agrarian Democrats, now called "reform agrarian Democrats," embraced Bryan, who pushed for agrarian reform, free silver, tariff reductions, and railroad regulation (S. Jones 1993).

The reform agrarian group consisted of representatives from the rural West and South (Broesamle 1973; Grantham 1983; Harrison 2004; Kent 1928; Link 1956; Scott 1963; Wiseman 1988). They strongly advocated government intervention in the economy through the expansion of the money supply and the creation of inflationary monetary policies that would help farmers who were burdened with large debts. In their view, the federal government needed to have the power to regulate markets and break up monopolies; accordingly, they backed increased railroad regulation and a powerful Interstate Commerce Commission (Goldman 1979; Gould 1978; Kazin 2006; Scott 1963). They also supported social and political reforms, such as women's suffrage and greater popular control of the government through the establishment of the initiative and referendum, primary elections, direct election of senators, and the publication of campaign expenditures.

In opposition, conservative Democrats favored high tariffs, a centralized private banking system, and the gold standard, while strongly opposing a silver platform (Broesamle 1973; Grantham 1983; Kent 1928; Sarasohn 1989; Wiseman 1988).[21] They united in opposition to William Jennings Bryan and his populist policies. As Kent states,

---

[20] In 1904 conservative Democrats were able to nominate Alton B. Parker for the presidency, after Bryan lost to Republicans the two previous presidential contests (1896 and 1900). However, Parker's substantial loss against Theodore Roosevelt in 1904 (37 percent of the popular vote against Roosevelt's 56 percent) diminished the power of conservative Democrats within the party.

[21] The silver platform was indeed adopted by the party in 1896, when Bryan won the nomination for the first time.

> In his subsequent campaigns he [Bryan] widened and deepened this sectional division between South and West on the one hand and East on the other.... The entire South and West were Silver; New England and the Middle Atlantic States were opposed [to a silver platform].... His anti-trust and government ownership of railroads campaigns were aimed at this section, designed to be popular in the South and West. (1928, 341–2)

Conservative Democrats also advocated states' rights and contested the expansion of federal discretionary powers, supporting minimal government intervention in the economy.

The Republican Party was divided between conservatives and progressives. Most of the Republican House members from states east of the Mississippi River, with the exception of Wisconsin, became part of the conservative wing of the party, while progressive Republican legislators primarily represented states west of the Mississippi River, plus Wisconsin (Chiu 1928; Gould 2003; Gwinn 1957; Hasbrouck 1927; Nye 1951; Schousen 1994; Reiter 1998). As Nye argues,

> The struggle was, in essence, a contest for control of the Republican party, to decide whether it would become a progressive party dominated by the Midwest, or a conservative party, dominated by the East. (Nye 1951, 272–3)

Progressives promoted the enactment of labor and social welfare programs and state intervention in the economy to correct for the unequal distribution of wealth and the exploitation of labor, especially child labor, by trusts and monopolies. They supported "neutral" or expert administration to replace the patronage and spoils system and pushed for broad regulatory reform to expand executive power over businesses and trusts, particularly the railroads. They favored a downward revision of the tariffs, which they argued were responsible for the increasing cost of living. Progressive Republicans were the first to promote conservation of natural resources and the creation of national parks.

In opposition to progressives, conservative Republicans were pro business and supported minimal state intervention in the economy, except when the intervention sought to protect the industrial system (Gerring 1998).[22] Conservative Republicans represented the industrial commercial core and opposed regulatory reform; they defended the rights of businesses to set their own prices, to keep their books private, and to negotiate labor contracts without interference from the government (Bensel 1984).

In Congress, the Republican Party controlled the House majority through 1911 (54th–61st Congresses), and then again in the 1920s. Until 1911, conservative Republicans held the power within the House, controlling it through one of their own, Speaker Joseph Cannon (R-IL). They also controlled the Senate

---

[22] Thus, they supported government intervention in favor of protective tariffs.

until 1913 through the "Senate Four": Nelson Aldrich (R-RI), William Allison (R-IA), Orville Platt (R-CT), and John Spooner (R-WI) (Stephenson 1930).

The progressives' main source of legislative influence and power from 1901 until 1909 was the presidency, where Theodore Roosevelt guaranteed that many of the policies they advocated became law. He frequently exerted executive authority to offset conservative opposition. In the 1908 elections, President Roosevelt and the Republican progressives supported William H. Taft, although progressives became dissatisfied with his policy preferences soon thereafter. Taft, with the help of conservative Republican Speaker Cannon (R-IL) in the House and conservative Republican Nelson W. Aldrich (R-RI) in the Senate, supported the enactment of a highly protectionist tariff law and continually attempted to dismantle the progressives' regulation and conservation program enacted during Roosevelt's presidency (Hechler 1940; Holt 1967; C. O. Jones 1968).[23]

In 1910, Roosevelt's dissatisfaction with Taft's opposition to progressive policies prompted him to embark on a tour of the West to support progressive candidates (Mowry 1958). It was during that trip, while in Kansas, that he announced his "all progressive" program, "New Nationalism," which he promoted by visiting forty states during the following year. Roosevelt declared his candidacy for president in February 1912; and upon losing the nomination to Taft, he called for the formation of a new party, the Progressive Party. With Taft and Roosevelt thus splitting the Republican majority, the Democrats won the presidential election of 1912 (Gerring 1998; Wilensky 1965).[24]

Democrats controlled Congress and the presidency during most of the 1910s. When Democrat Woodrow Wilson was elected president in 1912, reform agrarian Democrats gained a close ally in the executive (Grantham 1983; Harrison 2004; Link 1956; Wiseman 1988). Reform agrarian Democrats also controlled the House through Speaker James B. Clark (D-MO) between the 62nd and 65th Congresses (1911–1919).[25] Thus, between 1912 and 1919, and using the party caucus as the arena to gain the upper hand over conservative Democrats,[26] reform agrarians saw many of their policies become law as part of the New Freedom legislation. Included were the Federal Reserve Act; the Underwood Tariff, which dramatically lowered the tariff rates; and the

---

[23] Chapter 6 makes a detailed account of the politics and policies enacted during this period.

[24] The midterm elections of 1914 were disastrous for the Progressive Party, which lost many seats to Democrats. After much controversy, progressives finally returned to the Republican Party for the 1916 presidential election, when they nominated Charles Hughes, a candidate acceptable to both progressive and conservative factions. The 1916 election ended the role of the Progressives as a national party (Ekirch 1974; Nye 1951).

[25] Democrats held control of the Senate during the 63rd–65th Congresses (1913–1919).

[26] After the election of 1910, Democrats had adopted a caucus rule by which decisions made by two-thirds of the caucus were binding on all members. This rule helped the Speaker intraparty group, the reform agrarian Democrats, gain greater control of the caucus.

antitrust Clayton Act (Harrison 2004; Barfield 1965; Wiseman 1988). Reform agrarian Democrats lost control of the House and Senate to Republicans in the 1918 election and the presidency in the 1920 election.

Republicans again controlled Congress and the presidency during the 1920s. They regained the majority in Congress in the 1918 election, when conservatives supported Frederick Gillett (R-MA), a staunch conservative, for the Speakership. With his election, they became the Speaker group again. During the 1920s, progressive Republicans aligned with conservatives to support Warren G. Harding for president (Gould 2003; Hofstadter 1955).[27] He included progressives in his cabinet: Charles Evans Hughes from New York as secretary of state (not the choice of the more conservative elements of the party) and Henry C. Wallace from Iowa as secretary of the Department of Agriculture.[28] Harding also advocated many policies favored by progressives. For instance, in 1921 he signed the Sheppard Towner Maternity and Infancy Protection Act, which allocated federal monies to states for rural prenatal and baby care centers and supplied medical care for women and children.[29]

Upon Harding's death, Vice President Calvin Coolidge ascended to the presidency. He ran for the office in 1924, with strong endorsement from conservative Republicans. This faction also supported Herbert Hoover in 1928 and 1932. The endorsement of Hoover in 1932 drove many progressives away from the party. Hoover's electoral loss in 1932, in which he obtained 40 percent of the popular vote to Roosevelt's 58 percent, marked the end of conservative

[27] Even though Harding had been part of the conservative Republican faction, in the 1916 convention he strongly appealed for reconciliation with progressives, an action that gained him their endorsement.

[28] Wallace was an "outspoken editor of an Iowa farm journal, [whose] politics were moderately progressives ... [and] his liberal tendencies were obnoxious to the conservative wing" (Trani and Wilson 1977, 39).

[29] Another progressive policy supported by Harding was the establishment of the Veterans Bureau in 1921 as an independent agency. In 1921 Congress passed the Packers and Stockyard Acts, which enabled the secretary of agriculture to supervise packers and regulate and preserve competition among producers of livestock, poultry, and dairy products. This law made it more difficult for packers to control prices paid to the farmers. In 1922 the president signed the Grain Futures Act, which regulated the commodity exchanges on the basis of the Interstate Commerce clause. In the same year Congress enacted the Capper-Volstead Act, which legally protected cooperatives, exempting them from antitrust laws. Harding also supported several pieces of legislation intended to solve problems faced by farmers; progressives, a majority of whom represented rural constituencies, welcomed these laws. Harding signed the Farm Loan Act, which provided for further capital for federal land banks. The act was strongly opposed by Secretary of the Treasury Andrew Mellon, a procorporation and probusiness figure who represented the core of conservative Republicans. Congress also passed the Emergency Agricultural Credit Act, which provided short-term loan assistance to farmers. Furthermore, the president supported the extension for an additional year of the War Finance Corporation, which could underwrite farm credit and could make money available for farmers to buy seed in areas suffering from crop failures. The Federal Reserve Board was also expanded to include a representative for agriculture and farming concerns.

dominance of the presidential wing of the Republican Party for the next few decades.

3. 73rd–91st Congresses (1933–1971)

Conservative/southern Democrats and liberal/northern Democrats
Conservative Republicans and liberal Republicans

The Great Depression precipitated Democratic takeover of the House in the 72nd Congress (1931), and takeover of the presidency and Senate in the 73rd Congress (1933). The landslide victory of Roosevelt and the Democratic Party in 1932 left the Republican intraparty groups (conservative and progressive Republicans) in disarray. Rae argues that "during the 1930s the party's two major tendencies – western progressive and eastern and midwestern conservative – both appeared unable to cope with the advent of the New Deal" (1989, 25). Progressives from the West virtually disappeared during the 1930s; many candidates failed to win nomination within the party, while others lost their seats to Democrats. Many other progressive Republicans became Democrats of their own volition.

Within the Democratic Party, the intraparty dynamics during this time evolved into two groups: liberal/northern Democrats and conservative/southern Democrats. The southern Democratic delegation consisted of representatives from the eleven states of the ex-Confederacy plus the border states Oklahoma and Kentucky, while liberal Democrats were from the Northeast, Midwest, and West (Aldrich 1995; Brady and Bullock 1980; Burns 1963; Key 1949; Manley 1973; Moore 1967; Patterson 1966; Reiter 2001; 2004; Rohde 1991; Schousen 1994; Shelley 1977; Sinclair 1982; Deering and Smith 1984; Stang 1974).

Franklin Delano Roosevelt was elected president in 1932, in the midst of an unparalleled economic crisis that united the party behind his policies to stimulate economic growth, create government jobs, and regulate extensive sections of the economy. Although both Democratic intraparty groups initially supported Roosevelt's economic plan, by 1937 southern Democrats became increasingly uneasy with Roosevelt's policies (Black and Black 2002; Milkis 1993). The alliance among southern Democrats against representatives from the North and West strengthened when Roosevelt attempted to pack the Supreme Court and supported liberal candidates in the South during the Democratic primaries of 1938 (Black and Black 2002; Sinclair 1982).

Southern and northern Democrats differed ideologically on social policies, organized labor, and the role of the federal government in the economy. Northern Democrats supported increased government involvement in the economy and society at the expense of states' rights. They emphasized an economic agenda of redistribution, minimum wage, unemployment insurance, federal aid for education, and expansion of the size and scope of the welfare state (Milkis 1993; Lieberman 1998). In contrast, southern Democrats strongly opposed the creation of a comprehensive welfare state and the enactment of extensive regulatory reforms, although they favored federal assistance and welfare programs managed by the states (Black and Black 2002). Southern Democrats sought to prevent the expansion of federal powers in order to preserve the "southern" way of life and maintain the racial status quo. By advocating a small role for the federal government in social affairs, southerners intended to protect segregation and block racial and labor changes (Lieberman 1998; Manley 1973; Patterson 1967).

The position with respect to the New Deal was the main cause of division within the Republican Party (Rae 1989; Reinhard 1983; Weed 1994). Conservative Republicans strongly opposed New Deal legislation, government intervention in the economy, and the expansion of federal powers over the states. They also advocated rolling back the New Deal enactments. Senator Robert Taft (R-OH), son of President William H. Taft, was one of the main figures in the group, and led conservatives throughout the New Deal era and until his death in 1953. This intraparty group, which reasserted its influence within the party's congressional arm by 1938, was composed primarily of representatives from the Midwest, West, and South (Aldrich 1995; Burns 1963; Rae 1989; Reichard 1975; 1983; Rohde 1991; Schousen 1994; Sinclair 1982).

Liberal Republicans reemerged by the mid-1930s in urban centers in the East (Rae 1989). This wing of the party was based in New England and was composed mainly of representatives from the northeastern states (Aldrich 1995; Burns 1963; Rae 1989; Reichard 1975; Reinhard 1983; Rohde 1991; Schousen 1994; Sinclair 1982). Liberal Republicans attempted to move the party toward the ideological center by accepting and defending the New Deal. Nelson Rockefeller, governor of New York from 1959 until 1973, was one of the main leaders of this group.[30] Although liberal Republicans recognized organized labor and their rights, they tried to ensure that statutes would not be biased toward unions. They supported minimum wage increases and the enlargement of Social Security benefits and pushed for the expansion of federal powers over the economy, civil rights legislation, and environmental and consumer protection.

Although the ideological differences within each party were closely related to the New Deal's economic and social policies, they became more pronounced when racial, labor, and social welfare issues moved to the fore. Civil rights policies deeply divided the Democratic and Republican Parties (McMahon 2004). Liberal Democrats were the driving force behind the 1957, 1960, and 1964 Civil Rights Acts and the 1965 Voting Rights Act, and they supported labor union privileges. Southern Democrats opposed civil rights legislation as well as the expansion of the organized labor movement. For instance, southern Democrats were instrumental in enacting the Labor Management Relations Act in 1947, which stunted the growth of organized labor; later they joined

---

[30] Liberal Republicans were often called "Rockefeller Republicans."

Republicans to override President's Truman veto of the act (Katznelson, Geiger, and Kryder 1993).

Democrats controlled Congress for most of the 1931–1971 period. Republicans held the House majority only during the 80th (1947–1948) and 83rd Congresses (1953–1954). Liberal Republicans were the Speaker group in both Congresses and supported Speaker Joseph W. Martin (R-MA).[31]

Within the Democratic Party, southerners controlled the House until the early 1960s, when northern Democrats gained the Speakership and progressively expanded their influence. Southern Democrats were the Speaker group from 1931 until 1933, and again from 1935 until 1961.[32] The southern Democrats' second stronghold was the committee system, including the Rules Committee, which they controlled through committee chairs via the seniority rule (Goodwin 1959; Fenno 1973; Polsby, Gallaher, and Rundquist 1969; Robinson 1930). As a consequence, they opposed institutional changes that could scale back the seniority rule or empower the caucus at the expense of committee chairs.[33] Conservative southerners like Howard Smith (D-VA) and William Colmer (D-MS) successively served as chairs (1955–1973) of the powerful Rules Committee and were instrumental in defeating legislation proposed by northern Democrats.[34] Holding both the Speakership and influential committee chair positions helped them to block liberal legislation that would have threatened their interests. Furthermore, starting in the late 1930s, southern Democrats often united with conservative Republicans in both chambers of Congress in what is widely known as the "Conservative Coalition" (Manley 1973; Rae 1989; Schickler and Pearson 2009). Southern Democrats also controlled the majority in the Senate and most of its powerful committees (Foley 1980).

The first Speaker to be aligned with northern Democrats after the brief tenure of Rainey was Joseph W. McCormack (D-MA), who reigned from 1962 until 1971. Scholars agree in describing McCormack's Speakership as the

---

[31] Martin was also the minority leader when the party was in the minority from 1939 until January 1959, when conservative Republican Charles Halleck (R-IN) became the party leader. Martin was blamed for the big losses Republicans suffered at the polls in November 1958, which reduced their House delegation from 201 to 153.

[32] Except for northern Democrat H. Rainey's (D-IL) term as Speaker between 1933 and 1934, all Democratic Speakers between 1934 and 1961 were southerners: John Garner (D-TX) was the Speaker in the 72nd Congress (1931–1933), J. W. Byrns (D-TN) in the 74th Congress (1935–1936), William Bankhead (D-AL) in the 75th–76th Congress (1937–1940), and Sam Rayburn (D-TX) from the 76th Congress until his death during the 87th Congress (1940–1961).

[33] In 1949 and 1965 northern Democrats supported initiatives such as the enactment of the twenty-one-day rule, in 1961 they backed the enlargement of the Rules Committee, and in 1965 they sponsored additional rule changes that empowered the Speaker and altered the bicameral agreement process (Zelizer 2004) – all attempts to shift the balance of power in their favor.

[34] For instance, through their control of the Rules Committee, in 1961 southerners defeated the most important education bill passed by both chambers since 1862. In this case Rules Committee chair Howard Smith refused to form a conference committee.

period of northern Democrats' highest influence within the House (Polsby 2004). During this period, northern Democrats were able to leave their imprint through the enactment of the measures contained in the "New Frontier" and "Great Society" legislative programs. Essential for these enactments was congressional support of liberal Republicans, who provided pivotal help not only for several pieces of legislation but also for rule changes. In the 1960s, liberal Republicans formed the Wednesday Group in the House, a forum aimed to oppose the conservative Republican leadership and to promote liberal policies. In the Senate, liberal Republicans were crucial in helping northern Democrats to obtain quorum and filibuster-proof majorities.

Thus, while during most of the years between 1930 and 1970, southern Democrats controlled the congressional arm of the Democratic Party, northerners controlled the presidential wing. Indeed, all of the Democratic candidates in the period 1930–1970 were aligned with northern/liberal Democrats. That this intraparty group could prevail over conservatives in the election of presidential nominees dates from 1936, with the elimination of the Democratic Party rule that required presidential candidates to have the support of two-thirds of the delegates. Eliminating the rule effectively meant that presidential candidates no longer needed the support of southern delegates (Key 1949; Parmet 1976; Patterson 1967).[35] Thus, northern Democrats were able to secure the nomination of their candidates: Franklin D. Roosevelt in 1932, 1936, and 1940; Harry Truman in 1944 and 1948; Adlai Stevenson in 1952 and 1956; John F. Kennedy in 1960; and Lyndon B. Johnson in 1964.

They lost the presidency to liberal Republicans in 1952, 1956, and 1968. With the exception of Barry Goldwater in 1964, liberal Republicans were able to secure the nomination of a member of their faction in every presidential election in this period, largely because of the strong support of most northeastern governors. Rae explains that

> the east and the Midwest struggled for the party's presidential nomination … the Eastern section usually had the upper hand in this struggle because of its greater population, the influence of the governor and party bosses of the larger states and the power of the business community. (Rae 1989, 43)

Liberal Republicans coalesced behind Wall Street lawyers Wendell Willkie and Thomas E. Dewey, who won the Republican nominations in 1940 and 1944, respectively.[36] In both primaries, conservative Republicans supported Robert

[35] To abrogate this 100-year-old rule, northern liberals provided southerners with an apportionment concession. Starting in 1944, Democratic delegates would be apportioned on the basis of Democratic votes casts by states in elections rather than on population. This would mean that the most populous states (mostly in the Northeast, which were predominantly Republican) would not have more delegates per vote than southern states. The two-thirds rule elimination was opposed by thirteen states and favored by thirty-six states.

[36] Even though both lost to FDR, their candidacies were instrumental in reviving the liberal-progressive element within the Republican Party.

Taft (Neal 1984). Liberal Republicans won the presidency with Eisenhower's nominations in 1952 and 1956; conservative Republicans again supported Taft in the 1952 primaries.[37] In 1960, liberal Republicans supported Nixon's "Fifth Avenue Pact" with New York governor Nelson Rockefeller. With this pact, the Republican platform for the presidential election of 1960 adopted many issues from the liberal Republican agenda. In the presidential primaries of 1964, liberals supported Nelson Rockefeller and opposed the nomination of Barry Goldwater, whom conservatives supported.

Liberal Republicans' influence within the party began to wane in the 1960s, in large part as a result of the emergence and growing influence of the New Right, as reflected in the nomination of conservative Barry Goldwater in 1964. Indeed, liberals lost most of their governorships in the East, and Ronald Reagan's election as president of the Republican Governors Association in 1968 signaled a definite shift in power within the association to more conservative members.

4. 92nd–112th Congresses (1971–2013)

New Left Democrats and New Democrats/Blue Dogs
Moderate Republicans and the New Right

During the 1970s, 1980s, and 1990s, deep transformations within both parties occurred. The Democratic Party fractured between groups who wanted to move the party further to the left and groups who argued that the party needed to adopt a centrist position. At the same time, the conservative wing captured the Republican Party.

By the end of the 1960s, the power of northern liberal Democrats within the Democratic Party began to wane. Divergent positions over the Vietnam War, as well as the tumultuous 1968 election, fractured the Democratic Party. In the aftermath of the election, a number of Democrats, later called New Democrats, argued that the party needed to move to the center in order to retain the support of all regions. Another group, which emerged as the "New Left," included a significant number of women, youth, minorities, and anti–Vietnam War activists. They believed that the party needed to move to the left to present a real alternative to the Republican Party (Berry 1999; Shafer 2003; Zelizer 2004). A third group, the Blue Dogs, represented the most fiscally conservative element of the party. These intraparty groups shaped the divisions that currently exist within the Democratic Party.

---

[37] Even though many of Eisenhower's policies aligned with conservative Republicans', he did not dismantle the New Deal policies. On the one hand, Eisenhower pleased conservatives when he ended wage and price controls, abolished the Reconstruction Finance Corporation, and expanded the participation of private industry in development of atomic materials and facilities. However, in not dismantling welfare programs, Eisenhower also demonstrated his support for liberal policies; further, he also increased both Social Security benefits and the minimum wage (Rae 1989; Sundquist 1968).

The New Left gained dominance via changes in the presidential nomination process for which they had lobbied after the tumultuous 1968 convention (Ceaser 1979).[38] The new rules allocated delegates according to the number of votes that candidates garnered in primaries or caucuses, which guaranteed that each state's delegates would reflect its popular choice, not its politicians' choice. The reforms increased the number of New Left delegates, thus increasing the group's power in the nomination process. At the same time, the reforms removed traditional liberal-labor leaders from key positions as the main power brokers in the party (Soule and Clarke 1970; Polsby and Wildavsky 1976).

The New Left campaigned for secularism and progressive values. It embraced the causes of economically disadvantaged and disenfranchised groups such as minorities, women, the physically and mentally challenged, and, eventually, gays and lesbians (Layman 2001; Shafer 1988; Zelizer 2004). This cultural progressivism alienated various groups within the party, such as evangelical Christians, most of who left the Democratic Party by the end of the 1970s. The New Left also promoted middle-class suburban voters' interests, particularly on environmental and consumer protection issues (Landy and Levin 1995).

With respect to policy, the New Left advocated federal government intervention in the economy and society, endorsing health care reform based on universal coverage, the expansion of welfare, food stamps, and Head Start programs. It sought to democratize the policy process and reduce government corruption by encouraging citizen participation and reforming campaign finance. A big difference between the New Left and the defunct northern Democrat intraparty group was the New Left's comparative indifference to labor. Labor's demands were not at the top of the New Left's concerns, which contrasted with the traditional northern Democratic position.[39]

During the 1970s, Congress was the stronghold of the New Left. In the House, the New Left supported congressional reforms that reduced committee chairs' powers and dismantled the secrecy of committees. It also sought to increase the influence of the (liberal) Speaker and subcommittees (Zelizer 2004). It supported the 1970 Legislative Reorganization Act and a series of

---

[38] The selection of Hubert Humphrey as the presidential nominee in 1968 drew together the different elements in the New Left. This intraparty group was outraged at Humphrey's selection as the Democratic nominee because he had not competed in any of the primary elections; he won with the support of party leaders, who controlled enough votes to choose the presidential candidate.

[39] Only some of the trade unions and public interest groups that had been affiliated with the northern Democrats between 1930 and 1970 embraced the New Left. While the United Auto Workers (UAW) and the Americans for Democratic Action (ADA) affiliated with the New Left and supported George McGovern for president in 1972, other unions, including the American Federation of Labor–Congress of Industrial Organizations (AFL-CIO), opposed the New Left and McGovern's nomination. Overall, the influence won by the New Left within the party was at the expense of the power lost by the trade unions.

caucus rule reforms that weakened the power of southern Democrat commit-tee chairs.[40] Together, these reforms marked the end of southern Democrat dominance in the House.

In the 1980s, conservative Democrats reorganized in reaction to the New Left around what is now known as the New Democrats (Hale 1995). In 1985, southern/conservative Democrats founded the Democratic Leadership Council. Its aim was to move the party to the center and away from the image that the New Left had created (Baer 2000). The New Democrats tried to transform the party into one that advocated moderation and pragmatism, for the purpose of attracting middle-class suburban voters (Shafer 1988; Zelizer 2004).

The New Democrats also advocated reduced state involvement in the econ-omy and market-friendly policies (Shafer 2000). They viewed fiscal discipline and deficit reduction as the best means by which to spur economic growth. They also promoted integration in the international economy, free trade agree-ments (e.g., the North American Free Trade Agreement [NAFTA] and the General Agreement on Tariffs and Trade [GATT]), and higher spending on national security. The New Democrats tended to be probusiness, with a partic-ular emphasis on technology. The New Democrats adopted a moderate stance on cultural issues. They supported welfare and health care reform and cam-paigned for tougher crime legislation.

Many of the southern conservatives who remained in the Democratic Party organized around the Blue Dogs coalition in 1995.[41] Although they typically tended to represent rural regions and were more socially conservative than the New Democrats, many Blue Dogs were also members of the New Democrat coalition and supported its policies. The Blue Dogs were considered to be the most fiscally conservative members of the party.[42]

Starting in the 1960s, a new group, the New Right, emerged within the Republican Party.[43] It opposed liberal Republicans and attempted to restore the traditional conservatism of the party. While the New Right shared common

---

[40] The caucus reforms stipulated that 20 percent of the membership could demand a secret ballot on the selection of committee chairs. While the previous selection of committee chairs through an open voting system made it difficult for legislators to challenge existing committee chairs, a secret system enabled members of the New Left to challenge such chairs without fear of being punished. Furthermore, in 1974 the power to select committee members was moved from the Ways and Means Committee to the recently created Democratic Steering and Policy Committee chaired by Speaker Carl Albert (D-OK), enabling the New Left to replace a relatively conserva-tive Ways and Means contingent with a more liberal group.

[41] During the 1980s these conservative Democrats supported the Reagan administration's tax cuts, increases in military spending, and deregulation. They were called "boll weevil Democrats."

[42] During the 111th Congress (2009–2011), Blue Dogs reached their highest number, with more than fifty members in the House. However, they lost half of those seats to Republicans in the 2010 elections.

[43] The New Right's first demonstration of influence within the party was their successful back-ing of Arizona senator Barry Goldwater in 1964 as presidential nominee (Himmelstein 1990; Kolkey 1983).

ground on economic policies with traditional conservative Republicans, the two groups disagreed over other issues, such as foreign policy (Blumenthal 1986). For instance, although both opposed communism, conservative Republicans were isolationists, while the New Right favored assertive intervention in foreign affairs (Hodgson 1996). The New Right advocated free market policies and opposed growth of the federal government, especially in social and economic affairs.

The New Right coalesced in the Republican Study Committee founded in 1973, and later in the Conservative Opportunity Society, founded by Newt Gingrich (R-GA) in 1983. Both groups supported cuts in nondefense spending and advocated socially conservative legislation. The New Right opposed affirmative action, the feminist movement, and lesbian and gay rights activism and instead strongly supported what they defined as traditional American cultural values. Starting in the 1970s, and especially after *Roe v. Wade*, they were outraged at the New Left's support for abortion legislation and fought for the Republican Party to become the party of tradition and "family values."

On the opposing side were the liberal Republicans. They continued to lose representatives in Congress and, after the 1994 elections, coalesced around the Republican Main Street Partnership, a forum that united their very small membership in the House. Liberal Republicans were fiscally conservative, and supported a limited government, although they were liberal regarding social issues.

In the House, the New Left comprised the Speaker group until 1986, and supported Thomas (Tip) O'Neill (D-MA) as Speaker. After O'Neill's retirement in 1987, James C. Wright (D-TX) became Speaker. A moderate, Wright tried to steer the House in a centrist direction, although his objectives were cut short when he had to resign in 1989 in the midst of ethics charges. Between 1989 and until the Democrats lost the majority in the 1994 elections, the New Left became the Speaker group again, supporting Tom Foley (D-WA) as Speaker.

The New Left also controlled the presidential wing of the Democratic Party until 1992, although none of its candidates, with the exception of Jimmy Carter, won a national election. In 1968, the New Left supported both Eugene McCarthy and Robert Kennedy. It endorsed George McGovern for president in 1972, probably the most left-leaning candidate Democrats nominated since William Jennings Bryan in 1908 (Berry 1999; Gillon 1987). The New Left was instrumental in ensuring Carter's nomination in 1976, even though Carter's stances on social and welfare issues were more moderate than the New Left's. The New Left nominated Walter Mondale in 1984 and Michael Dukakis in 1988. However, with the exception of Jimmy Carter, who barely won the popular vote, none of the New Left candidates won in the general presidential elections (Milkis 1999).

In contrast, Republicans dominated the presidency until 1992. While liberal Republicans continued to lose influence during the 1970s and 1980s, they maintained control of the presidential wing of the party until 1976, nominating and winning with Nixon in 1968 and 1972, and nominating Gerald Ford and Nelson Rockefeller in 1976. The New Right supported Barry Goldwater in 1964, Ronald Reagan in the 1968 primaries, and John M. Ashbrook in the 1972 primaries. In 1976, in the primaries they again endorsed Ronald Reagan, who ultimately lost his bid. However, Ford's loss to Carter set the stage for the Republican nomination of a New Right candidate, Ronald Reagan, in 1980. Reagan fully embraced the New Right platform (Milkis 1999). In the 1988 primaries the New Right supported George H. W. Bush, who ran on a very conservative platform over liberal Republican Bob Dole.[44]

The New Right was responsible for the 1994 Republican congressional wins, largely because of the efforts of their leader, Speaker Newt Gingrich. Gaining the majority helped the New Right to solidify their dominance in the House. They centralized power in the leadership, established term limits for committee chairs, adjusted committee jurisdictions, and abolished three committees they felt served Democratic constituencies. These actions ensured that committee chairs would be loyal to the New Right and would promote the conservative agenda (Brennan 1995; Feulner 1983). Dennis Hastert (R-IL), who became Speaker in 1999, shared the New Right's ideological preferences.[45]

Democrats won the presidency again in 1992. In contrast to the New Left's previous prominence in presidential nominations, a New Democrat candidate, Bill Clinton, won the primaries in 1992.[46] Although the first years of Clinton's administration were not wholly in line with the Democratic Leadership Council's (DLC) and New Democrats' policy objectives, several New Democrat initiatives became law during Clinton's tenure, including comprehensive welfare reform, balanced budget requirements, and NAFTA (Milkis 1999; Skocpol 1996; Weaver 2000). The New Democrats also controlled the Democratic Party in the House, especially when Richard Gephardt became the minority leader in 1995.[47] Although Gephardt ultimately was able to draw Democrats together, redistricting removed most of the conservative Democrats from the Midwest, in part allowing the liberal contingent to take over the party again in the 2000s. Thus, the New Democrats were in firm control of the Democratic

[44] However, once Bush became president, the New Right opposed many of his policies, especially those regarding raising taxes; in 1990, 105 legislators followed Representative Newt Gingrich (R-GA) and voted against Bush's proposed tax increases.

[45] As *CQ Weekly* explained, Hastert became Speaker because his "standing as a trusted and stabilizing figure made him the consensus choice for Speaker just hours after the GOP nomination for the job was abandoned by Robert Livingston (R-LA), amid revelations of marital infidelity" (Carey 1999).

[46] The New Democrats pushed for changes to the Democratic presidential nomination process, which they felt was biased in favor of the Left. In 1988 they created Super Tuesday, a day early in the primary season when most of the southern states would hold their elections, aimed to give New Democrats an early push in the primaries.

[47] Richard Gephardt (D-MO) was never Speaker of the House but instead majority leader from 1989 until 1994 and then minority leader from 1995 until 2002.

Party in 2000 and nominated Al Gore, whom they already had supported in the 1988 Democratic primaries, for the presidency.

However, they lost to New Right Republican George W. Bush, whose "compassionate conservatism" introduced market mechanisms into education, health care, and Social Security. Bush took conservative stands on cultural issues like abortion, affirmative action, stem cell research, and gay marriage. The New Right, however, disagreed with his signature piece of education reform, "No Child Left Behind," and with his amendments to Medicare to cover prescription drugs for seniors (Greenstein 2003).

Indeed, the New Right became the governing establishment of the Republican Party. Zelizer (2010) calls this period of conservative dominance "modern conservatism":

> a period that began in the early 1980s when conservatives switched from being an oppositional force in national politics to struggling with the challenges of governance that came from holding power. (2010, 7)

In this sense, the New Right used presidential power (Ronald Reagan, George H. W. Bush, and George W. Bush) as the key mechanism by which to oppose Democrats and the federal agencies that the New Right sought to reform. The New Right controlled the House until 2006, and then again starting in 2011. The dynamics within the Republican Party are hard to predict, given the strength of new groups like the Tea Party, which have challenged the power of establishment conservative Republicans.

Within the Democratic Party, the New Left regained control of the House Democratic Party with the election of Nancy Pelosi (D-CA) as minority leader in 2002 and Speaker in 2007.[48] The change in leadership from New Democrats to the New Left raised concerns within the party, as noted in an article in the *New York Times*:

> The choice of Ms. Pelosi to replace Mr. Gephardt has stirred concern among the Democrats who helped steer the party to the center in the 1980s, and could fuel the ideological battle that seems to be brewing. After the party lost three presidential elections in a row [Carter, Mondale, and Dukakis], those Democrats argued for moderating views of social and national security issues to be competitive with Republicans. (Nagourney 2013)

The New Democrats became the non-Speaker group when the Democratic Party won the majority in 2006. Steny Hoyer (D-MD), the minority whip in 2003–2006 and 2011–the present and majority leader between 2007 and 2011, represented the group. New Democrats and the more conservative Blue Dog coalition frequently clashed with the New Left over fiscal policies and

---

[48] Nancy Pelosi (D-CA), a New Left Democrat, was elected minority leader over Martin Frost of Texas, a centrist supported by Steny Hoyer, another centrist Democrat.

party ideology, especially during the Bush administration (e.g., the Iraq War, the Republican bankruptcy reform bill).

In the 2004 primary campaign, many New Democrats supported Joseph Lieberman and John Edwards, while expressing antagonism toward Howard Dean. In the 2008 campaign, the New Democrats supported Hillary Clinton. The election of Barack Obama in 2008, as well as his reelection in 2012, were the first times the New Left successfully backed a presidential candidate since the election of Carter in 1976.

CONCLUSION

In this chapter, I explained in detail two factors of the American political system that profoundly affect power-sharing arrangements in the House. One of them is the separation of powers system stipulated in the Constitution. The presence of a president and a Senate whose approval is necessary to make laws creates incentives for House members to distribute power in some ways and not others.

The second factor is the continuing presence of distinct intraparty groups within the major parties since the very beginning of the Republic. Intraparty groups play a crucial role in primary campaigns, the presidential nomination process, and policy making within Congress. As I show in subsequent chapters, they also play a central role in negotiating the distribution of power within the House.

Both features are central to the theory I develop in Chapters 3 and 4. The presence of intraparty groups within parties, especially the House majority party, and the proximity of their preferences to those of the Senate and president, are key to understanding *when and why* House members choose particular rules and procedures. As I argue in the theoretical and empirical chapters that follow, House members' rule choices depend on the alignments of intraparty group preferences vis-à-vis those of the Senate and the president. Indeed, the critically important nuances of bargaining among constitutional actors depend heavily on the preferences of the intraparty groups.

3

A Constitutional Theory of Legislative Organization

House members know that their legislative success depends on the actions of the Senate and president.[1] This simple reality underlies the Constitutional Theory of Legislative Organization, which sets forth conditions under which changes in the preferences of the Senate and/or the president should induce a House majority to change its organizational rules so as to maximize legislative outcomes.

In this chapter, I develop a theoretical model that shows how the preferences of constitutional actors outside the House influence the House's internal power-sharing decisions; in Chapters 4 and 5, I derive the implications of the model for purposes of understanding, respectively, the timing and directionality of rule changes in the House.

THEORIES AND MODELS OF LAWMAKING
IN THE UNITED STATES

Scholars inevitably must decide which factors in their theories and models will be exogenous to all others. This decision is crucial, for it sets the terms of the "game" that the actors play. Prevailing theories begin with different assumptions about what is exogenous, which in turn leads to different model structures and thus widely varying conclusions about where the true power within the House lies.

Distributional theories argue that power rests on a committee system with property rights on its jurisdictions and a set of amendment rules that establish how others on the floor can amend the committee's bill (Shepsle 1979). Weingast and Marshall argue that

> the committee system provides substantial protection against opportunistic behavior ... [by institutionalizing] a trade among all the legislators, policy area

[1] The model presented in this chapter follows (Sin and Lupia 2012).

by policy area, for the right to select which points ... replace the status quo. (Weingast and Marshall 1988, 144–5)

The committee's gatekeeping powers and last-mover advantage rest on the committee's chance to review bills in conference committee (Shepsle and Weingast 1987). Thus, if the House or Senate introduces changes to a bill, the House conferees, who typically represent the committees with jurisdiction over the bill, get a "second crack" at it.[2] A game in which committees have an ex-post veto over the originally drafted bill guarantees equilibrium outcomes close to the committees' preferences.

Partisan theories assume the majority party to hold exogenous agenda-setting and proposal powers that guarantee policy outcomes close to the party median's ideal point (Aldrich 1994; Cox and McCubbins 1993). The game structure in Aldrich (1994), for example, assumes a party that selects a leader and provides him with a set of proposals from which he can choose. The party constrains the leader in that he can choose only proposals that a majority of the majority party prefers to the status quo and can win on the floor (1994, 320). If there is no outcome that meets both conditions, then the majority party will issue instructions to keep the gates closed (Aldrich, Grynaviski, and Rohde 1999, 5). As a result, legislative outcomes are always closer to the median member of the party (Aldrich 1994; Aldrich and Rohde 1997; 1998; 2000; 2001; Aldrich, Grynaviski, and Rohde 1999; Rohde 1991).

In the similar "cartel agenda model," the results rest on an additional assumption that senior members, who have fiduciary responsibility, hold institutional veto power within the House. In Cox and McCubbins's words (2005),

> the creation of multiple vetoes and the imposition of a minimal normative restraint on senior officeholder's behavior ... suffice to ensure that, whenever a majority of the majority party would like to see a bill blocked, some senior partners will in fact block it, either because they share the majority's views or because they feel a fiduciary obligation to do so.... They will have personal incentives to veto the bill and thus protect a majority from a roll. (Cox and McCubbins 2005, 42)

Thus, outcomes far from the majority party's preferences are never allowed on the floor.

Informational theories assume the minority party has the option to offer a motion to recommit, a procedural tool that allows the minority party to counter the procedural advantages of the majority (Krehbiel and Meirowitz 2002). In this sense, the motion is an

> institutionalized right granted to a minority (typically the minority party) to engage in a positive action to try to form a new majority and to do so at the end of the amendment process during floor consideration of legislation ... [the

---

[2] They argue this is the case because conference committee members "come principally from the committees of jurisdiction ... [and because] the conference report is considered [in the floor] under a closed rule as a take-it-or-leave-it proposal" (Shepsle and Weingast 1987, 95).

motion to recommit] functions as a significant damper on majority party power. (Krehbiel and Meirowitz 2002, 193, 200)

In this framework even when the first-mover advantage is granted to the majority party, the right to make final proposals gives the minority party the power to move outcomes close to the floor median.

Scholars have debated the veridicality of the various theories, on grounds that this or that theory begins with the wrong assumption about what can be taken as given. For example, some have questioned whether congressional committees actually have an ex-post veto power over legislation, noting that (i) the motion to go to conference is always subject to majority approval (Krehbiel 1991); (ii) the Speaker, not the committees, appoints conferees (Lazarus and Monroe 2007); and (iii) rules and precedents permit discharging a conference committee (Krehbiel 1991). Others have proposed that, in reality, the minority party does not have the last-mover advantage under the rules of the House: "The motion to recommit is not in order for most bills that reach the House floor ... the majority party has an *ex-post* veto over recommittal motions, in the form of points of order and ruling of the chair" (Cox, Den Hartog, and McCubbins 2006, 22). Roberts (2005) criticizes Krehbiel and Meirowitz (2002) for not accurately describing the motion to recommit process and failing to predict empirical patterns. In reality, he asserts, House rules allow the majority party to amend the motion to recommit, undermining the ability of the minority party to benefit from last-mover advantage.

The criticisms of the three prevailing theories of House rule making underline an important commonality: All make assumptions about House rules and organization that are open to challenge. To avoid this quagmire, I make no assumptions about the nature of House rule making itself. Instead, I begin with two realities of national policy making. First, the Constitution places House members into a "game" that is clearly specified and understandable, given more than two hundred years of history and experience. It is a game in which House members must account for two other constitutionally created actors, the Senate and president. Second, I assume that two intraparty groups exist within the majority party. Again, this assumption is rooted in history and experience, as I demonstrated earlier in Chapter 2. Including two intraparty groups within the majority party allows divergence of preferences within the party to affect bargaining; one of the intraparty groups within the House majority party can threaten to join the House minority party if its demands are not met.

In all, three notable attributes distinguish the constitutional bargaining model from previous models. First, the model includes the Senate and the president as key actors who participate in the legislative game.[3] Second, the model characterizes the House as composed of three factions, two belonging

---

[3] The decision to model the Senate as a unitary actor both simplifies reality and facilitates comparisons with perspectives on House power sharing that exclude the Senate. However, a future analysis should include an analysis of Senate factions, strategy, and rules changes.

to the majority party and the third representing the minority party. Finally, the model incorporates House factions' expectations about future legislative and interbranch dynamics at the time they are considering power-sharing changes. Given these model attributes, rules and procedures are endogenously determined by House factions, who anticipate the actions of two constitutionally established actors, the Senate and president.

THE MODEL: EXPLAINING CHANGES IN HOUSE ORGANIZATION

Reflecting the constitutional requirements of the legislative process, the actors – Senate, president, and House, itself composed of three factions – play *two distinct games* in succession. In the *power-sharing game,* House factions choose rules and procedures that distribute power among themselves, reflecting the bargaining process that occurs at the beginning of each new session of the House. Article I, Section 5 of the Constitution gives House members broad latitude to determine the chamber's power-sharing rules. Beyond implying that every two years the House must decide whether to adopt the same rules that governed the policy-making process during the previous Congress or to adopt new rules, Section 5 offers no instructions about the chamber's internal organization.

In the *legislative game,* the Senate, president, and House factions strive to find jointly acceptable legislative outcomes. This latter game consists of two stages. The first is a *bicameral agreement stage,* where House members and the Senate, the latter construed as an exogenous unitary actor with its own preferences, settle their differences. In the *constitutional stage,* the president, another unitary actor with its own preferences, approves or rejects legislative proposals made in the bicameral agreement stage.

To facilitate understanding of the model I describe later, Table 3.1 enumerates all of the relevant notation.

Although neither Senate nor president directly participates when the House negotiates rules, the two stages of the legislative game capture the notion that the Constitution gives House members strong incentives to anticipate bicameral agreements and constitutional stage dynamics when allocating power. In short, a constitutional theory clarifies how the requirements of Article I, Section 7[4] affect power allocation decisions made under Article I, Section 5.[5]

The game features a legislature with three House members, a Senate, and a president. I assume, from Chapter 2, three ideological factions in the House and label them F_1, F_2, and F_3. I focus on the case where no faction constitutes a majority of the House[6] and model the factions' preferences using two-dimensional ideal points ($F_1 \in R^2$, $F_2 \in R^2$, $F_3 \in R^2$); in particular,

---

[4] Article I, Section 7 says that to become laws, bills have to be approved by a House majority, by a Senate majority, and in case of a presidential veto, by two-thirds of the House and the Senate.
[5] Article 1, Section 5 says that "each House may determine the rules of its proceedings."
[6] That is, *max (%F1, %F2, %F3) < .5* and %F1 + %F2 + %F3 = 1.

TABLE 3.1. *Definitions of variables*

$F_1, F_2, F_3 \in R^2$	The ideal points of three House factions
F_1, F_2, F_3	We also use these terms as shorthand to refer to individual factions in the text. In examples, we sometimes refer to F_1 and F_2 collectively as the majority party and to F_3 as the minority party.
$\%F_i$	The percentage of the House that faction i controls, where $i \in \{1, 2, 3\}$
s	The Senate's ideal point, where $s \in \{F_1, F_2, F_3\}$
p	The president's ideal point, where $p \in \{F_1, F_2, F_3\}$
r_i	The reconciliation between House faction i and the Senate, where $r_i \in R^2$
q	The status quo policy, where $q \in R^2$
L	The outcome of the game's legislative process, where $L \in \{r_i, q\}$
$U_i(L)$	The policy utility to players with ideal point F_i from legislative outcome L. Denoted as $-\lvert F_i - L \rvert$ for simplicity. In reality, $$U_i(L) = -\sqrt{(x_{F_i} - x_L)^2 + (y_{F_i} - y_L)^2},$$ where x_d denotes the position of $d \in \{F_i, L\}$ on the horizontal axis of the two-dimensional policy space and y_d denotes the position of $d \in \{F_i, L\}$ on the policy space's vertical axis.
$c_i^k \in [0, 1]$	A power sharing offer from faction i to faction k, where $k \in \{1, 2, 3\}$.
CS	The constitutional set, where $CS \in R^2$
$v > 0$	The amount, in policy utility, by which r_i must beat q for the Senate to support an override of the president's rejection of r_i.
mid_i	The midpoint of the line connecting faction i's ideal point to that of the Senate.
sec_i	The point in the CS closest to mid_i when $mid_i \notin CS$.
π_x	A variable that breaks ties regarding player choices but does not affect outcomes. It represents player x's public stance, where $x \in \{Senate, president, F_1, F_2, F_3\}$. $\pi_x > 0$ denotes player x's desire to be seen supporting a particular outcome, even though the decision has no bearing on the outcome. $\pi_x > 0$ denotes player x's desire to be seen opposing the outcome, even though the decision has no bearing on the outcome. $\pi_x = 0$ denotes player x's indifference in that situation.

I assume simple linear utility functions. For faction $i \in \{1, 2, 3\}$ and legislative outcome $L \in R^2$, I denote faction i's policy utility as $U_i(F_i, L) = -\lvert F_i - L \rvert$, with the latter notation of spatial utility chosen for simplicity. I refer to F_1 and F_2 as the two factions of the House majority party and to F_3 as the minority party. These labels facilitate interpretation of the model's substantive implications.

Including three factions allows disagreement within the majority party to affect inter- and intraparty bargaining in the model. Furthermore, and as described in Chapter 2, many scholars – political scientists and, especially, historians – emphasize the importance of intraparty groups for understanding political dynamics in the United States.[7] Assuming that F_1 and F_2 collectively constitute the majority party allows the possibility that some majority party members will threaten to join the minority party as a means of withholding support when proposals by members of their own party generate discontent.

In what follows, I explain the dynamics within the power sharing and the legislative games. Then, through backward induction, I show how the two stages within the legislative game, the bicameral agreement and constitutional stage, influence House members' decisions regarding power sharing in their chamber.

The Power-Sharing Game

Article I, Section 5 of the Constitution empowers the House to design its own power-sharing arrangement but provides only minimal instructions on how to do it: "Each House may determine the rules of its proceedings, punish its members for disorderly behavior, and, with the concurrence of two thirds, expel a member." While the Constitution does not mandate majority approval for rules decisions, the House has traditionally adopted this convention; hence, I do the same in the model presented here.

Figure 3.1 depicts the model's power-sharing game. In it, F_1 moves first and has an opportunity to offer a power-sharing rule to F_2 or F_3. If F_1's proposal is rejected, then F_2 can make an offer to F_3. Successful rules require the support of two factions (i.e., a majority of House members). If no faction offers an acceptable rule, the game ends with legislative outcome $L = q$, where $q \in R^2$ represents a preexisting aggregate policy status quo.[8]

Offers take the following form: "If you, faction F_2, join with us, faction F_1, then together we shall commit to a power-sharing rule that is weighted as follows: With probability $c_1^2 \in [0, 1]$ the House shall act as if our faction's ideal point is its own and with probability $1 - c_1^2$ it shall act as if your faction's ideal point is its own." Here, subscripts denote the faction offering the rule and superscripts denote the faction to whom the offer is made.

I represent the rule as probabilistic for two reasons. First, I want to adopt the perspective of House members at those moments when they decide

---

[7] See, for example, Aldrich 1995; Brady and Bullock 1980; Burns 1963; Galloway 1969; Hasbrouck 1927; Nye 1951; Reiter 2001; 2004; Rohde 1991; Schousen 1994; Sinclair 1982.

[8] Whether or not F_3 offers a rule does not affect my conclusions about rule changes. To see why, note that if there is a rule that F_3 and either F_1 or F_2 most prefers, then F_1 or F_2 can simply offer it to F_3. In other words, all mutually beneficial rule changes that exist can be made in this game.

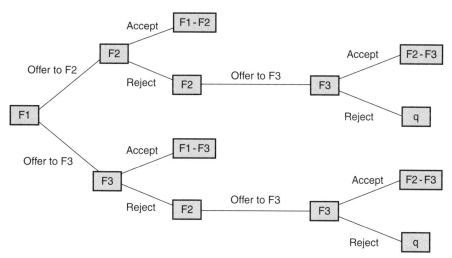

FIGURE 3.1. The power-sharing game.

whether or not to change the allocation of power in their chamber. At these moments, they are uncertain about which issues will arise and rely on probabilistic beliefs about how current power allocations will affect future legislative outcomes. Second, I seek to reflect that many House power-sharing rules are intended to persist for some period, typically the duration of the coming legislative term. So, to clarify the relationship between shifts in senatorial and presidential preferences and House-rule changes, I represent agreements that give one faction the power to set the agenda and another faction veto power over certain matters as analogous to a rule in which "your faction expects to control the legislative process (from the drafting and processing of bills to *ex post* controls on conference committees) c_i^2 percent of the time, while my faction expects to control it $100 - c_i^2$ percent of the time." In other words, rules are agreements that codify factions' relative power within a governing coalition.

Completing the power-sharing game's description requires a statement of how ties are broken. The default assumption is that a change in power-sharing rule requires more than indifference. Thus, in regard to reactions to an offer, if an offer to reallocate power yields the same utility as the status quo, it is rejected. If an offer from *F1* yields the same utility as an offer from another faction, it is accepted (i.e., if *F2* is indifferent between coalitions with *F1* or *F3*, it chooses *F1* to keep all power within the majority party). With respect to the decision to propose an offer, in contrast, if no offer provides the offering faction with greater utility than the status quo, then no offer is made.

Thus, House factions in the power-sharing game devise a set of rules and procedures that institute a distribution of power within the House. These agreements determine the factions' relative power to influence policy outcomes.

The Legislative Game

The legislative game has two stages, the bicameral agreement stage and the constitutional stage. Each stage represents future events that House members presumably consider when deciding whether or not to change the power-sharing rules that the previous legislature had in place. The bicameral agreement stage is a simple algorithm that characterizes basic attributes of congressional capacities to reconcile interchamber differences. The constitutional stage is a noncooperative game among the House, Senate, and president that follows the Constitution's rules for creating new laws.

Stage 1: Bicameral Agreement

The Constitution requires that the House and the Senate reconcile their differences before seeking presidential approval for legislation, but provides no instructions on how to do so. Many reconciliation methods have been used over the years, ranging from informal consultations to assembling a formal conference committee in which House and Senate delegates engage in sustained negotiations. That said, all bicameral agreement procedures share a common characteristic: They require approval by both representatives of the House and Senate.

Following this constitutional design, I represent interchamber bicameral agreement efforts as a bargain between the Senate's and House's chosen representatives. Shepsle and Weingast (1987) portray House-Senate negotiations as providing ex-post vetoes on House decisions. I extend their treatment by modeling House-Senate bargaining outcomes themselves as a function of the House's power-sharing rule. To see how a House power-sharing rule can affect a bicameral agreement, consider the Speaker's conferee selection powers.

When interchamber negotiations are conducted through conference committees, House Rule 1, Clause 11 gives the Speaker power to select conferees. Even after naming an initial set of conferees, the Speaker retains the right to subtract or add as s/he wishes and "there is no effective way to challenge the Speaker's choice of conferees in the House" (Longley and Oleszek 1989, 38). While the Speaker is not entirely unconstrained (i.e., if enough members are sufficiently displeased they can replace the Speaker or reduce her powers), House rules give the Speaker considerable latitude.[9] For example, Speaker Dennis Hastert (R-IL) chose thirteen Republican conferees to represent the House in negotiations over a managed-care package that he had worked hard to defeat in the House.[10] All but one of the conferees had opposed the House bill, and in the

---

[9] Lazarus and Monroe (2007) and Carson and Vander Wielen (2002) show empirically how speakers use their appointment power to manipulate conference committees to end up with outcomes closer to the party median.

[10] In October 1999, the House had overwhelmingly adopted a bipartisan bill that included a number of patient protections (e.g., allowing patients to sue their health plans in state courts) that the GOP leadership had consistently opposed. The bipartisan bill passed by a vote of 275–151.

end, Hastert was able to use his conferee selection power to kill in conference a bill that he had opposed and yet that had passed the House by a very wide margin (Carey 1999).

The House power-sharing arrangement determines the House's ideal point in this stage; that is, I assume that when power-sharing arrangements allocate resources and agenda power, they affect the likelihood that particular interests will be represented in a bicameral agreement. So, with probability $c_i^k \in [0, 1]$ the House's ideal point when negotiating with the Senate is also faction i's ideal point, and with probability $1 - c_i^k$ it is faction k's ideal point. I assume that the Senate seeks a bicameral agreement that is as close as possible to its ideal point, and that its ideal point, s, is in the set {$F1$, $F2$, $F3$}.

I now characterize the content of a bicameral agreement. One alternative would be to assume that either the House or the Senate has an advantage over the other to influence the content of the agreement. However, as Sin (2007) details, while some scholars have argued that the House prevails in negotiations (Steiner 1951), others contend that the Senate is more successful (Fenno 1966; Manley 1973). Still others (Strom and Rundquist 1977; Ferejohn 1975) claim that both chambers get their way when they have intense preferences.

Given this lack of scholarly consensus and the absence of procedural instructions in Article 1 Section 7, I represent attempts to reconcile differences between the House and Senate by a simple algorithm: "Split the difference if possible; otherwise recognize bargaining power." In this sense, the algorithm resembles the Nash bargaining solution (Nash 1950). This algorithm first draws a straight line between the ideal point of the faction representing the House and the ideal point of the Senate. If the midpoint of this line can prevail as the legislative outcome in the second stage of the legislative game, in which the House, Senate, and president approve the bill, then it is the *bicameral agreement*, $r_i \in R^2$, where i refers to the House faction that forged the agreement with the Senate (e.g., r_1 refers to an $F1$-Senate bicameral agreement). Otherwise, the algorithm searches the entire space for the point closest to the original midpoint that can prevail in the game's final stage. This point then becomes the bicameral agreement. If no such point exists, then there is no bicameral agreement and the game ends with $L = q$ as the legislative outcome.

In the model, a bicameral agreement is the representation of a set of bills that House members foresee when they allocate power. I do not intend for the set to represent a single bill, since my goal is to permit "anticipated legislative dynamics" as represented in the legislative game to influence decisions made in the power-sharing game. When modeling the bicameral agreement stage, I work from the perspective of House members who are playing the power-sharing game. Hence, I assume that House members use common knowledge about the Senate's and president's preferences to form expectations about the

---

A companion bill was also approved in the Senate, but it had no provisions granting patients the right to sue. Therefore, a conference committee was formed.

aggregate policy consequences of any possible power-sharing rule. The bicameral agreement in the model represents that expectation. In other words, the power-sharing game defines boundaries of the bicameral stage's bargaining set, while the final stage of the legislative game, whose outcome is explained later and is anticipated by players in the legislative game's bicameral stage, determines the set of feasible legislative outcomes.

Note that while a bicameral agreement must make both chambers better off than the status quo, it might benefit one chamber more than the other. Such asymmetric outcomes will occur when the status quo is much further from one of the chamber's ideal points than it is from the other. In such cases, the "distant" chamber has less bargaining leverage. In effect, the algorithm reflects the equal rights that Article 1, Section 7 gives to each chamber, while allowing bicameral agreements to be affected by bargaining power asymmetries that may stem from other aspects of a legislative context.

Thus, in the bicameral agreement stage the House and the Senate bargain over a legislative outcome that can be approved by a House and a Senate majority and signed by the president; or approved by supermajorities in the House and Senate. Who negotiates on behalf of the House depends on the power-sharing agreement decided in the first game. The design of this stage originates in the Constitution, which requires a majority of the House and the Senate to approve exactly the same bill, independently of the mechanism used to solve the differences between the chambers.

Stage 2: Constitutional Rules

Figure 3.2 depicts the extensive form of the legislative game's final stage. The House, Senate, and president consider the bicameral agreement r_i under a closed rule (i.e., $L \in \{r_i, q\}$). In what follows, I use the subscript r_i only when referring to a bicameral agreement between the Senate and a specific House faction. Otherwise, I simply use r.

The bicameral agreement needs the support of two House factions (i.e., a majority) to pass in the final stage. So, if two House factions and the Senate support the bicameral agreement, it goes to the president. Otherwise, the game ends with legislative outcome $L = q$. I assume that the House moves before the Senate. Since the model is one of complete information, this assumption is inconsequential.

If the bicameral agreement makes it to the president, he can approve or reject it. If approved, the game ends with outcome $L = r_i$. A presidential rejection causes the game to continue. I assume that the president, like the other players, seeks a legislative outcome that is as close as possible to an ideal point, p, where $p \in \{F_1, F_2, F_3\}$.

The game's final decision represents House and Senate reactions to a presidential veto. If neither chamber can generate sufficient support for an override, then $L = q$. If the override succeeds, then $L = r_i$. Mimicking the constitutional requirements for a congressional override of a presidential veto, an override in

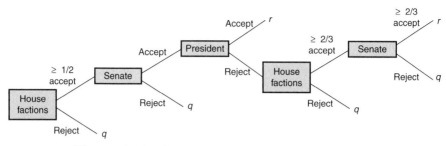

FIGURE 3.2. The constitutional stage.

the model requires the support of two-thirds of the members of each chamber. I represent this requirement in different ways for House and Senate.

For the House, an override requires the support of at least two-thirds of the membership; thus support of two of the three factions may not be sufficient. Rather, the size of the factions supporting the override must be greater than or equal to two-thirds of the membership. For example, suppose that factions F_1 and F_3 support an override. The override has sufficient support only if $\%F_1 + \%F_3 \geq 2/3$.

In comparison, I assume that, all else being equal, it is more difficult for the Senate to support an override than it is to support regular legislation, as it takes more votes to override a presidential veto (two-thirds) than to invoke cloture to end a debate and vote on the passage of a bill (three-fifths). I represent the Senate's supermajoritarian requirements by stating that the Senate supports an override only if r provides at least $v > o$ more utility to the Senate than q, where v is exogenous. In other words, a small change from q is not enough to elicit supermajority support in the Senate; an override requires that the bicameral agreement be substantially better for the Senate than the status quo.

EQUILIBRIUM PROPERTIES

The conclusions result from a subgame-perfect Nash equilibrium, whose existence and uniqueness are proven in Appendix B. In the model, a subgame-perfect Nash equilibrium consists of the following components: In the legislative game's final stage, players choose strategies that are best responses to the actions of all other players in this stage, and in the power-sharing game, House members choose strategies that are best responses to the actions of all other players, actions that are conditioned on common knowledge of the bicameral agreement algorithm and a belief that players will choose best responses in the final stage. Because I draw the conclusion on the game's extensive form via backward induction, I describe properties of the equilibrium in the same order.

The first proposition describes focal properties of the legislative game's final stage and produces the definition of a key concept, *the constitutional set*.

Proposition 1 (The Constitutional Set)

A new legislative outcome occurs if and only if one of the following conditions is met:[11]

- The Senate and president have distinct ideal points (here labeled s and p) and the House factions that share these ideal points prefer the bicameral agreement to the status quo; *or*
- The Senate and the president share an ideal point, and the House faction that shares this ideal point (here labeled Fi) and at least one other faction (here labeled $Fj \neq Fi$) prefer the bicameral agreement to the status quo; *or*
- The president prefers the status quo to the bicameral agreement, the size of the House faction that agrees with him (denoted $\%P$) is not large enough to prevent an override ($\%P < 1/3$), the Senate prefers the bicameral agreement to the status quo so much that it will support an override, and the House faction that is aligned with neither the Senate nor the president also prefers the bicameral agreement.

When House members decide on power-sharing rules, they are thinking ahead to the preferences of the Senate and the president, the other actors who also compose the constitutional set. As I show in the next two chapters, the constitutional set becomes very important when analyzing the timing and the directionality of new House rules.

Henceforth, I refer to the subset of the policy space that satisfies the conditions of Proposition 1 as the *constitutional set* (CS). An implication is that supplanting the status quo requires a bicameral agreement that is in the CS. Parts of the policy space that are not in the constitutional set are not viable legislative outcomes.

It is important to note that the CS need not be connected. The set of points that the president, the Senate, and a House majority prefer to the status quo need not overlap with the set of points that two-thirds of the Senate and two-thirds of the House prefer. In Figure 3.3, for example, $\%F1 + \%F2 > 2/3$.

The CS is the union of the shaded areas. The black area represents the set of policies that president, Senate, and a majority of House members prefer to the status quo. The gray area represents the set of policies for which the House and Senate will override a presidential rejection. The fact that these two areas are not connected alters the bargaining dynamics in an important way.

Instead of choosing a point on a continuous one-dimensional policy space, actors in this model can use the threat of a very different kind of outcome, say, the "override" subset of the CS, when bargaining with other actors. Substantively, disconnected constitutional sets are a consequence of the fact

[11] The final stage yields $L = r \neq q$ iff one of the conditions is met: (i) $s \neq p, |s - q| - |s - r| > 0$ and $|p - q| - |p - r| > 0$, (ii) $s = p = Fi, |s - q| - |s - r| > 0$, and $|Fj - q| - |Fj - r| > 0$, for $j \neq i$, and (iii) $s \neq p, \%p \leq 1/3, |p - q| - |p - r| \leq 0, |s - q| - |s - r| \upsilon > 0$, and $|Fj - q| - |Fj - r| > 0$ for $Fj \notin \{s, p\}$.

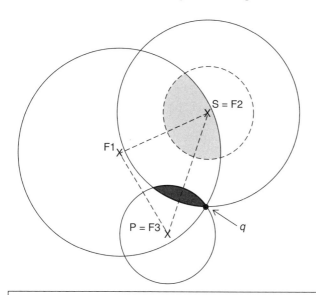

Policies unanimously preferred to status quo q by all House factions (F_1,F_2,F_3), the Senate, and the president

Policies sufficiently preferred to status quo q by House factions F_1 and F_2 (the majority party), and two-thirds of the Senate. Thus, approved by an override of a presidential veto.

FIGURE 3.3. Disconnected constitutional sets.

that Article 1, Section 7 allows laws to be made by two different types of coalitions – a House majority/Senate majority/presidential coalition *or* a House supermajority/Senate supermajority coalition. Knowing the shape of the CS, the House and the Senate negotiate a bicameral agreement. Let mid_i be the midpoint of the line connecting Fi, the House's ideal point, and s, the Senate's ideal point. This point "splits the difference" between the chambers' ideal points and is the default bicameral agreement. By assumption, if $mid_i \in CS$, then $r_i = mid_i$. When this midpoint is not in the CS, the algorithm searches for the point closest to mid_i that is in the CS. Call this "*second best*" point, sec_i. Therefore, $r_i \in \{mid_i, sec_i\}$ denotes the bicameral agreement. Appendix B includes a complete specification of the conditions under which each kind of bicameral agreement emerges.

The bicameral agreement's most important implication is as follows: Holding all House members' ideal points constant and shifting the Senate or president's ideal point, or both, the CS will change. The reason is that a change in the shape of the CS can affect whether or not the midpoint between a House faction's ideal point and the Senate's ideal point is in the new CS. As a result, changes in the shape of the CS can alter the values of current and potential House power-

sharing arrangements. Such alterations can affect all factions' bargaining leverage, which can change the outcome of the power-sharing game. Hence, changes
in the shape of the CS are the vehicle through which senatorial or presidential
preference shifts affect House power-sharing rules.

This takes us back to the House, where House factions, knowing the shape
of the CS as well as the Senate position in the bicameral agreement stage,
decide how to distribute power among themselves. Both stages of the legislative game influence the House's power-sharing choices.

I now characterize the decision made by House players in the power-sharing
game. Since the model joins two distinctively structured bargaining games, the
power-sharing game and the legislative game, where each stage allows a non-
trivial number of possible relations among variables, the number of possible
contingent relationships among variables in the model is large. Proving that the
game yields a unique equilibrium requires a full accounting of all such contingencies and thus makes the formal statement of power-sharing game equilibrium strategies quite long. Appendix B gives a full accounting. Here, I offer a
more intuitive presentation.

Consider the moment in the game when faction F_1 offers a new power-sharing rule to F_2 or F_3. First, F_1 considers the consequences of F_2 and F_3 rejecting
its offer and asks, "Will rejection lead to the continuation of the status quo
rules or to an agreement between F_2 and F_3?" Second, F_1 determines which
shares of power each faction will accept, taking into consideration that F_2 and
F_3 will each accept a power-sharing rule only if it provides at least as much
utility as either would gain from a rule that F_2 would later offer to F_3. Third,
if there exists a rule that is acceptable to F_2 or F_3, and that makes F_1 better off
than the status quo, then F_1 will offer a rule. Fourth, if there is more than one
such rule, F_1 offers the rule that maximizes its expected utility.

An example is depicted in Figure 3.4. In it, the president and Senate share
ideal point *(20, 34)* with House faction F_1. Factions F_2 and F_3 have ideal points
(40, 17) and *(0, 0)*, respectively. F_1 controls 40 percent of House members,
while F_2 and F_3 control 20 percent and 40 percent, respectively. The status quo
is located at *(20, 15)*. Two of the three possible reconciliations will be the midpoint of the line connecting the Senate's ideal point to that of the named faction,
$r_2 = (30, 25.5)$ and $r_3 = (10.4, 17.6)$. F_1 and the Senate share an ideal point, so
$r_1 = (20, 34)$ coincides with F_1. The president also shares F_1's ideal point.

The outcome in this game is a power-sharing arrangement between fac-
tions F_1 and F_2, where $c^*_{1^2} = .53$. Hence, $L = r_1 = (20, 34)$ with probability
.53 and $L = r_2 = (30, 25.5)$ with probability .47. To understand this outcome,
we need to look at the utilities, in the table below Figure 3.4. Note that if F_1
believed that F_2 would reject its offer, then F_1 could offer $c_1^3 = .24$ to F_3, which
F_3 would accept. Note that F_3 gains 23.4 more utils with a F_1-F_3 coalition
than with a F_1-F_2 coalition, while F_2 loses 9 utils with the F_1-F_3 coalition.

Although this offer makes F_1 worse off, as it loses 8.2 utils compared to
the F_1-F_2 outcome, it is better than what would happen if F_3 were to reject

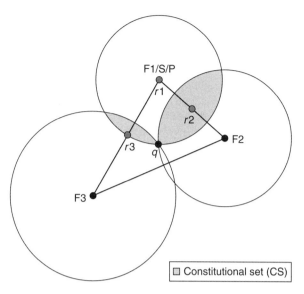

Utility for F1, F2, and F3, given the power-sharing arrangements

Powe-Sharing Arrangement	$U_{F1}(c_i^k)$	$U_{F2}(c_i^k)$	$U_{F3}(c_i^k)$
$c^*{}_1{}^2 = .53$	−6.2	−20	−48.4
$c_1{}^3 = .24$	−14.4	−28.9	−25
$c_2{}^3 = 1$	−13.1	−13.1	−39.4
q	−19	−20	−25

FIGURE 3.4. Power-sharing arrangement example.

the offer. *F2* would subsequently make an offer to *F3* where *F2* retained all power; *F3* would reject this offer because it makes him worse off than keeping the status quo, as *F3* loses 14.4 utils with the *F2-F3* coalition compared to the status quo. When *F1* or *F2* can credibly threaten to share power with *F3*, *F3*'s bargaining power influences the balance of power within the majority party (*F1* and *F2*).

CONCLUSION

Currently, prominent theories of House rule making center on (i) powerful committees (Shepsle 1979; Shepsle and Weingast 1987), (ii) the median member of the floor (Krehbiel 1991; Krehbiel and Meirowitz 2002), or (iii) the preferences of the majority party (Aldrich 1994; Aldrich and Rohde 2000; Cox and McCubbins 1993; 2005). Proponents of these theories reach different results, in part, because they emphasize particular institutional arrangements (i.e., committees have ex-post veto power, legislative minorities can offer motions to recommit, and majority parties have agenda-setting powers). Debates among the supporters of the various theories have reduced to debates over the relative importance of the arrangements in question. My approach to questions about how the House distributes power among its members has a different orientation. I do not make any specific assumptions about the rules and procedures that govern the House. I regard such decisions as endogenous to the choices legislators make in their first round of negotiations. As a result, my description of House bargaining dynamics differs from those described at the outset.

If House members are foresighted, then they have an incentive to consider the implications of Article I, Section 7 in the organizational decisions they make under Article I, Section 5. Consequently, shifts in the Senate's or president's preferences can and often will affect House-rule changes. A change in the ideal point of the Senate or the president can alter House factions' expectations about the legislative consequences of power-sharing rules, and anticipating those consequences can lead factions to change the rules to leverage power and legislative influence.

These conclusions are essential to predicting and understanding the timing and directionality of changes in the distribution of power in the House, the topic of the next two chapters.

4

Timing of House Organizational Changes

The importance of the Constitutional Theory of Legislative Organization I set forth in the preceding chapter stems from its implications for the timing and directionality of House power-sharing arrangements. House rules change predictably as the set of constitutional actors changes; rules and procedures that are optimal for legislating within one bargaining environment are not optimal in another. Indeed, I show in this chapter and the next, changes in the preferences of constitutional actors are essential to understanding when and why House majority party members entrust power in the Speaker and his or her supporters or distribute it more widely across the broader party delegation.

This chapter focuses on timing. I show formally and empirically that shifts in the Senate's and/or president's preferences increase the likelihood that the House adopts new rules. In the next chapter, I show how the new rules are designed to maximize the House's power within the changed context. What might appear as mere internal management is, in fact, forward-looking political calculation.

I first review existing theories and summarize their predictions about when new rules and procedures will be adopted. I then present my theory, show how it differs from existing theories, and, finally, analyze the adoption of major rules since 1879.

TIMING OF RULE CHANGES: CURRENT PERSPECTIVES

Extant theories on the timing of House-rule changes share a common assumption: Rational and strategic House members consider the preference configurations within their own chamber when deciding whether to adopt new rules for the upcoming congressional term. In other words, all theories assume that changes in House members' preferences largely determine the timing of rule changes.

In majoritarian theories, the preference that matters is the floor median, since final legislative decisions are made by a House majority. Krehbiel explains that

> the Majoritarian Postulate holds that objects of legislative choice in both the procedural and policy domains must be chosen by a majority of the legislature. (Krehbiel 1991, 249)

When the floor median changes, existing procedures and rules limit the new median member's capacity to meet its objectives, and so new organizational arrangements are adopted (Krehbiel 1991; Gilligan and Krehbiel 1989; 1990).

Other theories look to changes in House majority and minority party members' preferences to predict the timing of new rules. In the conditional party government model (Aldrich 1994; Aldrich and Rohde 1997; 1998; 2000; 2001; Rohde 1991), the majority party issues new rules in response to significant changes in the degree of intraparty homogeneity and interparty heterogeneity. When majority party preferences become more homogeneous and more dissimilar to the minority party preferences, then the majority party adopts new rules that advance its objectives. A related theory emphasizes changes in the relative capacities of majority and minority parties (Binder 1997). It stipulates that the timing of new rules depends on both changes in the size of the majority party and changes in the cohesiveness of the minority party relative to the majority party.

The party cartel theory (e.g., Cox and McCubbins 1993; 2005) posits that the majority party in the House manages the legislative process and strategically employs rules to capture the collective benefits of a coherent brand name:

> The House has structured the delegation of authority ... to ensure that the majority party has an advantage in setting the legislative agenda on both the floor and in the committee. (Cox and McCubbins 1993, 233)

Changes in rules are viewed as the result of changes within the House majority party; when its preferences change, the majority party adopts new organizational schemes and procedures to achieve the party's collective benefits.

Although the preceding works offer competing predictions of the timing of changes in House rules, all assume that rational and foresighted House members look only at the preferences of fellow chamber members when adopting rules designed to help them achieve their preferred policy outcomes. Assuming, as I do, that House members anticipate the preferences of other constitutional actors at the time they ponder rule changes generates different predictions about when such changes will occur.

CONSTITUTIONAL ACTORS AND THE TIMING OF RULE
CHANGES: EMPIRICAL IMPLICATIONS

In Chapter 3, I defined the subset of the policy space preferred to the status quo by the Senate, the president, and the House majority as the *constitutional set*

(CS); bills outside it are not viable legislative outcomes. I further showed that, even when holding the ideal points of House members constant, changing those of the Senate or the president alters the shape of the CS by changing the set of feasible legislative outcomes. The House rules that previously served the majority party most likely will no longer be optimal. Shifts in senatorial or presidential preferences, because they change the shape of the CS, cause the House to alter its power-sharing rules.

For instance, the shape of the CS changed considerably between the 110th and 111th Congresses. During the 110th Congress (2007–2009), the Democratic Party controlled the House and Senate majority while Republicans controlled the White House. At the beginning of the 111th Congress (2009–2010), a Democrat, Barack Obama, now occupied the presidency. This change in the CS meant that bills likely to become laws during the 110th Congress differed markedly from those likely to become laws during the 111th Congress. As noted in Chapter 1, the Democratic majority in 2009 made radical changes to the power-sharing rules that their same majority adopted in 2007, when it initially regained majority status. A power-sharing arrangement that served both factions of the House Democratic Party when dealing with a CS that included Republican president George W. Bush was no longer optimal when Democrat Barack Obama replaced him.

The Model's Implications for Timing: When Do House Members Adopt New Rules?

To understand how preferences of the Senate and the president create expectations among House members about what it will take to pass their preferred legislation, consider Figure 4.1, which depicts an initial distribution of constitutional actors' ideal points. In it, the president, Senate, and House faction $F2$ share the ideal point *(12, 12)*. House factions $F1$ and $F3$ have ideal points *(0, 24)* and *(30, 30)*, respectively. The status quo is *(24, 18)*. $F1$ controls 40 percent of the House, and $F2$ and $F3$ control 35 percent and 25 percent, respectively. Factions engage in power-sharing negotiations knowing that the bicameral agreement resulting from an agreement between $F1$ and the Senate will be $r_1 = (6, 18)$, and that resulting from an $F3$-Senate agreement will be $r_3 = (21, 21)$, with both bicameral agreements being midpoints between the Senate's ideal point and that of the relevant House faction ($F1$ or $F3$). Since the Senate and $F2$ share ideal point $r_2 = (12, 12)$, they will adopt it as the bicameral agreement.

The outcome of this game is a power-sharing arrangement between $F1$ and $F2$, where $c_1^{*2} = 1$, $F1$ represents the House in all bicameral negotiations, and $L = r_1 = (6, 18)$. This rule is sufficient to induce faction $F2$ to form a coalition with $F1$, rather than allowing power-sharing negotiations to continue. To see why, note that if $F1$ thought that $F2$ would reject $c_1^{*2} = 1$, $F1$ could offer to $F3$, $c_1^3 = .05$, which is the minimal offer from $F1$ that $F3$ would accept. Since $F2$'s

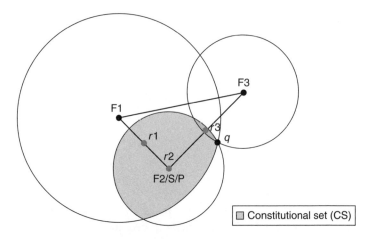

Utilities for F1, F2, and F3, given the power-sharing arrangements

Power-Sharing Arrangement	$U_{F1}(c_i^k)$	$U_{F2}(c_i^k)$	$U_{F3}(c_i^k)$
$c^*{}_1{}^2 = 1$	−8.5	−8.5	−26.8
$c_1{}^3 = .05$	−20.6	−12.42	−13.4
$c_2{}^3 = .05$	−21	−12.06	−13.4
q	−24.7	−13.4	−13.4

FIGURE 4.1. Timing of rule changes: example 1.

expected utility from this $F1$-$F3$ rule is less than the utility from $L = (6, 18)$, $F2$ accepts the offer from $F1$ described previously. $F1$, in turn, offers the rule to $F2$ because it prefers $L = (6, 18)$ to the policy consequences of the rule that would gain $F3$'s acceptance.

Suppose that an election shifts the Senate's ideal point from $F2$ to $F3$ and that all other ideal points remain constant. The shift radically reshapes the CS (Figure 4.2). Since $F3$ now shares the Senate's preferences, these preferences constrain any possible bicameral agreement. $F2$ remains aligned with the president and has enough members (35 percent of House membership) to prevent an override. Therefore, shifting the Senate's ideal point from $F2$ to $F3$ reduces the CS to the intersection of the set of points that both $F2$ and $F3$ prefer to q, a very small set.

This shift in the Senate's ideal point causes House members to seek a new power-sharing rule. The result is an $F1$-$F3$ coalition, where $c_1{}^3 = .50$. In other words, the game produces outcome $L = r_1 = (18, 24)$ with probability .50 and outcome $L = r_3 = (21.5, 21.5)$ with probability .50. These outcomes are sufficient for $F3$ to accept $F1$'s offer. Were $F3$ to reject the offer, then $F2$ would offer $c_1{}^3 = 1$, which would give $F2$ total control, $r_2 = (21, 21)$. While that outcome would make $F3$ at least as well off as accepting the status quo, $F1$ can make

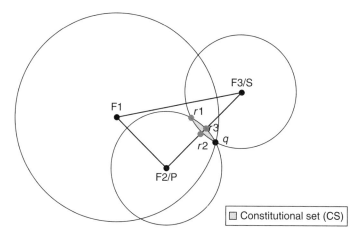

Utilities for F1, F2, and F3, given the power-sharing arrangements

Power-Sharing Arrangement	$U_{F1}(c_i^k)$	$U_{F2}(c_i^k)$	$U_{F3}(c_i^k)$
$c_1^{*2} = 0$	−21.2	−12.7	−12.7
$c_1^3 = .5$	−19.8	−13.4	−12.7
$c_2^3 = 1$	−21.2	−12.7	−12.7
q	−24.7	−13.4	−13.4

FIGURE 4.2. Timing of rule changes: example 2.

$F3$ marginally better off with the offer $c_1^3 = .50$ while making itself better off than it would be under a $F2$-$F3$ rule. Even though the policy preferences of all House members remain unchanged, the distribution of power among House factions changes substantially. While $c_1^{*2} = 1$ was an optimal arrangement when $F2 = s = p$, the shift in Senate preferences alters the rules that factions are willing to offer or accept.

The following proposition states the core empirical implication regarding timing:

> When a shift in the ideal point of the Senate or president (or shifts in both) changes the shape of the CS in such a way that it affects the value of at least one existing power-sharing rule for at least one of the three House factions, then the shift causes a rule change.

In other words, even holding constant every House member's ideal point, a shift in the ideal point of the Senate or the president can change the shape of the CS and, therefore, change the House's rules.[1]

In what follows, I test this proposition in multiple ways. First, however, I explain how I measure change in House rules.

---

[1] A change in only one faction's preferences can have a ripple effect; when one faction changes which rules it is willing to offer or accept, it reshapes the bargaining leverage of all factions.

HOUSE RULES: DEFINING THE UNIVERSE OF RULES
AND ORGANIZATIONAL CHANGES

To create my measure of rule change, I began with Schickler's original list of rules and procedures,[2] even though he coded his data for a different purpose, that is, to distinguish between rules "that were intended either to advantage the majority party and its leaders or to undermine them" (Schickler 2000, 271).[3] I then modified his data, first, by updating his list of rules and procedures through the 112th Congress;[4] second, by including rules and procedures that he did not take into account; and, third and most significantly, by analyzing the effect of rules on the distribution of power among the House majority party factions, not among the House majority and minority parties.[5] In this chapter I will focus on whether a particular Congress adopted new rules, leaving the discussion regarding the effect of the new rules for Chapter 5.

Because Schickler focuses on the majority party as a whole, and not on majority party factions, he does not include some rule changes I include. Certain rule changes would not affect the majority party's power as a whole, although they could reshape the distribution of power among factions within the majority party. From the perspective of the constitutional theory, therefore, such changes must be taken into account. For example, Schickler does not include the repeal of the Holman rule in his list because he argues that it did not affect the power of the majority party vis-à-vis the minority. I concur with his logic; for my theory, however, it is crucial to know that the repeal of the Holman rule affected the relative power of the factions within the majority party. First, the Holman rule empowered the members of the Appropriations Committee, who could add riders to appropriation bills that, if presented as single bills, would be vetoed by the president (Kiewiet and McCubbins 1991; Stewart 1989). When the House majority removed the rule, the power that had been vested in the members of the Appropriations Committee was transferred to the Speaker, who controlled the agenda and the introduction of amendments. Thus, even though the overall power of the majority party did not change, the distribution of power within the party did.

---

[2] Schickler relies on leading sources of congressional history of rules and procedures to create his impressive data set.

[3] Another important list of rules and procedures is provided in Binder (1997). Although her list overlaps significantly with Schickler's, they are not identical, and the emphasis is different. Whereas Schickler's focus is rules as they affect the majority party, Binder's list emphasizes the effect of rules on the minority party.

[4] Schickler coded new rules through the 104th Congress (1995–1996).

[5] For the time period in which my analyses overlap with Schickler's, he identifies thirty-three Congresses in which rule changes occurred; I identify thirty-six Congresses. My coding of the effect of rules differs from Schickler for ten Congresses. For more detail, see the online appendix. Of course, our coding should not overlap completely, given our very different purposes. While some rule changes did not affect the majority party's power vis-à-vis the minority party's, they did reshape the distribution of power between factions within the majority party.

TABLE 4.1. *Schickler and Sin's classification of changes and no changes in rules, by Congress*

	Sin: Changes in Rules	Sin: No Changes in Rules	Sin: Recent Congresses
Schickler: Changes in rules	33 Congresses (46th, 47th, 51st–54th, 60th–62nd, 64th, 66th, 68th, 69th, 72nd–74th, 79th–82nd, 87th, 89th–96th, 98th, 102nd, 103rd, and 104th)		
Schickler: No changes in rules	3 Congresses (49th, 67th, and 100th)	24 Congresses (48th, 50th, 55th–59th, 63rd, 65th, 70th, 71st, 75th–78th, 83rd–86th, 88th, 97th, 99th, 101st, 105th)	
Schickler: Recent Congresses not included in his analysis			7 Congresses (106th–112th)

For the period in which my analyses overlap with Schickler's, I identify thirty-six Congresses that changed their rules. By contrast, Schickler identified thirty-three Congresses. Table 4.1 summarizes the commonalities and differences between the two classifications. Appendix C presents a complete list of the rules and procedures considered in this study,[6] and Appendix D explains in detail the rules adopted during those three additional Congresses.

[6] I identified additional rule changes for some congresses that Schickler had already placed into the "rule change" category. Again, he did not include these rules because they were not germane to his majority-minority focus. One example is the changes to the Democratic caucus rules in the early 1970s. Although the rule changes did not affect the House per se, it did affect the distribution of power within the majority party. The new caucus rules authorized a secret ballot on committee chairs if 20% of the caucus demanded it, established a limit on the number of subcommittee chairs anyone could hold, and enacted the Subcommittee Bill of Rights. I included these new caucus rules in the list because they directly affected the distribution of authority within the House by altering the power of committee chairs and the membership and power of subcommittees (Bibby and Davidson 1972; Rohde 1974; Ornstein 1975). *Congressional Quarterly* stated that "DSG [Democratic Study Group] members agree that the reforms enacted in January and

My unit of analysis is a Congress, and the measure is whether the Congress changed at least one major rule. Binder (1997), Schickler (2000; 2001), and Cox and McCubbins (2005) all endorse this approach, arguing that there are too many problems inherent in trying to define what constitutes a single rule. In the words of Cox and McCubbins, this task fringes on the impossible because "each House rule is itself subdivided into clauses that are logically separable, and each clause often contains many potentially independent stipulations" (Cox and McCubbins 2005, 52). In following the lead of other scholars, I, like they, seek to reduce subjective interpretation.

Using the Congress as my unit of analysis also allows me to ignore the distinction between when the election occurs and when the legislature first convenes. This is important because, although since the passage of the Twentieth Amendment in 1933, there is (roughly) a two-month "lame duck" period between the general election and the subsequent convening of Congress, there was a much longer gap between the fall election and the first meeting of Congress previously.[7]

CONSTITUTIONAL ACTORS AND THE TIMING OF RULE CHANGES: EMPIRICAL ANALYSIS

The Constitutional Theory of Legislative Organization predicts the following: Suppose there is at least one shift in the ideal point of at least one of the House factions, the Senate, and/or the president; suppose, furthermore, that that shift reshapes the CS and, thus, the position of at least one bicameral agreement; then the shift may induce House members to change their power-sharing rules.

As an empirical matter, I use partisan change in one or more of the constitutional actors as a measure of CS change. The detailed research on House party factions, the Speakers, and the presidents (see Chapter 2) show this to be a good measure of CS change. However, I identified two instances where the partisanship of the House factions, Senate, and president did not change, yet the CS changed because the preferences of the newly elected president differed noticeably from those of his predecessor, who had been aligned with another faction of the majority party. One is the 61st Congress, when William H. Taft replaced Theodore Roosevelt; while Roosevelt was clearly aligned with the Progressive faction, Taft was closer to the conservatives. I review this case in depth in Chapter 7. The other is the replacement of Warren Harding with Calvin Coolidge, a case that I summarize in Appendix E.

February [1973] signaled a major change in the flow of House power and a major victory for the DSG itself" ("Democratic Study Group: A Winner on House Reforms" 1973).

[7] By taking each Congress as the unit of analysis, I also finesse the distinction between "normal" changes in control of a chamber that follow from general elections and a small number that took place within a Congress by the creation of vacancies and subsequent appointments or special elections and/or party switching by sitting members.

My empirical analysis proceeds as follows. First, I examine a single case, the 87th Congress's adoption of new rules in 1961. The new rules increased the membership of the Rules Committee, and thus decisively tipped the balance of power within the Democratic Party in favor of northern Democrats. Although focusing on a single case precludes making general statements that apply across Congresses, it facilitates in-depth exploration in a way that large-N quantitative studies cannot. I next analyze rule adoption from the 104th Congress (1995–1997) to the 112th Congress (2011–2013). The 104th Congress signals the return of the Republican Party to the House majority, after being in the minority for more than forty years. Therefore, changes in the CS during this period could be a result of changes in the partisanship of any one or more of the three constitutional actors: Senate, president, and/or House. A quantitative analysis of rule changes during these eighteen years will reveal whether a change in the partisanship of the Senate and/or president, even when the House majority party did not change, prompted the House to adopt new rules.

These time-limited data lack sufficient variability in factors representing alternative explanations of House-rule changes. The remaining three analyses, therefore, include the sixty-seven Congresses from 1879 to 2013. In the first of these three analyses, I use *Change in CS* as the key independent variable. It measures change in CS simply, as a change in the partisanship of any one of the constitutional actors. This variable bundles together different sources of change in the CS, on the premise that any CS change is a sufficient condition for a change in House rules, whether it was produced by changes in the partisanship of the House, Senate, or president or by any combination of the three. In the second of the three analyses, I use a different independent variable, *Shift in the Partisan Control of Constitutional Actors*, which distinguishes among the sources of the CS change. This more refined measure of CS change allows me to determine whether, as others have argued, changes within the House membership alone drive results. Finally, I show the percentage of times the House changed its rules, given the different sources of change in the CS. The percentages have the advantage of showing very clearly the number of Congresses that, after experiencing a particular change in the CS, changed their rules.

House Rule Changes, 1961

I begin with a single case: the rules adopted by the Democratic House majority early in the 87th Congress (1961–1963). The new House rules enlarged the House conservative-controlled Rules Committee from twelve to fifteen members. Peabody claims that

> by adding two pro-Administration Democrats and only one Republican to a
> committee previously dominated by two conservative southern Democrats and

the four Republican minority members, a six to six stalemate was converted to an eight-to-seven majority generally sympathetic to the needs of the Democratic leadership. (1963, 130)

This major redistribution of power in the House made it next to impossible for the Rules Committee's "conservative members [to] kill the president's New Frontier program" (Oleszek 2001, 119).

The composition of the House did not change significantly before or after the 1960 election. The DW-NOMINATE scores for the Democratic median in the House were −.259 in the 86th Congress, before Kennedy's election, and −.258 in the 87th Congress, after Kennedy's election (http://voteview.com/pmediant. htm). The minority Republican Party also did not change, with scores of .243 in the 86th Congress and .231 in the 87th Congress. Shifts in House member preferences do not explain why the 1961 House Democratic majority enlarged the Rules Committee.

So why, then, did the Democratic majority change the rules? The constitutional theory points to the presidential change in 1961, when liberal Democrat John F. Kennedy replaced Republican Dwight D. Eisenhower. Prior to Kennedy's election, when a Republican was president, a liberalization of the Rules Committee would not have facilitated the approval of liberal Democrats' preferred policies. Bills still needed to be within Eisenhower's win set. However, the election of Kennedy meant that, with the help of a liberalized Rules Committee, liberal Democrats were better positioned to transform their preferred policies into laws. As Oleszek anticipated, and my model now explains, Kennedy's election altered the CS, and, in turn, prompted changes in House rules.

House Rule Changes, 1995–2013

In the midterm elections of 1994, the Republican Party took over the House majority in what is now known as the "Gingrich Revolution," headed by soon-to-be Speaker of the House Newt Gingrich (R-GA). With this partisan change, control of the House majority once again became a matter of dispute between Republicans and Democrats, for the first time since 1955.

Changes in the CS during the eighteen years that followed the Republican takeover had diverse sources: changes in the partisanship of just the House, Senate, or president or changes in the partisanship of any two of these actors, that is, House and Senate or Senate and president. Looking in detail at these eighteen years is important to understanding which sources of CS change affected rules adoption. More to the point, are changes in the House majority the only ones that matter for rule adoption?

Table 4.2 reports the timing of rule changes, starting with the 104th Congress. The table shows that whenever the party of the House majority

TABLE 4.2. *Relationship between partisan change in constitutional actors and changes in rules, 1995–2013*

	President	Senate[a]	House[a]	Speaker (faction)	CS Change (source)	House Rules Change
1995–96 (104)	Clinton (D)	Rep. (+6, +6)	Rep. (+26, +38)	Gingrich (New Right)	Yes (House/Senate)	Yes
1997–98 (105)	Clinton (D)	Rep. (+10, +10)	Rep. (+20, +22)	Gingrich (New Right)	No	No
1999–00 (106)	Clinton (D)	Rep. (+10, +8)	Rep. (+12, +14)	Hastert (New Right)	No	No
2001–02 (107)	Bush (R)	both (0, +1)[b]	Rep. (+10, +12)	Hastert (New Right)	Yes (president/Senate)	Yes
2003–04 (108)	Bush (R)	Rep. (+3, +3)	Rep. (+24, +22)	Hastert (New Right)	Yes (Senate)	Yes
2005–06 (109)	Bush (R)	Rep. (+11, +11)	Rep. (+31, +28)	Hastert (New Right)	No	No
2007–08 (110)	Bush (R)	Dem. (+2, +1)[c]	Dem. (+31, +37)	Pelosi (Liberal)	Yes (House)	Yes
2009–10 (111)	Obama (D)	Dem. (+16, +16)	Dem. (+78, +76)	Pelosi (Liberal)	Yes (president)	Yes
2011–13 (112)	Obama (D)	Dem. (+6, +6)	Rep. (+49, +49)	Boehner (Conservative)	Yes (House)	Yes

Notes: [a] Seat margin at opening and end of each session shown in parentheses.

[b] U.S. Senate control in the 107th Congress switched multiple times. On January 3, 2001, the Senate convened with 50 Republican and 50 Democratic members, and Democratic vice president Al Gore was able to break ties as president of the Senate. The January 20 inauguration of George W. Bush gave the role of tiebreaker to Vice President Richard Cheney, switching formal control from the Democrats to the Republicans. On May 24, 2001, however, Vermont senator James Jeffords left the Republican Party and began to caucus with the Democratic members as an "independent," switching Senate control back to the Democratic Party. On October 25, 2002, Democratic senator Paul Wellstone died in a plane crash, leaving behind a Senate of 49 Democrats and 49 Republicans, with Jeffords still the tiebreaker. On November 5, 2002, Republican Norm Coleman won the election to the 108th Congress for the seat vacated by Wellstone. However, the day before, Minnesota governor Jesse Ventura, of the Reform Party, appointed independent Dean Barkley to serve the remainder of Wellstone's term. Unlike Jeffords, Barkley caucused with neither major party, leaving Democrats in control 49 + 1 to 49 to 1. The November general election for the 108th Congress coincided with a special election in Missouri to fill its (Class 1) Senate seat for the remainder of the 107th. In January 2001, Democrat Jean Carnahan had been appointed to fill the vacancy caused by the death of her husband, Mel, in yet another plane crash in October 2000 (his November 2000 election was posthumous). Republican Jim Talent defeated Carnahan in both the general and special elections and was seated on November 25, 2002, creating Republican Party control of the Senate for the conclusion of the session (50 to 48 + 1 to 1).

[c] The 110th Congress opened with 49 Republican and 49 Democratic senators, plus two members elected as independents who nonetheless caucused with the Democrats – Bernie Sanders of Vermont and Joe Lieberman of Connecticut – giving them formal control of the chamber.

(110th and 112th Congresses), Senate majority (108th Congress), or president (111th Congress) changed hands, the House made important rule changes. A change in the CS generated by a change in only one, and any one, constitutional actor was sufficient to prompt the House majority party to change its internal distribution of power. A change in the partisanship of more than one constitutional actor (104th and 107th Congresses) also brought about House-rule changes. When no constitutional actor's partisanship changed – the 105th, 106th, and 109th Congresses – neither did House rules change. In short, a change in the House majority party alone is sufficient but not necessary for the adoption of new rules.

A shift in the partisanship of the Senate and/or the president, even when the House majority ideal point remains constant, almost always reshapes the CS, and creates a strong incentive for a change in the House's power-sharing rules. It is next to impossible to explain this pattern in the timing of rule changes without taking into account that foresighted House members anticipated the consequences of a change in the preference of the Senate and/or president when deciding whether to reallocate power among themselves.

My next analyses cover all Congresses and incorporate factors representing alternative explanations of legislative organization.

House Rule Changes, 1879–2013

Most of the existing literature on House organization argues that changes in the ideological compositions of the House majority and minority parties, as measured by roll call data, explain the adoption of new House rules. Although scholars share a unitary focus on the House, they disagree on which ideological changes are most fundamental. Some scholars emphasize the House median, others emphasize party medians, and still others emphasize levels of party homogeneity and party size. By including these other scholars' measures, I account for the possibility that there was a meaningful change in the majority party's overall ideological composition along the liberal-conservative dimension, even though the partisanship of the House majority party did not change.[8] For example, competing theories would argue that, when the House majority remains constant, new rules are adopted not because the Senate's or president's preferences change but, rather, because the House majority party becomes more extreme or moderate, or more or less homogeneous. In the analyses that follow, I include the following measures of changes in House members' preferences.[9]

---

[8] All these measures are based on DW-NOMINATE scores, which measure preferences expressed through roll call votes.

[9] The data for the covariates are based on DW-NOMINATE. I followed Schickler's (2000) lead in how to construct each variable.

Change in House median (Schickler 2000; 2001) captures changes, from one Congress to the next, in the relative distance of the floor median to the majority and minority party medians. As the chamber median moves closer to the majority party median, and further from the minority party median, House-rule changes that advantage the majority party are more likely to occur. Constructing the measure entails taking the difference in the absolute values of the distance between (i) the floor median and minority party median and (ii) the floor median and majority party median, that is, Abs(Median floor – Median minority) – Abs(Median floor – Median majority).

Four covariates, *Change in party homogeneity, Change in party polarization, Change in party capacity, and Change in majority party size*, capture changes in majority party membership between two Congresses. *Change in party homogeneity* is the ratio of the standard deviation of majority party members and the standard deviation of all floor members (Cox and McCubbins 1993; 2005; Aldrich and Rohde 2000; 2001). It measures changes in the preference homogeneity of House majority party members; the higher the homogeneity level and thus the consensus within the party, the greater the likelihood of new rules that delegate power to the Speaker. *Change in party polarization* (Aldrich and Rohde 2000; 2001) measures the change in the difference between the majority and minority party medians between Congresses. It hypothesizes that large changes in the distance between party medians increase the probability of major rule adoption. *Change in party capacity* (Binder 1997) measures the difference in strength between the majority and minority parties from one Congress to the next, which depends on the size of the party and the degree of ideological cohesion.[10] *Change in majority party size* measures changes in the proportion of members belonging to the majority party. Dion (1997) argues that the smaller the majority, the more likely it is to change (and use) the rules to achieve its objectives.

The analyses in this section begin with the 46th Congress (1879–1881). With this Congress, the House majority party began enacting rules to empower itself to shape chamber business, a practice that has since continued. Starting in 1879, the majority party founded "the modern structure of agenda power in the House – in which access to the floor is regulated by the Rules Committee and the delegation of privilege to selected committees" (Cox and McCubbins 2005, 50). The sixty-seven Congresses from 1879 until 2013 cover a variety of CS changes.

I use two different measures of CS change. The first measure, *Change in CS,* is a dichotomous variable. Whenever there is a partisan change in any one or

---

[10] More specifically, Party Capacity is the difference between majority and minority party capacity. Majority party capacity is equal to the Majority Party Rice Cohesion score, which is calculated as the degree of division within the majority party, times the percentage of majority party membership in the House. Minority Party capacity is calculated in the same way.

more of the three constitutional actors – House majority, Senate majority, and/
or president – from one session to the next, *Change in CS* takes a value of 1.
Combining changes in each individual constitutional actor's partisanship, this
variable assumes that any change in the CS is sufficient to induce House members to adopt new rules.

However, distinguishing the source of the CS change is necessary to pit my
theory against others, all of which argue that changes within the House majority party are the key to predicting the adoption of new House rules. The second
measure, *Shift in the partisan control of constitutional actors,* distinguishes
among the following possibilities: (i) shift in the House majority party, but no
shift in the Senate's majority party and the president's party; (ii) shift in the
House majority party and shift only in the Senate's majority party, or the president's party, or in both the Senate's majority party and the President's party;
and, (iii) no shift in the House majority party, and shift in the Senate's and/or
president's party.

Table 4.3 presents the results using my first independent variable, *Change
in CS*. This analysis is crucial because it directly tests a prediction of the constitutional theory that a change in the CS, no matter the source, increases the
likelihood of rule changes in the House. The estimates in the models are based
on logistic regression.[11]

The first model includes only my *Change in CS* variable. It shows that a
change in the CS has a strong effect on the adoption of new House rules;
this change increases the odds of rule change by a factor of 8.25. The other
models include *Change in CS* with other combinations of factors that measure
change in the ideological composition of the House. Regardless of specification,
Change in CS strongly affects the timing of major rule changes in the House.
Indeed, *Change in CS* is the only variable that consistently reaches statistical
significance, regardless of how many other covariates are included.[12] The finding that a change in the CS affects the likelihood of new rules comports with
the Constitutional Theory of Legislative Organization.

Supporters of current theories might object that changes in the House majority party are driving the results, since *Changes in CS* bundles different sources of
CS change. To address this possibility, I substitute *Shift in the partisan control*

---

[11] The time series nature of the data is a reasonable worry. In this case, I assume that the probability of rules change is constant across Congresses, controlling for the covariates. If, instead, the
data follow some sort of dynamical logic, one would posit that the probability of rule changes is
not constant, but driven by a function wherein adjacent periods are more similar to one another
in baseline probabilities than periods far apart. Both Schickler (2000) and Binder (1997) have
argued that there is no sensible theory of dynamics of rule change: "there are no theoretical reasons to expect…autocorrelation or heteroscedasticity…the historical records lends no evidence
that past reforms have been mimicked by subsequent majorities or that there have been any
learning effects from one Congress to the another" (Binder 1996, 16).

[12] I also conducted a likelihood-ratio test for the *Shift* variable to test whether the coefficient associated with the variable is zero. The null hypothesis that the coefficient associated with the *Shift*
variable is equal to zero can be rejected at the .01 level.

TABLE 4.3. *Logit estimates for changes in House organization, given a change in the CS, 1879–2013*

	Model 1	Model 2	Model 3	Model 4	Model 5	Model 6	Model 7	Model 8	Model 9	Model 10
Change in CS	2.11***	2.17***	2.18***	2.24***	2.14***	2.21***	2.23***	2.13***	2.21***	2.21***
	(.57)	(.60)	(.60)	(.62)	(.59)	(.61)	(.62)	(.61)	(.62)	(.63)
Change in House median		3.95	4.14	6.54		3.74	6.31		3.56	6.64
		(2.15)	(3.42)	(3.81)		(2.17)	(5.99)		(2.14)	(6.17)
Change in party homogeneity						-2.64	1.08	-.02	-1.77	3.84
						(4.61)	(7.36)	(5.07)	(4.66)	(11.62)
Change in party polarization					9.79		5.77	9.00	6.58	6.34
					(8.08)		(8.32)	(8.26)	(8.18)	(8.55)
Change in party capacity			-.000					.003		.001
			(.003)					(.002)		(.006)
Change in majority party size				-.05	.04		-.06			-.09
				(.07)	(.04)		(.11)			(.16)
Constant	-.61	-.61	-.61	-.62	-.64	-.61	-.64	-.61	-.64	-.63
	(.36)	(.37)	(.37)	(.37)	(.37)	(.37)	(.37)	(.37)	(.37)	(.38)
Log likelihood	-37.72	-35.88	-35.88	-35.72	-36.38	-35.71	-35.26	-35.96	-35.39	-35.21

Note: DV: At least one major rule change in a Congress. Cell entries are logit estimates; standard errors in parentheses

*** p < .01, ** p < .05, N = 67.

of constitutional actors for *Change in CS. Shift in the partisan control of con-stitutional actors* differentiates the source of the CS change.

Shift in the partisan control of constitutional actors has four categories: *Change in House–Stable Senate and president, Change in House–Change in Senate and/or president, Stable House–Change in Senate and/or president,* and *No change in the CS,* the latter serving as the reference category. I also include the same measures of change in House membership that I included in Table 4.3, that is, *Change in House median, Change in party homogeneity, Change in party polarization, Change in party capacity,* and *Change in major-ity party size.* Table 4.4 shows the results.

The first model includes the logit estimates for the *Shifts* variable only. The estimate for change in the House majority party does not reach statistical sig-nificance, suggesting that changes in the partisanship of the House majority are not driving the results reported earlier (Table 4.3). The coefficient in the second row shows that a change in the House majority party combined with a change in the partisanship of the Senate and/or president increases the odds of new rule adoption by 7.3. These results still do not pit the constitutional theory against others because it bundles together changes in House partisanship and partisan change of another constitutional actor. However, the third row shows that even though the House majority remains unchanged, shifts in the parti-sanship of actors outside the House appreciably shape rule changes. A change in the partisanship of the Senate majority or the president increases the odds of a rule change by a factor of 9.2. This result is important because it shows that the effect of *Change in CS* is not driven by change in House partisanship, as competing theories presume. House members take into account changes in the partisanship of the Senate and the president in their decisions on whether to adopt new rules.

Models 2–8 include different combinations of additional variables that control for changes in the ideologies of House members. None of them – *Changes in the House median, party capacity, party homogeneity, party polarization, or majority party size* – accounts for the timing of changes in House rules. Even after controlling for other variables that might account for new rule adoption, the *Shift* variable still predicts change in legislative organization.

These results show that even after including factors that capture ideological changes within the House, a change in the Senate and/or president is key to predicting the timing of House rule adoption. The separation of power struc-ture imposed by the Constitution is crucial to understanding the timing of House internal management decisions.

Table 4.5 reports the percentages of Congresses that adopted new rules under each of the four categories of the *Shift in the partisan control of consti-tutional actors* variable. I compare the three different sources of CS change to cases in which no shift in partisanship of the constitutional actors occurred. The constitutional theory predicts that any of the three situations should bring

TABLE 4.4. *Logit estimates for changes in House organization, 1879–2013*

	Model 1	Model 2	Model 3	Model 4	Model 5	Model 6	Model 7	Model 8
Change House, stable Senate, and president	1.99 (1.17)	2.4 (1.25)	2.4 (1.28)	2.73** (1.3)	2.67** (1.32)	2.43 (1.32)	2.65** (1.33)	3.63** (1.67)
Change House, change Senate and/or president	1.99** (.86)	1.81** (.89)	1.8** (.92)	1.95*** (.95)	1.83** (.94)	1.69 (.89)	1.88** (.96)	1.16 (.97)
Stable House, change Senate and/or president	2.21*** (.73)	2.32*** (.76)	2.32*** (.76)	1.69*** (.64)	2.28*** (.75)	2.33*** (.76)	2.29*** (.75)	2.27*** (.76)
Change House median		4.15 (2.19)	4.01 (3.45)	5.93 (3.88)	3.9 (2.21)		4.54 (3.56)	
Change party homogeneity					-3.11 (4.94)		-3.59 (5.34)	
Change party polarization						11.3 (8.82)		15.4 (9.7)
Change party capacity			.000 (.004)				-.000 (.004)	.005 (.003)
Change majority party size				-.07 (.07)		.05 (.04)		-.009 (.06)
Constant	-.61 (.36)	-.61 (.37)	-.61 (.37)	-.68 (.41)	-.61 (.37)	-.65 (.37)	-.62 (.37)	-.64 (.38)
Log likelihood	-37.69	-35.66	-35.75	-37.21	-35.54	-36.18	-35.52	-35.05

Note: DV: At least one major rule change. Cell entries are logit estimates; standard errors in parentheses
*** p < .01, ** p < .05 N= 66.

TABLE 4.5. *Percentage of major rule changes, given different sources of shifts in the partisan control of constitutional actors, 1879–2013*

Shift in the Partisan Control of Constitutional Actors	Outcomes
Shift in partisan control of the House majority, stable Senate majority, and president's party 5 out of 67 Congresses (7 percent)	80 percent of Houses change major rules
Shift in partisan control of the House majority, and Senate majority and/or president's party 10 out of 67 Congresses (15 percent)	80 percent of Houses change major rules
Shift in partisan control of the Senate majority and/or president, stable House majority party 18 out of 67 Congresses (27 percent)	83 percent of Houses change major rules
No shift in partisanship in House majority, Senate majority, or president 34 out of 67 Congresses (51 percent)	35 percent of Houses change major rules

about rule changes. Most notably, it predicts that a shift in the Senate's and/or president's partisanship will effect changes in rules even when the House's partisanship does not change.

The last row shows that in the thirty-four Congresses where no shift in the partisanship of the House majority, Senate majority, or president occurred, that is, where the CS remained relatively constant, the House changed rules only 35 percent of the time. In contrast, the House adopted new rules when there was a change in the partisanship of the House majority 80 percent of the time. Similarly, it adopted new rules in 80 percent of the cases where a change in the partisan control of the House, Senate, and/or president occurred. The results reported in the third row of Table 4.5 are the most illuminating of all. Of the eighteen Congresses where only the Senate majority and/or the president's party changed, the House adopted new rules 83 percent of the time. The contrast of this percentage with the 35 percent percentage is striking, since existing theories implicitly predict that these two percentages should be similar. Changes in the preferences of the Senate and the president are key to understanding the timing of new rules in the House.

The preceding results show that once a shift in the partisan control of the Senate or the presidency is taken into account, existing explanations of the timing of new House rules no longer hold. These results diverge markedly from conventional wisdom and illustrate the critical importance that other institutional actors play in the House's internal decisions regarding rules.

CONCLUSION

I tested the timing of new rules and procedures with data that cover the period 1879–2013. In all of the analyses, I found that changes in the partisanship of the Senate and the president had an effect on the adoption of new rules. When House members are considering which rules will help them attain their preferred laws, they apparently think immediately about the preferences of the Senate and the president. Normally, a shift in the preferences of the Senate or the president will bring about rule changes.

5

The Senate and White House Shadows: Centralization and Decentralization of the Rules of the U.S. House, 1879–2013

In Chapter 3, I formally derived empirical implications of how changes in the constitutional set (CS) affect the timing of House rule adoption. The model generated a key prediction: A House majority adopts new rules and procedures primarily when changes in the preferences of constitutional actors alter the set of bills that can become law. In Chapter 4, I presented empirical evidence in support of this claim. I showed that when the partisanship of the House majority, Senate majority, and/or president changes, the likelihood that the House will adopt new rules increases.

In this chapter, I derive and test implications regarding the nature of the rules that House members adopt after changes in the partisanship of constitutional actors. I show that after a change in the CS that affects the likelihood of approval of at least one bicameral agreement, the alignment of the preferences of constitutional actors – Senate, president, House majority party factions, and House minority – strongly influences whether the new rules centralize power in the Speaker and his or her faction or decentralize it across the two majority party factions.

I first review existing theories' predictions about the directionality of new rules. Then I use the model developed in Chapter 3 to show that the positions of the Senate and the president, relative to the two majority party factions and the minority party, affect the directionality of House rules. I state the conditions under which, after a change in the partisanship of constitutional actors, the majority party will centralize authority, and offer two distinct predictions about when it will decentralize it. Last, I test these implications with historical data covering the period 1879–2013.

THE DIRECTIONALITY OF RULE CHANGES: CURRENT PERSPECTIVES

When discussing extant research on the timing of rule changes in Chapter 4, I noted a key assumption underlying existing theories of House power-sharing arrangements: Only the preferences of other House members matter when the House chooses rules to organize itself. That same characterization applies to research on directionality. Extant theories implicitly assume that the House of Representatives is an isolated entity whose members choose and revise rules without anticipating the likely behavior of other constitutional actors.

The ideological balance-of-power theory (Schickler 2000; 2001), essentially an extension of the majoritarian theory, posits that the directionality of new rules adopted in the House depends on changes in the relative distances between the House floor median and the median of each of the two House parties. Here, the median legislator on the floor is the pivotal decision maker:

> When [the House floor median] moves closer to the median member of the majority party, she will favor rule changes that enhance the majority party's agenda control. By contrast when she moves closer to the median member of the minority party, she will favor rule changes that limit the majority party's agenda control. (Schickler 2000, 270)

From the ideological balance-of-power perspective, any time the position of the median legislator changes, the old status quo is out of equilibrium and the "floor median will oppose rule changes that pull outcomes away from her favored policies and will instead seek changes that bring outcomes more closely in line with her preferences" (Schickler 2000, 271).

In the conditional party government model (CPG) (Aldrich 1994; Rohde 1991; Aldrich and Rohde 1997; 1998; 2000; 2001), rules and procedures that strengthen the power of the House majority party leaders become more likely when, after an election, (i) the preferences of the majority party become more homogeneous and (ii) those preferences become more distinct from those of the minority party. As Aldrich, Rohde, and Berger (2002, 19) posit,

> The greater the extent to which legislators' preferences satisfy the CPG condition, the more (potential) incentive they have to empower their party in the chamber.

If a significant portion of the House majority party shares common objectives, new rules will strengthen the power of the leadership, causing likely outcomes to move toward the party median. Conversely, when the preferences of House majority party members become more heterogeneous, then new rules will weaken the power of the majority leaders.

The partisan capacity theory (Binder 1997) posits that new rules adopted in a particular Congress will be more likely to create minority party rights when, after an election, the House minority party has increased in size and become more cohesive relative to the House majority party. A strong minority party needs fewer members of the majority party to form a winning coalition than a weak minority needs. In contrast, the House majority party will be more likely to adopt rules that suppress minority party rights when the minority party's capacity for obstructionism in the House has increased and the majority party has become larger and more cohesive than the minority party.

In all of these theories, the sole explanation of directionality in rule changes is a change in the ideological distances among House members only. Different authors use different measures – distances between the floor median and the two party medians, distance among all majority party members, and so on – but explanations do not extend beyond the House itself.

Such explanations are limited. Incorporating the Senate and the president in the analysis and analyzing the House majority party in terms of its factions reveal that the House majority party chooses rules on the basis of its policy expectations, given the whole array of preferences of the various actors.

THEORY: EXPLAINING THE DIRECTIONALITY OF RULE CHANGES

I characterize heterogeneity within the majority party by assuming the presence of two factions within the majority party. Even though this is an approximation to reality – as American parties have sometimes had more than two distinct factions – assuming only two simplifies the model without distorting the basic logic of the strategic interaction.

Scholars have demonstrated the value of asking whether new rules centralize or decentralize power within the majority party (Cox and McCubbins 2005). New rules that centralize power in the Speaker and the faction ideologically closer to him give the Speaker greater capacity to make unilateral decisions regarding the flow of legislation and the assignment to committees within the House. New rules that decentralize power remove authority that was previously conferred on the Speaker and distribute it among the House majority intraparty groups. I refer to the House majority party faction with preferences closer to the Speaker as the *Speaker group* and the House majority party faction with preferences further from the Speaker as the *non-Speaker group*. The two factions are crucial to identifying and understanding the directionality of rule changes. I show, in the following, that after a change in the partisanship of the House majority, Senate majority, and/or president, the nature of the rules the House majority adopts depends on the ideological positions of the Senate and the president vis-à-vis the two House majority party factions and the House minority party.

My model generates three empirical implications regarding the directionality of rule change. It predicts when the majority party will centralize authority and it makes two distinct predictions about when it will decentralize authority.

Centralization of Power – Empowering the Speaker

The model predicts that centralization of power in the Speaker and his intraparty group will occur under two conditions after a change in the CS that affects the location of at least one bicameral agreement: The non-Speaker group (the group with preferences furthest from the Speaker's) now prefers the Speaker's ideal point to the status quo; and it now has an ally in the Senate and/or president that increases the likelihood of policy outcomes within its win set. The first condition resembles a key condition of both the Conditional Party Government Theory (CPG, Aldrich and Rohde 2000) and the Party Cartel Theory (PC, Cox and McCubbins 2005). Because it incorporates changes in the Senate and presidency, the second condition is less straightforward. I discuss the two conditions in turn.

Delegation of power is a typical principal-agent problem. On one hand, and as extensive scholarship in political science shows (Cox and McCubbins 1993; 2005; Kiewiet and McCubbins 1991; Lupia and McCubbins 1998), delegation of power to the Speaker yields benefits to both majority intraparty groups. Most notably, it helps the majority party to overcome collective action and coordination problems by using the time and resources available to the party leadership. When the leadership enjoys greater power, the majority party is better equipped to take decisive action to achieve its policy goals.[1] For example, Cox and McCubbins argue that "majority party members delegate to party leaders the authority to manage legislative resources and the legislative process in order to solve the cooperation and coordination problems they face, including maintaining the value of party label" (2005, 23).

Delegation can also be costly, however, as centralization of agenda-setting power can move policy in the ideological direction of the person to whom power is delegated (McKelvey 1976; Romer and Rosenthal 1978). The agent may behave opportunistically, manipulating the content and course of policy outcomes away from the preferences of the principal. When considerable power is delegated to the Speaker and his/her faction, members of the non-Speaker faction might find the House pursuing legislative outcomes that are far from its preferences.

When, then, would the non-Speaker faction agree to delegate power to the Speaker and his or her faction? The first condition, earlier, implies that the non-Speaker group will agree to centralize power in the Speaker when it prefers the ideal point of the Speaker to that of the status quo. As the CPG theory predicts, the more homogeneous are the preferences within the majority party (and the further the distance from the status quo), the greater will be the centralization of power in the Speaker.

I show in the following that even when the preferences of the two majority party groups are heterogeneous and divergent, the Speaker and non-Speaker groups may still agree to centralize. This will happen when the non-Speaker group sees an ally in the Senate and/or president. The non-Speaker group

---

[1] In this sense, party leaders create focal points, structure the agenda, and increase the effectiveness of the party by streamlining the approval of bills and reducing opportunity and transaction costs, for example, saving legislators' time and energy (Cox and McCubbins 1993, 2005; Kiewiet and McCubbins 1991; Lupia and McCubbins 1998).

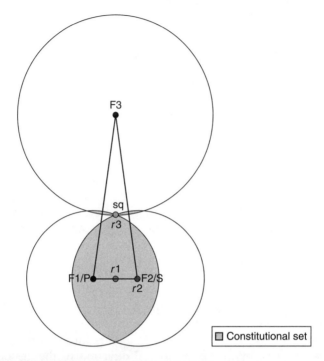

Utilities for F1, F2, and F3, given the power-sharing arrangements

Power-Sharing Arrangement	$U_{F1}(c_i^k)$	$U_{F2}(c_i^k)$	$U_{F3}(c_i^k)$
$c_1^{*2} = 1$	−7.5	−7.5	−48
$c_1^3 = 0$	−19.5	−19.7	−30
$c_2^3 = 0$	−19.5	−19.7	−30
q	−19.5	−19.7	−30

FIGURE 5.1. Centralization of power in the Speaker: homogeneous majority party.

knows that the Senate and/or president will hold up or amend House bills that move policy too far away from its preferences, and thus it can accept a power-sharing arrangement that centralizes power in the Speaker faction.

Figures 5.1 and 5.2 illustrate when centralization should be most likely to occur. Assume *F1* and *F2* are the two majority party factions. Furthermore, assume that *F1* is the faction that is aligned with the Speaker and holds all agenda-setting power (i.e., Speaker faction), while *F2* is the non-Speaker faction. *F3* represents the minority party.

Figure 5.1 depicts the initial distributions of the various constitutional actors' ideal points. Assume that, after an election in which the partisanship of one or more constitutional actors has changed, the president now shares an ideal point with the majority party faction *F1(13, 0)*, while the Senate has the

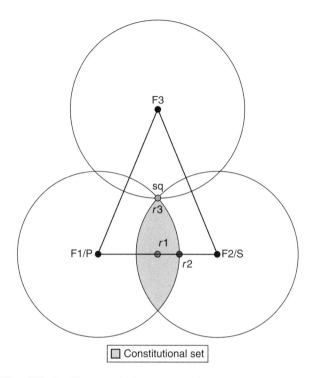

Constitutional set

Utilities for F1, F2, and F3, given the power-sharing arrangements

Power-Sharing Arrangement	$U_{F_1}(c_i^k)$	$U_{F_2}(c_i^k)$	$U_{F_3}(c_i^k)$
$c_{*1}^2 = 1$	−20	−20	−48
$c_1^3 = 0$	−27	−27	−30
$c_2^3 = 0$	−27	−27	−30
q	−27	−27	−30

FIGURE 5.2. Centralization of power in the Speaker: heterogeneous majority party.

same preferences as the majority party faction F_2 *(28, 0)*.[2] F_3 has ideal point (20, 48). The status quo is at (20, 18). F_1 controls 37 percent of the House, and F_2 and F_3 control 36 percent and 27 percent, respectively.[3]

At the beginning of the new Congress, the three factions engage in power-sharing negotiations, knowing that the bicameral agreement[4] resulting from

---

[2] In the model, I assume that the Senate and the president "share" an ideal point with one of the House factions. Although this assumption simplifies the analysis, in a broad set of conditions these actors have similar, though not identical preferences.

[3] For the cases I am considering here, two factions are required to make a majority.

[4] A bicameral agreement is the representation of a set of bills that House members foresee when they allocate power. I do not intend for the set to represent a single bill, since my goal is to permit

the bargain between F_1 and the Senate would be r_1 (20.5, 0) and that resulting from an F_3-Senate agreement would be r_3 (20, 18), with both bicameral agreements being midpoints between the Senate's ideal point and those of the relevant House factions.[5] Since the Senate and F_2 share ideal point r_2 (28, 0), they will adopt it as the bicameral agreement.

The outcome of this game is a power-sharing agreement between the majority party factions in which F_1 keeps all power to set the agenda and represents the House in all bicameral negotiations. The expected legislative outcome is $L = r_1$. The table below Figure 5.1 shows the utilities for each of the factions arising from the different power-sharing arrangements. To see why F_2 would agree to such a distribution of power, note that if F_2 rejects the offer, F_1 will offer $c_1^3 = 0$ to F_3, which F_3 will accept.[6] F_2 also knows that the only offer F_3 would accept from F_2 is $c_2^3 = 0$. Both distributions of power are worse for F_2 than the one F_1 offers.

Furthermore, note that F_1's actions are constrained by the Senate's preferences because any agreement needs the approval of the Senate to become law. Even if F_1 has enough institutional power to determine House outcomes unilaterally, r_1 still needs to be in the Senate's, and, consequently, F_2's, win set. Thus, F_2 agrees to delegate power to F_1 because it can take advantage of the benefits of delegating power in the leadership without facing policy costs, as it knows that it prefers r_1 to sq. This is the case represented by the CPG theory, where the distance among the members of the House majority party is the driving force behind delegation of power in the leadership.

This result also helps to clarify how the Constitutional Theory of Legislative Organization differs from CPG and PC theories. The relative distances among House factions and the Senate and president are the driving forces in the former. I show that even when the majority party becomes heterogeneous, the non-Speaker faction agrees to delegate power to the Speaker as long as it can count on an outside ally that constrains the actions of the Speaker.

To see how the constitutional theory result is independent of the distance between the preferences of F_1 and F_2, consider Figure 5.2. Assume that, after an election, the ideal points of F_1 and F_2 have changed to (0, 0) and (40, 0), respectively, while the positions of the Senate and the president with respect to the factions remain constant. The president still shares the ideal point of F_1, while the Senate shares that of F_2. The ideal point of F_3 and the status quo also remain constant.

As a result of the reshuffle in the House majority membership, the majority party factions are now twice as far from each other. Substantively, this

---

"anticipated legislative dynamics" as represented in the legislative game to influence decisions made in the power-sharing game.

[5] See Chapter 3 for a characterization of bicameral agreements.

[6] Subscripts denote the faction offering the rule and superscripts denote the faction to whom the offer is made.

increased distance represents greater heterogeneity of preferences within the majority party, since the ideal point of F_I is much further from F_2. The CPG theory (Aldrich and Rohde 2000), for instance, predicts decentralization of power, since the greater level of heterogeneity within the majority party makes delegation costlier; some members of the majority party cannot trust a powerful Speaker who has preferences so far from their own.

However, drawing the Senate and the president into the analysis reduces the importance of changes in House members' preferences. Indeed, the result of the game is similar to the one where the ideal points of F_I and F_2 are much closer to each other: F_I keeps all power to set the agenda and $L = r_I$ (20, 0) 100 percent of the time.

But why would F_2 still delegate all power to F_I, with its dissimilar preferences? The answer is simple: F_I's actions are constrained by the Senate's preferences because any agreement needs the approval of the Senate to become law. Even if F_I has enough institutional power to determine House outcomes unilaterally, r_I still needs to be in the Senate's, and, consequently, F_2's, win set. Incorporating the preferences of the president and the Senate in the model shows that a shift in the majority party membership does not suffice to produce a change in the distribution of power within the House.

This result implies that even when the level of majority party homogeneity is low, House factions are far more likely to centralize power in the Speaker when the non-Speaker group is aligned with the preferences of the Senate and/or president. Recognizing the relative positions of these actors with respect to House factions furthers understanding of when the House will likely adopt rules that increase the power of the Speaker and his or her associated group.

Decentralization of Power – Revolting against One's Own Leader

The model predicts that decentralization will occur under two distinct conditions. The first condition is described in this section and the second in the following section.

In the first case, the non-Speaker faction (F_2) pushes for new rules that decentralize power within the majority party when, after a change in the CS that alters the location of at least one bicameral agreement, the Speaker's ideal point (F_I) is worse than the status quo for F_2, and both the Senate's and president's ideal points are closer to the Speaker group's preferences than to the non-Speaker group's. The non-Speaker group will force a rule change to gain agenda-setting powers because the potential costs of delegating power to the Speaker increase dramatically when it prefers the status quo to the Speaker's preferences and it lacks an ally in the Senate and/or president. Indeed, the Speaker's capacity to make laws very close to his/her ideal point and far from the non-Speaker group's is considerable when the Speaker faction enjoys the support of the president and Senate.

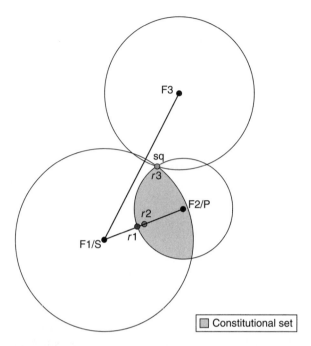

Utilities for F1, F2, and F3, given the power-sharing arrangements

Power-Sharing Arrangement	$U_{F1}(c_i^k)$	$U_{F2}(c_i^k)$	$U_{F3}(c_i^k)$
$c^*{}_1{}^2 = 1$	−10.1	−18.3	−45.5
$c_1{}^3 = 0$	−30.8	−18.3	−22.5
$c_2{}^3 = 0$	−30.8	−18.3	−22.5
Q	−30.8	−18.3	−22.5

FIGURE 5.3. Directionality of rule changes: centralization of power.

Figures 5.3 and 5.4 illustrate this result. Again, assume that $F1$ and $F2$ are two factions of the majority party in the House. $F1$, the Speaker faction, holds the Speaker position and all agenda-setting power. $F2$ is the non-Speaker faction, and $F3$ the minority party.

In Figure 5.3, the Senate shares preferences with the majority party faction $F1$ (o, o), while the president has the same ideal point as the majority party faction $F2$ (27, 9). $F3$'s ideal point is (25, 46) and the status quo is (18, 25). Factions engage in power sharing negotiations, knowing that the expected policy outcome of the next period would be $r1$ (9.6, 3.2) if $F1$ were to represent the House in negotiations with the Senate and the president and $r2$ (13.5, 4.5) if $F2$ were to represent the House in such negotiations. Note that even though $F1$'s preferences are far from $F2$'s, $F1$'s actions are constrained by the

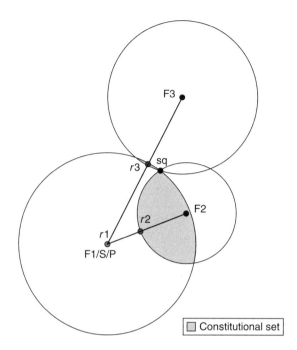

Utilities for F1, F2, and F3, given the power-sharing arrangements

Power-Sharing Arrangement	$U_{F1}(c_i^k)$	$U_{F2}(c_i^k)$	$U_{F3}(c_i^k)$
$c^{*2}_1 = .29$	−10.1	−18.3	−45.8
$c_1^3 = 0$	−30.2	−21.5	−22.5
$c_2^3 = 0$	−14.2	−14.2	−43.1
q	−30.8	−18.3	−22.5

FIGURE 5.4. Directionality of rule changes: decentralization of power.

president's preferences because any agreement between the House and the Senate needs the approval of the president to become law. Substantially, even if *F1* has enough institutional power to determine House outcomes unilaterally, *r1* still needs to be in the president's and *F2*'s win sets. The outcome of this game is a power-sharing agreement of the majority party factions; *F1* keeps all power to set the agenda and represent the House in negotiations with the Senate and president, and *L = r1* 100 percent of the time. Note that *F1*'s offer is sufficient to induce *F2* to coalesce with *F1*, thus bringing power-sharing negotiations to an end. The table shows the utility for each of the factions of the different power-sharing arrangements.

Suppose that election results shift the president's ideal point from *F2* to *F1*, while everything else remains constant (Figure 5.4). That is, even though the president's party does not change, his preferences change substantially, and, therefore, so does his alignment with the internal majority party factions.

As Figure 5.4 shows, the shift radically changes the location of the bicameral agreements with the Senate. F_1 now shares the Senate's and president's policy preferences. If F_1 were to keep all power during the new congressional period, the expected policy outcome would be r_1 (0, 0), which coincides with F_1's ideal point. This policy move is possible because the president's preferences do not constrain F_1's actions anymore, and thus F_1 has both the incentive and the capacity to make laws that coincide with his policy preferences.

How will F_2 adapt to this preference environment? Anticipating the future, F_2 knows that if F_1 were to keep all power, she can take actions that would reduce F_2's welfare. The capacity to structure an effective institutional remedy to the problem of an unconstrained F_1 is the primary means by which F_2 can prevent changes in policy outcomes that would significantly reduce her well-being. As the factions' utilities show, the shift in the president's ideal point affects F_2's preferred power-sharing arrangement. The result of this game is a rule in which $L = r_1$ (0, 0) with probability .29 and $L = r_2$ (13.5, 4.5) with probability .71. The new rule represents a reallocation of House power in which both factions in the majority party have a significant probability of representing the House in negotiations with the Senate and president.

To understand these results, consider that in Figure 5.3, F_2 collected the benefits of delegating power to F_1 while also overcoming the problems of delegation by having an outside ally, the president, who constrained F_1's actions. Even though a conflict of interest between F_1 and F_2 gave the Speaker faction the incentive to act against the wishes of the non-Speaker faction, F_1 still needed to pursue policies that enhanced F_2's welfare. However, when F_2 lost the only ally that could restrain policy outcomes (Figure 5.4), F_1 gained the capacity to follow his preferred policy proposals. Under these circumstances, the non-Speaker group cannot rely on an outside ally to constrain the set of policies preferred by the Speaker. Decentralization of power in the House is the mechanism by which F_2 can induce an otherwise defiant F_1 to take his interests into account. The new rule gives power to F_2 so that F_2 can also hold sway in the political battles over the legislation in question. As a real-world matter, this situation has always evoked a fierce battle in the House between the two intraparty groups.[7]

While the Speaker group does not want to give the non-Speaker group more power, the latter forces decentralization of power by threatening to unite with the minority party to change the rules. Indeed, cases in which both the Senate

---

[7] Indeed, the congressional debates leading to decentralization of power when both the Senate and the president are closer to the Speaker faction are acrimonious and reveal deep divisions within the party regarding the proposed rule changes.

and the president are closer to the Speaker's preferences than to those of the non-Speaker group constitute the very few cases in the history of rule adoption in which the House majority party was rolled by an alliance of members of its own party and the House minority party (Cox and McCubbins 2005).[8]

With the rule change, the non-Speaker group gains bargaining power over the Speaker group and now acts in tandem with the Senate and the president. The non-Speaker group can threaten to ally with the minority again if its policy preferences are not taken into account, a credible threat that induces the Speaker to change his behavior so as to keep the majority in the House intact.

Situations in which the Speaker group, the Senate, and the president are aligned ideologically and are able to move policy toward their shared ideal are the only situations where a group in the majority party will side with the opposition to change the rules.

Decentralization of Power – Empowering Outliers

Now suppose a change in the shape of the CS alters at least one bicameral agreement and the opposition party controls both the Senate and presidency. Then the majority party will decentralize by delegating power to party outliers, defined as those legislators who hold more extreme preferences than other members of the House majority party on issues of importance to the chamber. The rationale for empowering outliers and giving them an effective veto in House negotiations with the Senate and president rests in their capacity to reject Senate proposals that moderate members themselves could not credibly reject.

The result stems from straightforward rational anticipation. By constitutional design, the House, Senate, and president all have veto power over policy proposals (bills), wherever they originate. If, after an election, the opposition ends up controlling the Senate and presidency, bargaining leverage for the House majority party arises from those House members whose threats to reject proposals from the Senate and the president will be viewed as credible.

Suppose, for example, that the House majority party is considering a bill proposed by the Senate, which the other party controls. Although moderates might feel inclined to go along with the bill because they have not publicly rejected it, an extremist who is committed strongly and publicly to an opposing position can respond as follows: "I am unable to accept your proposal and I would prefer that we produce no legislative outcome rather than accept the concession you propose." Majority party House moderates who prefer a stronger version of the bill or, at worst, the status quo, would achieve a better

---

[8] I should note that this condition, where both the president and the Senate are closer to the Speaker group, is rare. The reasons underlying this fact are probably related to the internal party politics decided in a previous game, outside the public arena.

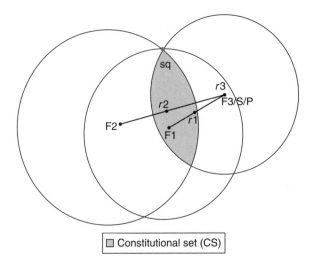

Utilities for F1, F2, and F3, given the power-sharing arrangements

Power-Sharing Arrangement	$U_{F1}(c_i^k)$	$U_{F2}(c_i^k)$	$U_{F3}(c_i^k)$
$c_1^{*2} = 0$	−16	−20.9	−40.5
$c_1^3 = 1$	−18	−45.3	−18
$c_2^3 = 1$	−16	−20.9	−40.5
q	−50.2	−51.5	−46.1

FIGURE 5.5. Directionality of rule changes: outlier result.

outcome by sending extremist members of their party, rather than themselves, to negotiate with a Senate that prefers weakening the status quo.[9]

Figure 5.5 illustrates this result. Assume F_1 and F_2 are two factions of the House majority party, and F_3 is the minority party. Assume that after an election in which the preferences of at least one constitutional actor changed, the Senate and the president share preferences with the House minority party. Their shared ideal point is to the right of the two majority party factions' ideal points. At the beginning of a Congress, F_1, whose ideal point (30, 0) is located toward the center of the figure, must contemplate the kind of offer it will make or accept when negotiating a distribution of power with F_2 (0, 5). Looking ahead to the negotiation with a Senate and a president now dominated by the opposition party, F_1 expects that by controlling the negotiations with the Senate and the president, it can increase the likelihood that the expected policy outcome for the next Congress will be r_1 (45, 10).

---

[9] Here, I invoke negotiation metaphorically and do not propose a theory of conference committees.

A question arises: Can faction F_1 benefit by delegating power to a less centrist faction? The answer is "no," as long as the other faction is the minority party and it shares the Senate's and president's ideal points. If F_3 were to represent the House when bargaining with the Senate and the president, then the expected policy outcome would be $L = r_3$ (60, 20), an outcome further from faction F_1's ideal point than is r_1. What about F_2? Its ideal point is to the left of F_1. If its members are given power to control the agenda and negotiate with the Senate and the president, then the expected outcome is r_2 (20, 12.5). This point is closer to F_1 than is r_1. F_1 receives higher policy utility (−16 utils) when F_2 negotiates with the Senate and president than when F_1 itself does (−18 utils). As a result, the best offer F_1 can make entails giving F_2 all of the negotiating power.

This result is intuitive, and begins, again, with the fact that by constitutional design, the House, Senate, and president all have meaningful veto power over bills. When the opposition controls the Senate and the president, the relatively centrist House faction gains greater policy utility by having preference outliers represent them in negotiations with the Senate and the president. Such dynamics explain the otherwise inexplicable phenomenon that members of the majority party sometimes choose to yield substantial power to their party outliers.[10]

This result suggests an intriguing rationale for the role of committee outliers. Moderates and outliers on the same side of an issue may agree that both benefit if outliers are in charge of negotiating.[11] Indeed, the result implies that when House majority intraparty groups negotiate a distribution of power, they both may gain by appointing preference outliers to positions on powerful House committees, whose members are likely to be negotiating with the Senate and the president.[12] This observation reinforces Epstein and O'Halloran's (1999) empirical finding that the selection of House committee members is influenced by the preferences of the president and the Senate. They find that ideal points of select House committee members "tend to move counter to those of the President" (171), and that preference outliers are more numerous on House committees under conditions of divided government.

---

[10] This result parallels Kedar's (2005) party-balancing claim. Kedar examines the behaviors of spatially oriented voters in parliamentary elections. Of interest is the case where a voter expects a party A to be in government and is contemplating whether to vote for a party B or a party C. Suppose party B's ideal point is closer to that of the voter. Kedar reasons that the voter will have an incentive to vote for party C instead if she believes that postelection coalition bargaining will yield an A-C coalition that produces policies closer to her ideal point than would an A-B coalition. Empirically, she finds evidence of such voting in several countries.

[11] For instance, in the 2011 Republican Party example detailed in Chapter 1, the consequence of delegating power to outliers is pulling the bill closer to the ideal points of both majority intraparty groups.

[12] Consider, in this regard, the appointment in 2011 of Ron Paul (R-TX) for the first time in his twenty-five-year career as chairman of the House Financial Services' Subcommittee on Domestic Monetary Policy and Technology, which controls the Federal Reserve, an institution Paul wants to abolish. The House majority decided on an outlier for the position precisely when the opposition controlled the Senate and the presidency (see Chapter 1).

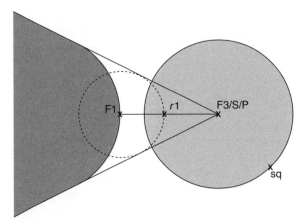

FIGURE 5.6. Range of outliers.

FIGURE 5.6. Range of outliers.

Figure 5.6 shows the range of outliers that may benefit the party when the Senate and president share the same ideal point as the House minority party, $F3$.[13]

The dashed circle around $F1$ represents the set of legislative outcomes that provide $F1$ with greater policy utility than $r1$, the midpoint between $F1$ and the Senate. To simplify the presentation, I consider the case where $F1$ can either keep all agenda-setting power for himself, ensuring that he will be in control of House outcomes, or transfer power to another intraparty group, ensuring that the negotiations with the Senate will be managed by the other majority faction. The shaded and nonshaded ranges of Figure 5.6 show what combination of preferences will yield an outcome that faction $F1$ prefers to $r1$, that is, the bill that will emerge if $F1$ keeps all power to himself. If the other majority party faction is located in the nonshaded range, then faction $F1$ gets greater policy utility by controlling negotiations with the Senate and the president. If, however, the faction is anywhere in the shaded range, then faction $F1$ can have greater policy utility by yielding agenda-setting control.

Note that the shaded range extends considerably to the left. This occurs because both the extreme and moderate factions benefit if they produce House policy outcomes that are in this far-left range, which they know must be inside the Senate's and president's win set (the circle surrounding S). Since the Senate and president can credibly veto any point outside their win set, any outcome produced by the negotiation between the "outlying" Senate faction and the presidential faction will be closer to $F1$ than is $r1$.

The Constitutional Theory of Legislative Organization demonstrates that when the Senate and the president share the ideal point of the minority party,

---

[13] The ideal point of the third faction does not appear, because it is not needed for purposes of this example.

the majority party can transfer substantial power to outliers and still benefit from the outcome. The relatively centrist House faction gains greater policy utility by having preference outliers represent them in negotiations with the Senate and the president.

EMPIRICAL IMPLICATIONS: THE DIRECTIONALITY OF RULE CHANGES

Given a change in the partisanship of constitutional actors, the House majority will adopt new rules that are driven by a strategic effort to maximize influence over policy.

In summary, my model makes three precise predictions:

- When, after changes in the CS, the non-Speaker group prefers the Speaker's ideal point to the status quo, or it has an ally in the Senate and/or president that guarantees policy outcomes within its win set, the majority party factions will agree on new rules that empower the Speaker.
- When, after changes in the CS, the Speaker faction's ideal point is worse for F_2 than the status quo, and both the Senate's and the president's ideal points are closer to the Speaker's preferences than to the non-Speaker's, the non-Speaker faction will push for new rules that decentralize power within the majority party.
- When, after a change in the CS, the House majority party factions face a Senate and a president controlled by the opposition party, both factions will agree on decentralization by empowering party outliers. In this case, decentralization serves to increase the House majority party's bargaining power.

EMPIRICAL ANALYSIS: DATA AND MEASUREMENT

To test these predictions, I created a data set that includes, as explanatory variables, measures of change in the configurations among the constitutional actors and, as the dependent variable, a measure of the direction of rule changes in Congress. The data set covers the period 1879 to 2013.

Measuring the Positions of Constitutional Actors: House Factions, the Senate, and the President

The model's predictions regarding the directionality of new rules depend heavily on the array of preferences that exist across all the constitutional actors at the beginning of a new Congress. In the empirical analyses that follow, I use a categorical variable to designate the positions of the two House majority party groups and the minority party vis-à-vis the Senate and president. In turn, this requires estimating the position of each constitutional actor for each congressional session. My strategy consists of first identifying the House majority party factions and their relative positions as well as the position of the House minority party. I then identify the House majority party faction with which each of the House Speakers was more closely aligned. With all of this established, I characterize the positions of the president and Senate vis-à-vis the House majority party factions and the House minority party.

In Chapter 2, I explained how I identified all intraparty groups and their members for every Congress between the 46th and the 112th Congresses, and the position of the Speaker and the president with respect to House majority party factions. Appendix A shows the ideological stances of majority party factions with respect to the Speaker and the president for the period 1879–2013. In brief, I followed a substantive and labor-intensive path.[14] For factions, I relied heavily on leading sources on parties and party factions in history and political science, distinguishing the factions on the basis of two factors: their ideologies, defined as their preferences about the role and scope of the government in the economy and society, and the geographical areas they represented. To estimate the Speaker's preferences, I also used leading sources on House Speakers to classify their positions within their own parties, focusing on how these sources characterized the Speaker before he was elected, including his/her policy preferences and support within the party in his quest to become Speaker. Moving to the president, if his party was the same as the minority party in the House, I coded them as similar. If the president belonged to the same party as the House majority, I used the American presidency series published by the University of Kansas, as well as leading studies of each president, to classify whether the president was closer to the Speaker or non-Speaker group.

The last step was to identify the positions of the Senate with respect to the House majority factions and the House minority party. For this task, I used Common Space scores, which are based on roll call data and can be compared across chambers.[15] Even though this is not a perfect measure, I did not find an extensive literature that focuses on the Senate and that identifies Senate factions. There are some references to the "Senate four" during the 1900s or the Senate "farm bloc" during the 1920s, but these are rare exceptions.

---

[14] I decided not use DW-NOMINATES to identify the members of each intraparty group for various reasons. First, there is some arbitrariness in where scholars put the cutoff points that divide moderates from other members of the party; different scholars do it in different ways. Second, the measure is based on bills that made it to the floor and that received a roll call, which are not appropriate for my endeavor because the very topic I want to study, the distribution of power in the House, determines the fate of bills. At the end of the day, bills considered on the floor are endogenous to the distribution of positive and negative agenda-setting power. Third, there is an accumulated literature, both in history and in political science, that offers in-depth information on the nature of intraparty groups.

[15] To this end, I used Common Space DW-NOMINATE scores with bootstrapped standard errors in one dimension (Carroll et al. 2009).

If the Senate majority was in the hands of the House minority party, I classified it as such. When the House and Senate majority were controlled by the same party, I classified the position of the Senate majority with respect to the House majority factions. To simplify matters, I decided to focus on the Senate pivot, the legislator whose vote is needed to invoke cloture and end a filibuster. I made this decision because even though the Constitution requires only a majority of the Senate to pass a bill, Senate rules on debate mean that bills effectively need supermajorities to pass (Koger 2010; Wawro and Schickler 2006).[16] Thus, I measured the distance of the Senate pivot to the median of each of the factions. Although three-fifths of the Senate membership is the number required since 1975, from 1917 until 1975 two-thirds majority was required to impose cloture.[17] To pinpoint the pivot between 1879 and 1917, when there was no written rule, I followed Wawro and Schickler (2006), who identify the pivot with the strict majority, a procedure that allows the exact filibuster pivot to change as new states were incorporated into the Union. Additionally, Wawro and Schickler claim that the bare majority was still successful in passing bills during the few decades after cloture reform because the costs to obstructionists were still too high (2006, 95). To be conservative, I coded the filibuster pivot from the 65th until the 69th Congress (1917–1923) as the strict majority.[18] After calculating the ideological distances between the Senate pivot and House faction medians with Common Space scores, I coded whether the Senate filibuster pivot was ideologically closer to the Speaker faction or the non-Speaker faction.

Using the predictions derived from the model, I distinguish among three situations: first, when, after an election, either the Senate or the president, or both, move closer to the non-Speaker group than to the Speaker group; second, when, after an election, both the Senate and the president move closer to the Speaker group (i.e., both are far from the non-Speaker group and close to the Speaker group); and third, when, after an election, the House minority party gains control of both the Senate and presidency. When there was no change in the partisanship of any constitutional actor, I coded the result as no change in CS.

[16] Once a senator receives recognition on the floor, said senator may address the chamber for as long as he or she wishes, and a simple majority of the Senate is insufficient to end the debate. In the contemporary Congress, rule XXII requires a three-fifths of the Senate vote to invoke the "Cloture Rule" to end a filibuster.

[17] For this period, the filibuster pivots "were the 33rd and 67th percentile senators" (Wawro and Schickler 2006, 26). Until the 85th Congress (1957–1958) the total membership of the Senate was ninety-six senators so the filibuster pivot was at the 64th percentile from the most liberal senator if the House majority was Democratic and at the 33rd percentile from the most liberal senator if the House majority was Republican.

[18] I estimated the pivot for each Congress at the time when the new House rules were enacted. For the cases when new rules were adopted more than once in a singular Congress, I calculated the filibuster pivot for each case. However, differences in the pivot within the same Congress never led to a change in the faction aligned with the Senate.

Rules and the Distribution of Power within the Majority Party: Coding Centralization and Decentralization of Power in the House

I view rules as agreements that codify the relative power of the House majority party factions (Cox and McCubbins 2005). Accordingly, I distinguished rules as centralizing power in the Speaker's faction, decentralizing power by redistributing it between the two majority party factions, or having no effect. The "no effect" classification covers three cases: No new rules were adopted, the new rules differed in only minor ways from the ones they replaced,[19] or the new rules were adopted too late in a given period to affect the distribution of power during that particular Congress.[20]

To create my measure of rule change, I began with Schickler's original list of rules and procedures, even though he coded his data for a different purpose, that is, to distinguish between rules "that were intended either to advantage the majority party and its leaders or to undermine them" (Schickler 2000, 271).[21] I then modified his data, as explained in Chapter 4, first, by updating his list of rules and procedures through the 112th Congress;[22] second, by including rules and procedures that he did not take into account; and, third and most significantly, by analyzing the effect of rules on the distribution of power among the House majority party factions, not between the House majority and minority parties.

For the period in which my analyses overlap with Schickler's, he identifies thirty-three Congresses in which rule changes occurred; I identify thirty-six Congresses. My coding of the effect of rules differs from Schickler's for ten Congresses. For more detail, see Appendix F. Of course, our coding should not overlap completely, given our very different purposes. While some rule changes did not affect the majority party's power vis-à-vis the minority party's, they did reshape the distribution of power among factions within the majority party. Thus, I coded rules as centralizing power in the Speaker's faction, redistributing it between the two majority party factions, or having no effect.

To classify rule changes as centralizing power, decentralizing it, or having no effect, I relied on general congressional histories and leading sources on congressional rules and procedures and their assessments regarding the effect of rules on the distribution of power within the majority party.[23] If at least two

---

[19] In the 90th Congress, the twenty-one-days rule was replaced with other rules that kept the distribution of power within the House majority party constant. See Appendix F for more information on this case.

[20] There is one case that fits the category: the 60th Congress. The Republican majority adopted the Calendar Wednesday rule during the last days of the Congress. Thus, the rule had no effect on the 60th Congress per se. See Appendix F for more information on this case.

[21] Another important list of rules and procedures is provided in Binder (1997). Although her list overlaps significantly with Schickler's, they are not identical, and the emphasis is different.

[22] Schickler coded new rules through the 104th Congress (1995–1996).

[23] Alexander 1916; Bolling 1964; Cooper 1988; Damon 1971; Galloway 1969; Hasbrouck 1927; Josephy 1980; Oleszek 2001; Riddick 1949; Smith 1989; Zelizer 2004. For the most recent period, I relied on the *CQ* weekly account for each Congress that details the most relevant rule changes.

TABLE 5.1. *Number of Congresses in which the House changed its internal organization, by type of rules adopted, 1879–2013*

Change in House Rules	N	%
No change in rules	28	42
Rules decentralized power	8	12
Rules centralized power	31	46
Total	67	100

sources agreed that new rules favored one faction or increased the power of the Speaker, then I coded each rule change as such. Appendix C presents the coding and the list of the rules and procedures included in this study.

Table 5.1 summarizes the rule changes that the House made over the period of study. Twenty-eight out of sixty-seven Congresses did not change their rules and procedures. Nearly 50 percent of all Congresses (thirty-one Congresses) centralized power in the Speaker, while only 12 percent (eight Congresses) decentralized power across the majority party groups.

ANALYSIS

My theory predicts that rule changes will centralize or decentralize power in the House majority party as a function of changes in the alignments among the two House majority party factions, the minority party, the Senate, and the president.

Accordingly, the primary independent variable of interest has four categories: (i) no change in the CS; (ii) change in the CS, with the Senate *and/or* president moving closer to the non-Speaker faction than to the Speaker faction; (iii) change in the CS, with the Senate *and* president moving closer to the Speaker faction than to the non-Speaker faction; and (iv) changes in the CS, with the House minority party taking control of the Senate majority and presidency. My model predicts that the House will adopt no new rules when the CS does not change after an election. It also predicts that new rules that centralize power in the Speaker group will be adopted in those Congresses that fall into category (ii) and new rules that decentralize power will be adopted in Congresses that fall into categories (iii) and (iv).

I conduct two analyses, with the latter more directly pitting the constitutional theory against competing ones. First, I simply calculate the percentages of Congresses that centralize, decentralize, or do not change rules under each of the categories of the independent variable and illustrate the findings with an example. This analysis of the directionality of rule changes is suggestive only, since it fails to account for alternative explanations that hold prominence in the literature. The second analysis predicts the likelihood of centralization and decentralization of power in the House taking into account variables that other scholars have used. Finding that the constitutional theory still holds would increase confidence in the validity of the theory that the relative positions of constitutional actors affect House members' decisions regarding the nature of the rules they adopt. Most convincing of all would be to find that variables measuring the constitutional theory are significant, while variables measuring alternative theories are not.

No Changes in CS

Table 5.2 shows the percentages of Congresses that changed their rules and procedures under each category of my independent variable. First, for all the Congresses in which the CS remained constant – the House majority party, the Senate majority party, and the president's party did not change – the House adopted the same rules as those of the preceding Congress 65 percent of the time. This finding, which was also reported in Table 4.5, supports the constitutional theory prediction that when the preferences of all actors, and therefore the CS and bargaining environment, remain constant, the House will not feel compelled to adopt new rules and procedures.

Change in CS and the Non-Speaker Group Gained an Ally (Allies) in the Senate and/or President (Senate and/or President Closer to the Non-Speaker Faction Than to the Speaker)

Now consider what transpires when there is a change in the partisanship of the House majority, the Senate majority, and/or the president after an election. From Chapter 4, we know that the likelihood that the House majority party will adopt new rules increases after a change in the CS. In the previous section, I showed theoretically that the nature of the rules adopted depends on the relative positions of the Senate and president with respect to the House majority party factions and the minority party.

The second row of Table 5.2 shows that when a change in the CS takes the form that the Senate and/or the president becomes ideologically closer to the non-Speaker group, the House majority party adopts new rules centralizing power in the Speaker 84 percent of the time. This very high percentage means that the non-Speaker group agrees to centralize power in the hands of the Speaker when it gains an outside ally that constrains the behavior of the Speaker. Because bills need to consider the preferences of all constitutional actors, the non-Speaker group can enjoy the benefits of delegating power to the leadership while still approving legislation close to its ideal point.

An example can be found in the 111th Congress, which I introduced in Chapter 1. In 2009, after a change in the partisanship of the president, the House Democratic majority adopted new rules that centralized power in the hands of liberal Speaker Nancy Pelosi (D-CA). One of those rules relaxed

TABLE 5.2. *Distribution of Congresses by nature of the change and preference alignment of constitutional actors, 1879–2013*

	Change in House Rules			
	No change	Decentralization	Centralization	Total
No shift in partisanship of House majority, Senate majority, and/or president's party	65%	3%	32%	100%
Shift in partisanship of House majority, Senate majority, and/or president's party and				
Senate and/or president closer to the non-Speaker group than the Speaker group	12%	4%	84%	100%
Senate and president closer to the Speaker group than the non-Speaker group	33%	67%	0%	100%
Senate majority and presidency controlled by the House minority party	33%	67%	0%	100%

the strict "pay-go" rules that the same majority had adopted just two years earlier. The pay-go rules established that any budget decision had to be deficit neutral, so that mandatory spending increases or tax cuts had to be offset with tax increases or spending cuts elsewhere. Under the new rules, the majority could attach an emergency designation – an act of war or terrorism, a natural disaster, or a prolonged period of low economic growth – to a spending bill and exempt it from the "pay-go" requirements. In addition, the new rule allowed legislators to link exempted bills with other bills that did not meet the waiver requirements.

Why did Democratic majority factions relax the very rules they had adopted only two years earlier? We now can understand more clearly than in Chapter 1 why the Democratic majority relaxed those rules. First, the rule changes correspond to a change in the president's partisanship. Rules that were useful with a Republican in office simply were not useful when a Democrat replaced him. More to the point, why did the new rules centralize power in the Speaker? Why did the non-Speaker group, the moderate and conservative Democrats, go along with the changes? After all, these fiscally conservative members of the

Democratic Party knew that the relaxed rules would increase the power of the Speaker and the liberal group affiliated with her. Moderate and conservative Democrats accepted the relaxed rules because they could count on a Senate that was closer to their preferences than to those of the liberal Democrats. Because bills need the approval of the Senate, moderates and conservatives knew that any bill pushed by Pelosi and her faction had to be within the range of acceptability of the Senate pivot. They were willing to increase the Speaker's power and take advantage of the benefits of delegation because the presence of an outside actor with preferences closer to their own gave them confidence that legislation would not be overly skewed toward the liberal wing of the party.

Change in CS and Senate and President Move Closer to the Speaker Group (Non-Speaker Group Has No Outside Allies)

Consider, in contrast, what happens when, after a change in the partisanship of at least one of the constitutional actors, the non-Speaker group loses its outside ally. Table 5.2's third row shows that when both the Senate and the president become closer to the Speaker group than to the non-Speaker group, a House majority decentralizes power in 67 percent of these cases. As a real-world matter, these episodes are marked by a confrontation between the Speaker and non-Speaker group.[24] While the Speaker group does not want to give the non-Speaker group more power, the latter forces decentralization of power by uniting with the minority party to change the rules. By decentralizing power, the non-Speaker group gains agenda-setting power and can exert control over policy outcomes.

An iconic example, discussed at length in Chapter 6, is the revolt against Republican Speaker Joseph Cannon (R-IL) in 1910. I show there how a constitutional actors' perspective generates an interpretation of the Cannon episode that differs greatly from the currently prominent one.

Change in CS and the House Minority Party Gains Control of President and Senate

My theory predicts that the House majority party has a strong incentive to decentralize power to increase the majority party's leverage when bargaining with the opposition. By giving power to outliers, the House majority party becomes more credible in its position when negotiating with the president and Senate. In this regard, the last row of Table 5.3 shows that after a change in the partisanship of constitutional actors such that the House minority party

---

[24] These constitute the very few cases in the history of rule adoption in which the House majority party was rolled by an alliance of members of its own party and the House minority party (Cox and McCubbins 2005).

TABLE 5.3. *Multinomial logit estimates for models of changes in House organization, 1879–2013*

	Model 1	Model 2	Model 3	Model 4
	Centralization vs. no changes in rules	Centralization vs. no changes in rules	Decentralization vs. no changes in rules	Decentralization vs. no changes in rules
Primary hypotheses				
Shift in partisanship of House majority, Senate majority, and/or president's party and				
Senate and/or president closer to the non-Speaker group than the Speaker group	2.59***	2.64***	1.99	.63
	(.72)	(.89)	(1.54)	(2.27)
Senate and president closer to the Speaker group than the non-Speaker group	–15.27	–16.73	3.78***	4.73**
	(2925.9)	(6422.7)	(1.59)	(2.08)
Senate majority and presidency controlled by the House minority party	–15.26	–15.45	3.78***	4.82**
	(2068.9)	(1270.8)	(1.34)	(2.15)
Change House median		10.9		–8.99
		(7.7)		(16.7)
Change party homogeneity		5.47		8.74
		(13.89)		(26.7)
Change party polarization		–1.96		32.6
		(12.4)		(24.01)
Change party capacity		–.000		.003
		(.008)		(.011)
Change majority party size		–.049		.018
		(.198)		(.40)
Constant	–.69	–.81**	–3.09	–3.86***
	(.37)	(.42)	(1.02)	(1.25)
Log likelihood	–44.30	–37.30	–44.30	–37.30

Note: N = 67. Standard errors in parentheses
**p < .05, ***p < .0.

now controls both the Senate and the president, new rules decentralize power in 67 percent of the cases.

Two examples, one from congressional history and one from contemporary politics, illustrate the advantage to the House majority party of decentralizing power in party outliers. First is the repeal and readoption of the Reed rules in the 52nd and 53rd Congresses (1891–1895). The Reed rules had first been adopted by a Republican controlled House in 1889, when the partisanship of the House majority and the president's party changed from Democrats to Republicans. The Reed rules significantly curtailed the power of any group of House members to obstruct business, hence serving to centralize power in the majority party leadership.[25] In 1891, the Democratic Party took over the House, while the Senate and the presidency remained under Republican control. This new House majority immediately abolished the Reed rules, giving any minority the capacity to thwart and delay the legislative process. However, just two years later, the same House Democratic majority readopted the Reed rules.

Why would the same majority abolish rules that it would embrace again just two years later? What accounts for these reversals? The constitutional theory helps to understand these seemingly inexplicable occurrences. In 1891, the newly elected Democratic majority faced an opposition-controlled Senate and president. By abolishing the Reed rules and allowing any minority to oppose legislation, the majority bestowed additional authority on outliers, increasing their bargaining power against a Senate and presidency controlled by the opposition. However, the 1893 bargaining environment differed, with the Democrats regaining control of both Senate and presidency. Empowered outliers were no longer needed to bargain with the Senate and president, who now were allies, not foes. The same Democratic majority therefore readopted the Reed rules so as to centralize power in the speakership.

A more recent example is from the 112th Congress (2011–2013), which I also introduced in Chapter 1. In January 2011, Republicans became the majority party in the House and immediately abolished the Gephardt rule, which automatically increased the debt ceiling upon passage of a budget resolution, allowing House members to avoid a politically unpalatable vote on raising the debt ceiling.[26] With the rule's elimination, the House now *had* to hold a separate vote on the debt issue, thus giving the most fiscally conservative members of the Republican conference, the outliers, the power to oppose any increase in the debt. We know that this rule change had significant implications

---

[25] In particular, the Reed rules lowered the quorum necessary for the Committee of the Whole and allowed a majority to close debate. Furthermore, the Reed rules gave the Speaker power to deny recognition to those legislators intending to delay the legislative process, and they enabled the Speaker to count, during quorum calls, all those members present in the chamber who would not answer to the call (this maneuver was called the disappearing quorum and was used to block business in the House).

[26] Under the rule, any budget resolution adopted by the House automatically triggered a separate debt ceiling measure that was without delay sent to the Senate.

for how members of Congress would address the weak economy. Why did the Republican leadership make this rule change? Abolishing the Gephardt rule gave Republicans needed bargaining leverage against the Democrats, as outliers could credibly condition their vote on the debt ceiling on additional concessions from the White House in the form of major budget cuts. Indeed, as a consequence of the rule change and its effect on Republicans' bargaining leverage, Republicans were able to strike a deal to reduce the budget by $1.2 trillion.[27] Thus, decentralization of power at the beginning of the 112th Congress heightened Republicans' bargaining power with a president and a Senate controlled by the Democratic Party.

All in all, the percentages in Table 5.2 are consistent with the constitutional theory, which situates and analyzes institutional changes in the House as part of a broader bargaining environment. However, there might be other factors, especially those emphasized in the existing literature on House organization, that largely determine whether rules centralize or decentralize power. Accordingly, I next incorporate information about dispersion within House factions in my statistical analysis.

Multinomial Analysis

The following analyses include measures that other scholars have shown to be major explanations of rule changes. All these measures are designed to capture changes in the composition of the House membership, on the assumption that rule changes are largely a matter of internal management.

Change in House median (Schickler 2000; 2001) captures changes in the floor median relative to the minority and majority party medians, predicting that the closer the floor median is to the majority party median, the higher will be the probability of centralization of power. Four covariates, *Change in party homogeneity*, *Change in party polarization*, *Change in party capacity*, and *Change in majority party size*, capture changes in majority party membership.[28] *Change in party homogeneity* (Cox and McCubbins 1993; 2005; Aldrich and Rohde 2000; 2001) measures changes in preference similarity

---

[27] The deal first created a committee with superpowers to make recommendations about the $1.2 trillion in budget cuts. However, because that committee ultimately was not able to reach an agreement, automatic budget cuts across the board went into effect on March 2013.

[28] The data for the covariates are based on DW-NOMINATE. I followed Schickler's (2000) advice on how to construct each variable. Change in *House median* represents the differences in the distances between (i) the floor median and the minority party median and (ii) the floor median and the majority party median. *Party homogeneity* is the ratio between the standard deviation of the majority party members and the standard deviation of the floor. *Party polarization* is the difference between the majority and minority party medians. *Party capacity* is the difference between majority and minority party capacity. *Majority party capacity* is equal to the *Majority party rice cohesion* score, which is calculated as the degree of division within the majority party, times the percentage of majority party membership in the House. *Minority party capacity* is calculated in the same way.

among majority party members; if the preferences of majority party members become more homogeneous, scholars have shown, then the rule changes will centralize power. *Change in polarization* (Aldrich and Rohde 2000; 2001) measures preference changes across parties; the more distinct parties become, the higher the probability of centralization. *Change in party capacity* (Binder 1997) measures the difference in strength between the two parties; the smaller the difference in party capacity between majority and minority, the more likely that the House will decentralize power. The idea is that a stronger minority party needs fewer members of the majority to form a winning coalition, and, therefore, the members of the majority will lend support to the minority in exchange for assistance in passing preferred bills. *Change in majority party size* measures the change in the proportion of members belonging to the majority party (Dion 1997). Dion argues that a smaller majority will be more cohesive and will adopt rules that centralize power in the leadership.

Table 5.3 reports multinomial logit estimates that compare the likelihood of centralization or decentralization vis-à-vis no changes in rules. It shows that partisan alignments among constitutional actors, not changes in the House membership, are the driving factor in House organization decisions.

The parameter estimates in Model 1 compare the likelihood that legislators will adopt new rules that centralize power in the Speaker to the likelihood of adopting the same rules that were in force during the previous Congress. The only coefficient that significantly affects centralization of rules in the hands of the Speaker faction is one corresponding to a change in the CS, specifically where the Senate pivot and/or the president moves closer to the non-Speaker faction. The odds of adopting new rules relative to adopting no new rules are 13.3 times greater when, after a CS change, the Senate and/or the president is closer to the non-Speaker group.

Model 2 incorporates the variables that account for changes in the ideological composition of the House. Even after controlling for such ideological changes, the CS variable is still significant.[29] Indeed, when the Senate and/or president is closer to the non-Speaker group, the odds of new rules that centralize power in the Speaker are fourteen times higher than the odds of no change in rules. By contrast, changes in the House median, majority party homogeneity, level of party polarization, party capacity, and majority party size do not affect the likelihood of centralization of power in the Speaker.

Models 3 and 4 look at the likelihood that legislators will adopt new rules that decentralize power within the majority party relative to adopting no new rules. Consistent with the constitutional theory's expectations, the estimates in

[29] Multicollinearity is not a problem in these data. The VIF for the predictors is below the accepted number of 10 (if higher than 10, there is moderate correlation in the data) and the tolerance for these variables is always higher than .10, also the accepted norm. The condition number of 6.06 is also low (when the condition number is greater than 15 multicollinearity is a concern; Belsley, Welsch, and Kuh 2004), meaning that collinearity is not a problem in the data.

Model 3 show, first, that the likelihood of decentralization of power increases when, after a change in the CS, the president and Senate pivot are now closer to the Speaker faction than to the non-Speaker faction. It also shows that decentralization is more likely to occur when, after a change in the CS, the House minority party now controls the Senate and the presidency. Those results also hold in Model 4, which incorporates competing theories' variables. Indeed, the odds of decentralization relative to no changes in rules are forty-four times greater when the Senate and the president are closer to the Speaker faction and when the Senate and the presidency are controlled by the House minority party. Including the additional variables increases the odds of decentralization by a factor of 113 when the Senate and the presidency are now closer to the Speaker group, and by a factor of 124 when they are both controlled by the House minority party.

All in all, the results reveal that after a change in partisanship of constitutional actors, the alignment among the Senate, president, House majority faction, and minority party has a significant impact on House members' decisions to decentralize power in the House.[30] Furthermore, even after controlling for additional variables, the constitutional theory variables are still significant, thus showing that changes in the distribution of preferences within the House do not affect the probability that different types of rules will be adopted.

Overall, the empirical analysis supports my theoretical expectations. Changes in the preferences of constitutional actors influence House members' decisions to change rules.

CONCLUSION

The framework developed in Chapter 3 very naturally extends to deal with how – and not only when – House rules change, broadly, in response to changes in the array of the preferences among the Senate, the president, and House intraparty groups. A change in the House, Senate, or president can create incentives for the majority party to adopt new rules and procedures, and the theory set forth here predicts how such preference change induces centralization or decentralization of power. When choosing rules, legislators

---

[30] Because the number of cases in the analysis is relatively small (sixty-seven cases) and the use of asymptotic analysis may be inappropriate, I also conducted Fisher's exact test to analyze the association between two events. With Fisher's exact test, the significance of the deviation from a null hypothesis can be calculated exactly, rather than relying on an approximation that would become exact only in the limit as the sample size grows to infinity. The drawback is that this test tells me only whether two events are related, but does not tell me how they are related. The p-value of the Fisher's exact test for the independent variable is 0.0011 when the dependent variable is a dichotomous variable, where 1 means change in the House, Senate, or president and 0 its absence. When the dependent variable distinguishes between centralization and decentralization of rules, the p-value is 0.00012. Both results suggest that changes in the constitutional setting and the specific relationship among House parties, the Senate, and the president are closely related to changes in House rules and procedures.

strategically decide which rules and procedures are optimal given different bargaining environments.

House rules do not necessarily enhance or undermine the power of the majority party in the House; rather, the rules they enact, or fail to enact, affect the balance of power within the majority party. When majority party rule-making decisions are viewed from the perspective of alignment among the intraparty groups and the Senate and president, the types of rules that will be adopted in the House are predictable.

The empirical analysis was based on an original database that included the positions of the Senate pivots, presidents, and House factions. The data cover the whole period, from 1879 to 2013. I showed that rules that centralize power in the Speaker are more likely when the non-Speaker group has an ally in the Senate and/or the president. When, after a change in the partisanship of constitutional actors, the non-Speaker group loses that outside ally, or when the Senate and the president are controlled by the opposition, the probability of decentralization of power increases.

6

New Rules for an Old Speaker: Revisiting the 1910 Revolt against Speaker Cannon

The revolt against Speaker Cannon in 1910 is one of a handful of events in congressional history widely regarded as having been transformative. A coalition of Democrats and progressive Republicans changed the existing power-sharing arrangement by stripping Cannon's membership on the powerful Rules Committee and doing away with his power to select its members. Routinely cited as the single most noteworthy case of decentralization of power in the House, the revolt holds a prominent place in the literature on rule changes and legislative leadership. The vast scholarship on the subject explains the revolt as a consequence of Cannon's dictatorial management of the House and manipulative use of committee assignments.

Given the general consensus on the causes of the uprising, the Cannon revolt is a particularly demanding case to test my theory. Can a change in the preferences of constitutional actors, and thus a change in the constitutional set (CS) and the types of bills likely to become law, explain the timing of the revolt and the direction of the rule changes that accompanied it? I propose that it can. I argue that with the election of a conservative president in 1909, William H. Taft, Progressive Republicans lost their presidential ally, Theodore Roosevelt. For more than six years, Roosevelt had been an ally who effectively influenced the type of policies that became laws, blocking the enactment of conservative bills that the Speaker and the Senate preferred and promoting the approval of progressive ones. Before 1909, progressives could enjoy the benefits of delegation (i.e., a powerful Speaker who could quickly push bills through the floor), without worrying about policy shifts toward the conservative side.

However, as I show in detail in the following, the presidential election meant a change in the alignment among constitutional actors. Even though Roosevelt and the progressives initially supported William H. Taft, progressives came to realize, between the election and the inauguration, that Taft would not be the legislative ally Roosevelt had been. Indeed, Taft's first year as president included the enactment of one of the most conservative tariff laws in American history (the Paine-Aldrich tariff law), and the push in Congress for the sanctioning of laws that would have dismantled the progressive program enacted during Roosevelt's presidency. In what follows I show that while progressives were content to serve under a powerful Speaker who, after implicit or explicit bargaining with their presidential ally, pushed for progressive bills, they were not willing to stand by while a powerful Speaker pushed through a conservative agenda.

My discussion proceeds as follows. I first briefly summarize the sequence of activities leading up to the revolt. I then review the prevailing interpretation of the revolt and conclude with several questions that the prevailing interpretation cannot answer. Finally, I argue that anticipated changes in policy outcomes arising from changes in the CS are the underlying mechanism that explains both the timing and the substance of the rule changes that the "Cannon revolt" comprised.

THE REVOLT AGAINST SPEAKER CANNON

Joseph Cannon (R-IL) was elected Speaker for the first time in 1903, and he served in that position continuously until 1911, when the Democratic Party took control of the House. His powers were ample; he controlled the House floor, appointed members to all committees, and designated committee chairs. This included the powerful Rules Committee, to which Cannon appointed himself as chair. The famed revolt took place in March 1910, just before an election that broke a fourteen-year run of Republican majorities.

Important to the revolt is to understand factional politics within the Republican Party. The party was divided between progressives and conservatives.[1] Progressives favored the enactment of labor and social welfare programs and state intervention in the economy. They also supported a downward revision of the tariffs; regulation of business and corporations, especially railroads; conservation of natural resources; and creation of national parks. In contrast, conservative Republicans advocated minimal state intervention in the economy, except when that intervention aimed to guarantee a protective tariff system. They were probusiness and opposed government regulation of prices, accounts, and labor conditions.

Progressives had first attempted to claw some powers back from Cannon almost a year before the better known incident, at the end of the 60th Congress (1907–1909). Progressives demanded the enlargement of the Committee on Rules, the abolishment of the Speaker's power to choose committee members, and a calendar day in which they could present nonprivileged legislation (Hechler 1940). However, three days before the conclusion of the 60th Congress, Cannon negotiated a compromise granting progressives a calendar

---

[1] See Chapter 2 for an in-depth review of progressives and conservative Republicans.

day so that each committee would be called to bring up bills that had not been granted a special rule by the Rules Committee. "Calendar Wednesday" was intended to give progressives limited capacity to set the legislative agenda and bring their preferred issues to the floor. As Jones (1968) states, "There were strong hopes that it [Calendar Wednesday] would limit Cannon's powers" (C. O. Jones 1968, 625).

However, Calendar Wednesday's design rendered it inherently weak. For instance, a simple majority could waive Calendar Wednesday, so it was relatively easy for a group of conservative Republicans to do away with it whenever they wanted. When, a few days later, the 61st Congress convened to decide on its rules and procedures, progressives, who were not appeased by Cannon's initial offering, attempted to dilute the power of the Speaker. To prevent any sweeping change in the distribution of power, Cannon supported yet another limited change in rules: an updated Calendar Wednesday that required a two-thirds majority to waive the calendar and thus made progressives' votes pivotal to suspending it. The revised Calendar Wednesday also created a consent calendar to make it easier for members to secure consideration of noncontroversial legislation. In concession to the House Democratic minority, the new rule also guaranteed the minority party a motion to recommit a bill to the committee.

Disappointed with Calendar Wednesdays, progressives launched a stronger revolt in the 61st Congress. On March 17, 1910, George W. Norris (R-NE) introduced a resolution to strip Cannon of his membership – and, thus, obviously, chairmanship – on the Rules Committee. This resolution eliminated Cannon's control over the committee's composition. Norris strategically introduced the resolution as "privileged by Constitution" in the same manner that an immediately prior resolution about the census had been introduced.[2] He made the argument that since the Constitution authorizes the House to make its own rules, the resolution was privileged.[3] With many of Cannon's Irish supporters absent, celebrating St. Patrick's Day, he blocked the motion with a point-of-order debate. That debate extended over several days, considered both the merits of the resolution and whether it was in order, and featured repeated failed attempts by Cannon supporters to adjourn. After

[2] The subject of the census resolution was noncontroversial. It changed the census form so that it would inquire about the nationality and mother tongue of foreign nationals.

[3] More specifically, he posited that even though he did not believe that the census proposition had been in order, given that the proposition had been adopted, it followed that the adoption of his "rule change" resolution was also justified: "But this must follow, as a logical result, it seems to me, in that case that the privileged nature of the resolution did not depend on its being reported by a committee or considered by a committee, but it was privileged, if privileged at all, because the Constitution made it so. No committee consideration, no committee report, would all to or take away from its privileged nature. I am not responsible for the position in which the House has placed itself; but to be consistent, it seems to me this resolution would have to be held privileged the same as the others" (*Congressional Record*, March 17, 1910, 3293).

two acrimonious days, on St. Joseph's Day, Cannon ruled that the resolution was not in order. However, a House majority, consisting of progressive Republicans and Democrats, overruled him. Norris then moved the previous question. After more heated debate, the Norris resolution was adopted, thus removing the Speaker from the Rules Committee. With that removal, Cannon lost all power to select its members.

PREVAILING INTERPRETATION OF THE REVOLT

How do scholars explain the revolt? In general they consider it a landmark in congressional history, representing the high-water mark in the accumulation of power in the hands of the House Speaker (Cox and McCubbins 1993; C. O. Jones 1968; 1970; Peabody 1976). Conventional wisdom centers on Cannon's "excessive leadership" as the source of the revolt (Bolling 1968; Cooper 1988; Galloway 1969; C. O. Jones 1968; Peabody 1976; Peters 1990; Riddick 1949). Before it, Speaker Cannon could deny recognition on the House floor and appoint members to all committees as well as designate their chairs. This included the powerful Rules Committee, of which Cannon selected himself as chair. Galloway (1969) argues that "these powers in combination were so far-reaching that the speaker came to be considered as an officer second only in power and influence to the President of the United States himself" (Galloway 1969, 136).

In his groundbreaking study on the limits of leadership in the House, Jones argues that Cannon's powers were centered on two pillars, his chairmanship of the Rules Committee and his control of the membership of other important committees. Jones writes that "a frequent complaint [among House members] was that the Speaker abused House Rule X, which gave him the power to appoint the standing committees" (C. O. Jones 1968, 620). Ripley (1967) claims that Cannon used his powers to

> promote his own legislative preferences and to stifle the preferences of progressive Republicans and Democrats.... Cannon maintained strict control over the committee chairmen and would not hesitate to bypass them, or demote them, if they disagreed on important legislation. He used committee assignment to promote men whom he trusted. (Ripley 1967, 19, 90)

Other influential studies of Cannon's speakership reach the same conclusion. Polsby, Gallagher, and Rundquist (1969) assert that the "the insurgent's successful challenge to Cannon's leadership in 1910 laid heavy stress upon his arbitrary use of the Speaker's power of appointment." According to Rohde (1991, 4), Cannon

> used his powers ... as a vehicle for rewarding allies and punishing dissidents. Control of the Rules Committee permitted him to determine which bills got to the floor, and his power as presiding officer enabled him generally to dictate their fate once there. (Rohde 1991, 4)

After reviewing the enormous literature on Cannon, Rager (1998) summarizes that Cannon was "an unbending autocrat who ruled the House with an iron hand" (Rager 1998, 64).

IS THE PREVAILING INTERPRETATION CORRECT?

This brief review of the sequencing of events surrounding Cannon's ouster raises questions about the validity of the prominent interpretation of the revolt.

- With respect to timing:
  - If Cannon's authoritarianism was sufficient reason to oust him, why did House members decentralize power only after Cannon had been serving as the Speaker for more than six years? Cannon had been elected as Speaker in 1903, after all, seven years prior to the revolt.
  - Given that Cannon tried to appease progressives at the end of the 60th and the beginning of the 61st Congresses with rule changes designed to increase their agenda setting power, why did progressives nevertheless revolt a year later?
- With respect to the direction of the rule changes:
  - If the main impetus for the revolt was Cannon's power over committee assignments and his dictatorial management of the floor, why did the revolt only address Cannon's powers with respect to the Rules Committee? After the revolt, Cannon still controlled the floor and could select members and chairs of all committees other than the Rules Committee.

In the remainder of this chapter, I argue that the constitutional theory can answer these pivotal questions, whereas the currently prominent perspective on the Cannon revolt cannot. A change in the partisanship of the president, and the consequent new alignment among president, Senate, minority party, and House majority party factions, explain both the timing of the revolt and the rule changes that, dramatically, decentralized power in the House.

TIMING OF THE REVOLT: WHY DID THE PROGRESSIVES REVOLT
ONLY AFTER CANNON HAD BEEN SERVING AS THE SPEAKER
FOR MORE THAN SIX YEARS?

I argue that the key element to explaining the timing of the revolt is the change in the CS; in 1909 conservative Republican William Howard Taft became the twenty-seventh president of the United States, replacing progressive Republican Theodore Roosevelt. This presidential transition represented a sweeping change in the shape of the CS. Two related but distinct questions are pertinent in this section. First, why did the revolt not happen before the CS change in 1909? Second, why did the revolt not happen immediately after the CS change? I take each of these questions in turn, looking into the alignment of preferences, and the policies enacted before and after the CS change in 1909. Note that changes in the CS as well as in the preferences of constitutional actors are key, because they determine the set of policies that could be enacted into law.[4]

Why Not a Revolt before the 1909 CS Changes?

The essence of the constitutional theory I developed in previous chapters is that rules respond to changes in the CS. There were, however, no changes in the CS between 1903, when Cannon became Speaker, and 1909, so from the point of view of this theory, there is no puzzle. Theodore Roosevelt was the president during these six years, and the Senate and the House were controlled by the Republican Party. Even the House membership remained fairly constant during the period as the Republican Party gained seven seats in the 1902 mid-term and forty-four in the 1904 election, and lost only twenty-eight seats in the 1906 midterm and four seats in the 1908 election (Ornstein, Mann, and Malbin 1999). Remember that alternative explanations of rule changes focus precisely on House membership changes. Changes in the position of the floor median (Schickler 2000; 2001) or party medians (Binder 1997; Aldrich and Rohde 2000) cannot explain the timing, as there was little such movement in the 61st Congress. Figure 6.1 shows the scores from the 57th to the 61st Congress (1901–1911).

The change in floor and party medians in the 61st Congress is minimal and does not differ from the changes observed since the 58th Congress (1903–1905), when Cannon became Speaker.[5]

Figure 6.2 reports majority party homogeneity and party polarization for the 57th–61st Congresses. The change in party homogeneity is minimal, and it actually increases in the 61st Congress. Existing theories will predict centralization of power in the Speaker, not a revolt. With respect to polarization, the changes are again very small. Between the 60th and 61st Congresses, the change is half the size of the change between the 59th and 60th Congresses, when no rule changes occurred. Put simply, these figures show that changes in the preferences of House membership cannot account for the revolt.

---

[4] This analysis parallels Valelly's (2009) study of the Reed rules, in which policy outcomes play a central role. He argues that the enactment of the Reed rules stems from House Republicans' preferences about the structure of the party system. That is, centralization of power in Speaker Reed in 1879 was not the result of preference homogeneity in the Republican Party or the preferences of the floor median. Rather, it was the result of particular policy preferences of the majority party. In this case, the new rules were the mechanism that would allow the majority to enact bills that could regulate House elections in the southern United States.

[5] Majority and minority party medians are fairly constant throughout the ten-year period. Floor medians change slightly, but the change from the 58th to the 59th Congress (+.056) is greater in magnitude than the change from the 60th to the 61st Congress (−.049). However, there are no changes in the rules in the 59th Congress. Thus, the change in floor median cannot justify the revolt.

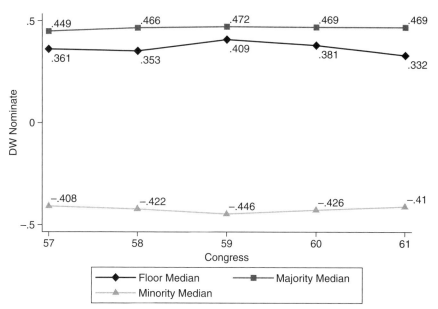

FIGURE 6.1. Floor median, majority party median, and minority party median in the House, 57th–61st Congresses.

Second, there was no revolt before the 1909 CS change because the alignment of preferences among president, Senate, minority party, and House majority party factions was such that delegation of power in the Speaker was convenient for the majority party. The constitutional theory predicts that House majority party factions will agree on delegating power to the Speaker and his faction when they can count on an outside ally to restrict the type of policies that become laws. I showed that no matter the ideological distance between majority party factions, if the expected laws are within the non-Speaker group's preference set, the latter will agree to support a powerful Speaker because it can still enjoy the benefits of delegation without worrying about the Speaker's behavior. President Roosevelt was an ally for progressives (the non-Speaker group), a friendly president who blocked the enactment of conservative bills and promoted the approval of progressive ones. With a powerful ally outside the House, progressives could enjoy the benefits of delegation, in this case a powerful Speaker who could quickly push bills through the floor, without worrying about policy shifts toward the conservative side. In exchange for conservative support of the progressive program, Roosevelt guaranteed conservative Republicans at least the status quo on policies they cared about.

An analysis of the legislation enacted during Roosevelt's presidency offers insight as to why progressives in the House did not revolt before 1910. If anticipated policy change is the underlying mechanism linking constitutional actors

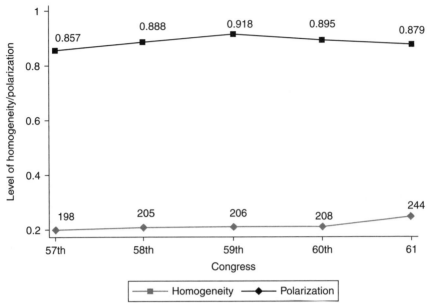

FIGURE 6.2. Majority party homogeneity and party polarization, 57th–61st Congresses.

with rule changes, then the policies enacted during the six-year period while Cannon was Speaker and Roosevelt was president, the 58th (1903–1905), 59th (1905–1907), and 60th (1907–1909) Congresses, should reflect progressives' preferences. Indeed, a closer look at the policies reveals that issues of vital importance to progressives, such as social welfare, corporate regulation, and natural resource conservation, were regularly on the agenda and often became law.

Table 6.1 lists the "progressive" enactments during the 1903–1909 period and supplements the list with comments on the individual items' legislative importance.

I use the ranking developed by Clinton and Lapinski (2006), who employ an item-response model to create measures of legislative significance. Their measure is based on a comprehensive data set that includes 37,766 public statutes passed between 1877 and 1994 and on "elite evaluations (20) of the importance of public enactments at different points in time" (2006, 233). The authors also document the "amount of attention Congress devotes to each statute, whether a conference committee was required, and the session in which the legislation was introduced" (2006, 233).

The six laws referenced in Table 6.1 are not only among the most important measures enacted during each of the corresponding Congresses; some of them also rank very high among all statutes enacted between 1877 and 1994.

TABLE 6.1. *Important legislation enacted while Cannon was Speaker and Roosevelt was president*

Year Enacted	Law	Mean Significance[a]	Rank among Measures Enacted in the Same Congress	Rank among All Measures Enacted between 1877 and 1994
58th	Transfer Act (HR 8460)	.504	1st	549th
59th	Pure Food and Drug Act (S 88)	1.956	1st	3rd
59th	Hepburn Act (HR 12987)	1.743	2nd	14th
59th	Meat Inspection Act (HR 18537)	1.018	3rd	171st
60th	Employer Liability Act (HR 20310)	.853	2nd	287th
60th	Child Labor Act (S 4812)	.348	3rd	700th

[a] Clinton and Lapinski built the ranking using an item-response model to create a measure of legislative significance. The measure is based on a comprehensive data set that includes 37,766 public statutes passed between 1877 and 1994 and incorporates "elite evaluations (20) of the importance of public enactments at different points in time" (2006, 233). They also use information regarding the "amount of attention Congress devotes to each statute, whether a conference committee was required, and the session in which the legislation was introduced, to extend the ratings to statutes unmentioned by the raters" (2006, 233). For a detailed explanation of the methodology see Clinton and Lapinski (2006).

Thus, the legislation enacted in this period is not trivial; much of it shaped the U.S. economy and society. A detailed examination of those policies helps to understand why progressives tolerated a "dictatorial" Speaker for more than six years. In policy terms, they were getting much of what they wanted. I review three policy areas: regulation of corporations, conservation of natural resources, and social welfare. I also look into the tariff schedule, the policy area that Roosevelt did not touch as part of his implicit bargaining with conservative Republicans.

Regulation of Corporations

Dismantling trusts and regulating corporations engaged in interstate commerce were significant components of the progressives' legislative agenda, and the Roosevelt administration addressed them both (Gould 1974; 1991; 2001; Hechler 1940; Hofstadter 1963; Mowry 1958). First, Roosevelt pursued more than thirty-five antitrust actions against the oil, tobacco, meatpacking, and other industries, exerting strong executive action by directing the Justice Department to take antitrust measures where needed (e.g., against J.P. Morgan's Northern Securities Company and Rockefeller's Standard Oil Company).[6]

Second, in 1906 Roosevelt signed the Hepburn Act, a landmark piece of legislation that significantly increased railroad regulation. The act strengthened and expanded the power of the Interstate Commerce Commission (ICC) to review and establish "just and reasonable" maximum rates, to examine railroad company accounts, and to supervise extensively the railroad industry. Roosevelt was a key force behind the passage of this legislation, as Gould explains:

> Much of the language of the bill was framed in the Justice Department ... the passage of the Hepburn Act culminated two years of effective and purposeful presidential leadership.... If it had not been for Theodore Roosevelt ... there would not have been any railroad legislation of any kind. (Gould 1991, 164)

Third, at the same time that the Hepburn Act became law, two other important pieces of industrial regulation legislation moved through Congress. One was the Pure Food and Drug Act of 1906, which, according to Carpenter,

> bears an immense institutional legacy. It authorized the regulations of food and pharmaceutical products now carried out by one of the nation's most powerful federal agencies, the Food and Drug Administration. (Carpenter 2001, 2)

The other was the Meat Inspection Act of 1906, which gave the Department of Agriculture the power to inspect all meat purchased in interstate commercial transactions and oversee the conditions in meatpacking houses.

These distinctively progressive measures, which provided protection for citizens through federal government regulation, became law in spite of a conservative-dominated House and Senate, and only because Roosevelt supported them. Progressive John Nelson (R-WI) points to the president as being the force behind the progressive legislation:

> It is true that the railway rate bill, the pure-food bill, and the meat inspection bill had been favorably acted upon by Congress, but is there a man here who does not know that these great measures for the betterment of conditions among the people were forced through this House by the "big stick" in spite of the rules and the Speaker. (*Congressional Record*, 61st Congress, Second Session, 3305)

With Roosevelt in the White House, the policies pushed by Cannon were within the progressives' acceptance set.

---

[6] Even though the Sherman Antitrust Act had been enacted in 1890, the enforcement of antitrust statutes had been lacking, as the Justice Department had not taken any serious action against mergers and combinations. For instance, President William McKinley had not pursued any case of antitrust during his almost five years in the White House, even though hundreds of consolidations of trusts that reshaped the American economy had occurred.

Conservation of Natural Resources Program

Progressives also favored natural resource conservation (Stradling 2013). As Skowronek explains, "Roosevelt's conservation initiative aimed to end the unrestrained destruction of the nation's resources and to begin ... the constructive management of resources" (1993, 250). Through executive orders, Roosevelt created the Wildlife Preserves and the Forest Reserves, which devoted millions of acres of federal lands to the National Forest Reserves, despite the probusinesses preferences of conservative Republicans, who opposed such measures.[7] Through executive orders, the president created the Country Life Commission and the National Conservation Commission and appointed the Inland Water Commission, which was entrusted to prepare a plan for the conservation of river systems.

The Transfer Act of 1905 shifted the responsibility for management of national forests from the Department of Interior to the Department of Agriculture.[8] It also allowed the Forest Service to make its own appropriations by creating a special fund created from the sale of forest products, the use of forestlands, and the lease of waterpower. Carpenter (2001) argues that "the 1905 law was pathbreaking in several ways [and] it released the Forest Service from dependence on congressional appropriations" (Carpenter 2001, 282). Through other enactments, Congress also granted the chief of the Bureau of Forestry, Gifford Pinchot, the power to set Bureau regulations and the right to enforce those regulations and make arrests for violation of laws in forest reserves and national parks.

Social Welfare Acts

Other key progressive bills that became law while progressives had an ally in the presidency include a 1908 Child Labor Law for the District of Columbia, which regulated the employment of children, and a Committee on Child Labor law, enacted during the 59th Congress, that gave the secretary of commerce and labor the responsibility to investigate the child labor problem. The latter was very important as it provided the necessary funds for conducting a federal study on child welfare, whose results were key for the establishment of the U.S. Children Bureau in 1912, the first bureau to be headed by a woman, Julia Lathrop. Furthermore, two Employer Liability Acts that established workmen's compensation measures for work-related injuries became law in 1906 and 1908, respectively, a strong progressive response to the high number of railroad deaths.[9]

---

[7] In 1907 when Congress banned the creation of new national forests except by laws approved by Congress, Roosevelt released an executive order that created twenty-one new national forests immediately before signing the bill (Skowronek 1993).
[8] Gifford Pinchot was the chief of the Bureau of Forestry. He was a Yale educated and German trained scientist who "became one of Roosevelt's most trusted confidants ... [and] is widely credited for the 'greening' of Roosevelt" (Carpenter 2001, 278)
[9] The first act was invalidated by the Supreme Court.

The Tariff Schedule

Roosevelt bargained for the votes of conservative Republicans in both chambers in all the areas enumerated previously, in exchange for his compromise to maintain the status quo regarding the current tariff schedules.

The tariffs traditionally had been a contentious issue within the party. Although the Republican Party coalition was initially based on high tariffs that protected the manufacturing belt of the Northeast and the raw materials produced in the Midwest and West,[10] by the beginning of the twentieth century progressives from the Midwest and West banded together to support a decrease in the tariff. The severe increase in the costs of living, especially in the prices of manufactured products, made the high tariffs less attractive. Sanders argues that

> in the presence of rising prices and rapacious trusts, protection seemed less golden. Its benefits accrued mainly to eastern manufacturers and their bankers and, to a lesser extent to vulnerable wool, fruit, timber and sugar-beet producers in the west, but the midwestern farmer got little out of the Republican system. (Sanders 1999, 219)

In light of these trends, progressives repeatedly solicited Roosevelt's support to revise the tariff schedules.[11] During his entire tenure, however, Theodore Roosevelt would not accede to these demands. Skowronek (1993) posits that Roosevelt

> bargained away his proposal for a special commission to report on the tariff in return for conservative support for his much-heralded initiative on railroad regulation.... Roosevelt had used this troublesome issue [the tariff] to his best advantage by gaining some much needed leverage with the Old Guard.... The agreement worked effectively enough in the House where Speaker Joe Cannon facilitated action on a bill the President liked. (1993, 242, 249)

Thus, the tariff review was part of Roosevelt's bargaining with conservative Republicans; Cannon and his intraparty group supported progressive policies in exchange for preservation of the status quo on tariffs (Chamberlain 1946; Gould 1974; Hechler 1940; Mowry 1958; Sanders 1999).[12]

---

[10] For instance, Sanders explains that Republicans forged unlikely coalitions by creating tariff schedules that protected "hide producers in the west and the Corn Belt and footwear manufacturers in the northeast, sugar refiners in the northeast and sugar-beet growers in the midwest and west, and iron-ore extractors in Michigan-Minnesota and steel manufacturers in Pennsylvania and Ohio" (1999, 218). The high tariffs mostly penalized the South, which had to pay high prices for manufactured goods while its export markets for tobacco and cotton were restricted by other countries in retaliation for the high tariffs the United States imposed on their products.

[11] The current Dingley Tariff Law (1897) imposed an average of more than a 50 percent tariff on products imported from other countries.

[12] For example, Roosevelt's successful campaign in favor of what became the Hepburn Act was predicated on the implied threat of a tariff revision (Gould 1974, 58).

Ultimately, this bargaining between Roosevelt and conservatives was to their mutual benefit; it enabled progressives to pass their preferred legislation, which they highly valued, and at the same time allowed Cannon and the conservatives to keep tariffs at current levels, an issue extremely salient to this faction. Thus, under this bargaining agreement facilitated by Roosevelt, progressive policies were approved in the House, where the powerful Speaker could push them without interference of the more conservative elements of the party.

A closer look at enacted policies, then, reveals that, despite Cannon's iron-hand control of the House, important progressive policies were enacted. The presence of progressive president Theodore Roosevelt guaranteed the enactment of bills that were within the progressives' win set. Progressives did not mind delegating power to a Speaker as long as they had an ally outside the House that would negotiate on their behalf. Indeed, a powerful Speaker guaranteed that the policies negotiated with the president would fly through the legislative process and avoid hurdles in the House. Thus, progressives had no incentive to seek out a redistribution of power before the CS change in 1909.

Why Did the Revolt Happen a Year after Taft's Election?

If the CS change is the key element to understanding the revolt, we would expect progressives to have pushed for changes in rules right after Taft's election. Indeed, twice progressives attempted to revolt, at the end of the 60th Congress and at the beginning of the 61st. However, as explained previously, conservative Republicans, who offered the creation of Calendar Wednesday and then a modification to make it more workable, preempted both attempts.

It is important to note that while Roosevelt and the progressives initially supported William H. Taft, progressives came to realize, between the election and the inauguration, that Taft would not be the legislative ally Roosevelt had been. Although Taft had promised Roosevelt to keep his advisers, Taft's new cabinet not only lacked progressives, it also leaned heavily toward corporate interests (Gould 1974, 88). For another thing, in the immediate aftermath of Taft's election and before the inauguration, Taft did not support Roosevelt in disputes with Congress over conservation policies. These actions signaled to progressives that they had lost the ear of the White House, thus reducing limits on what policies conservatives could pass.

Cannon recognized progressives' worries and sensed their unease. That awareness explains why, three days before the end of the 60th Congress, Cannon granted progressives the Calendar Wednesday, when committees could bring up unprivileged bills to the floor. Cox and McCubbins (2005) argue that

> in order to forestall an even worse outcome, the regular Republicans offered a resolution to institute a Calendar Wednesday. (Cox and McCubbins 2005, 60–1)

Binder (1997) explains that "supporters of the new rule intended to weaken majority leaders' control of the agenda and to ensure actions on bills preferred by Democratic minorities and /or Republican progressives" (Binder 1997, 133).

Calendar Wednesday was strengthened when the 61st Congress convened. Progressives attempted to revolt, and Cannon, with the support of Democrats, backed yet another limited change in rules aimed to guarantee progressives further institutional power to set the agenda, a power that progressives had previously bargained with conservatives through Roosevelt.[13] However, progressives soon realized that those rules, even though a useful tool to influence the agenda, were not enough to block conservative policies.

Indeed, contrary to progressives' preferences, conservative Republicans enacted one of the most conservative tariff laws in American history. Furthermore, they tried to enact laws that would have dismantled the progressive program enacted during Roosevelt's presidency.

I now discuss, in greater detail, the events during the first year of Taft's presidency that led progressives to revolt.

The Payne-Aldrich Tariff Act

The most important enactment during the year between Taft's inauguration and the revolt was the Payne-Aldrich Tariff Act. In March 1909, Taft called a special session of Congress to revise the tariff. The Republican platform, owing to the strong influence of progressives, had pledged to reduce the tariff schedules. The bill was debated for three weeks on the House floor, and Cannon allowed the offering of amendments to 90 percent of the bill. The initial version of the bill that passed in the House had progressive support, as it significantly reduced the rates that had been set by the 1897 act. In the Senate, however, conservative Republicans introduced more than eight hundred amendments, all of which either kept the tariff at 1897 levels or increased it. Chamberlain (1946) argues that "the increases had been dictated by special interests, which were powerful enough to write almost any tariff schedule they might choose" (Chamberlain 1946, 107).[14] When a Conference Committee convened, six of the nine conferees that Cannon selected were protectionists, and the bill that came out of the committee included all of the Senate's amendments.

In August 1909, the highly protectionist Payne-Aldrich Tariff bill became law.[15] A month after the enactment of the tariff bill, in a speech at Winona, Minnesota, Taft posited that

> I am bound to say that I think the Payne Tariff Bill is the best tariff bill that the Republican Party ever passed. (September 17, 1909)

---

[13] By supporting Cannon and not the progressives, the minority party obtained a new rule, the ability to make a motion to recommit legislation.

[14] For instance, Senator Aldrich, with the support of conservative Republicans, was able to benefit the Northeast by increasing the duties on wool, silk, and cotton manufacturers to a level higher than those established in the Dingley Tariff Act.

[15] The Payne-Aldrich Tariff bill ranks first in significance among those passed in the 61st Congress. It ranks second in importance with a mean significance of 2.120 among all statutes enacted between 1877 and 1994 (Clinton and Lapinski 2006).

Progressives were outraged by the bill and strongly lobbied for a presidential veto, stating that Taft "seems to have surrendered absolutely to Aldrich" and that "we might as well get ready to make our fight without him" (Cumming to Bristow, September 25, 1909, Bristow papers; cited in Hechler 1964). The Payne-Aldrich Tariff Act was the first sign that policies on the most significant issues in the country were moving in a conservative direction. Outside Congress, progressive-leaning publications chronicled the impact of the act, essentially moving the intraparty struggles within the House into the public arena. Many articles directly linked the change in presidential preference with the precarious state of progressive ideology and influence. A writer for *Success Magazine*[16] described the legislative battle over the tariff bill as follows:

> Five months of Congressional vocalization saw the reduction advocates pushed backwards from every position they had taken, and the tariff unchanged – except where it had made worse. ... The reductionists ... had fought so long and so furiously without a suspicion they were battering a stone wall with their bare fists. Business preferred the tariff as it was; Business had its will. (*Success Magazine*, January 1910)

The editor of *Collier Magazine* asserted: "If Roosevelt had been in the White House, the tariff bill as it stands to-day would have been a very different thing" (*Collier Magazine*, June 12, 1909, 43).

Progressives also lost their battle to include income tax legislation in the Payne-Aldrich Tariff bill. In the House, Democrats, supported by progressives, presented an income tax amendment to supplant the losses in revenue given the lower tariffs expected with the new bill.[17] However, conservative Republicans fiercely opposed the enactment of an income tax (*Congressional Record*, 61st Congress, 1420–1421), and to avoid it, they supported Taft's proposed solutions: the creation of a tax on the earnings of corporations and the approval of a constitutional amendment that would give Congress the power to levy an income tax.[18] Although progressives generally opposed the corporation tax because it could easily be passed on to consumers, this time they supported it

---

[16] *Success Magazine* was a progressive publication founded by Orison Swett Marden in 1897. Although it was initially created as a publication to inform, educate, and promote material success, around 1905 Marden began to publish numerous "exposure" articles, among which the most famous were extensive attacks on Speaker Joseph Cannon (especially Judson Welliver's article "The End of Cannonism" in January 1910). In addition to the pieces critical of the Speaker, topics covered in the magazine included exposés of child labor practices, political corruption, and trusts. Due to financial difficulties, the magazine folded in 1911.

[17] At this time most of the federal income was from tariffs. As the tariffs were on imported goods, this kind of taxation was heavily regressive (individuals with low income spend a higher proportion of their income than the rich on consumption goods). The income tax proposed by Democrats and supported by progressives had the objective of taxing wealth from stocks and bonds, which was not taxed either in the federal tariff or in the states' property taxes.

[18] Conservative Republicans were confident that the constitutional amendment would fail to achieve enough states' ratification.

because it included a provision by which the accounts of corporations would be published and accessible to the public.[19]

Therefore, just five months after Taft's inauguration, the tariff duties had been increased to levels that were higher than they had previously been. Furthermore, the possibility of enacting an income tax had been thwarted by the adoption of a corporate tax that progressives believed could be easily passed on to consumers. These two outcomes, higher tariffs and a corporate tax, meant an increase in the prices of goods and, consequently, in the cost of living, both of which directly affected the progressives' constituencies. Indeed, both issues were thus central in contributing to the revolt against Speaker Cannon. Progressive policies would not fare any better over the following six months, as the Speaker and his intraparty group relentlessly challenged the policies enacted under Roosevelt.

Taft's Program on Regulation and Conservation

At the same time that the Payne-Aldrich bill became law, conservative Republicans were preparing to dismantle the regulatory policies established by Roosevelt. What follows is a detailed analysis of the legislative process behind Taft's proposals regarding the regulation of corporations. Detailed attention to the process is important because the regulatory bill introduced, debated, and pushed by the Taft administration during January, February, and part of March 1910 dismantled the regulatory framework established by Roosevelt and was highly procorporation, yet the bill that emerged from Congress after the revolt differed greatly. Progressives had been excluded prior to the revolt; afterward, they were able to influence the content of the bill to a great extent.

Immediately after the enactment of the Payne-Aldrich Tariff Act, the president formed a Special Railroad Committee to investigate interstate commerce legislation and propose new railroad regulation. Progressives felt apprehensive about the future bill as (i) the members of the Special Railroad Committee had close ties with corporations, (ii) the attorney general had held numerous conferences with the lawyers for the big railroads, and, (iii) the president himself met privately with six of the leading businessmen in American railroads. Writing to a colleague, progressive senator Joseph Bristow (R-KA) noted that, in reference to the railroad legislation,

> I have no faith whatsoever in getting the President to stand with us against Root, Knox, Wickersham and Aldrich and company, and from present indications it seems to me that we are confronting the bitterest fight we have yet been in. (Bristow to Albert Cummins, October 30, 1909, cited in Hechler 1964)

Newspapers interpreted the situation similarly. The *New York Times* wrote that

---

[19] As I explain later, a few months after the approval of the bill, Republicans devised a strategy to render this provision null.

they [progressives] fear that the bill to accomplish the President's purposes, coming from corporation lawyers like Wickersham, Knox and Root will strengthen
the position of corporations.... They are afraid – after what they saw him do
in the tariff fight – that he will be persuaded by the designers. (*NYT*, October
19, 1909)

By the end of January 1910, Representative Charles Townsend (R-MI) introduced the bill in the House, and Stephen Elkins (R-WV) in the Senate.[20] The
bill confirmed the worst fears of progressives. First, it proposed the creation
of an Interstate Commerce Court, composed of five members appointed for
life, which would have exclusive jurisdiction over railroad matters. The president considered the court to be the best remedy for the long litigation arising from decisions of the Interstate Commerce Commission (ICC). However,
progressives argued that the creation of the Commerce Court was unwise, not
only because railroads would be able to influence the selection of court members but also because the massive power of the railroads would be focused in
a single judicial entity.

The bill drafted by the administration weakened the ICC, establishing that
all suits against the orders of the ICC would be given to the Department of
Justice, excluding the ICC and interested parties from any participation in the
suits.[21] The bill also prohibited the representation of the plaintiff shipper by
separate counsel. Progressives were outraged by these provisions, claiming that
they would seriously impair the efficiency of the ICC, leaving it with little more
power than that of making recommendations.

With respect to the rate agreement among railroads, the bill required that
when agreements were entered into and put into practice, copies of the agreement and the classification made therein should be filed with the ICC, for the
commission's subsequent inspection. However, the bill made no provision to
allow the ICC to review the agreements, and did not provide a procedure by
which the ICC could express its disapproval of the rate agreements. Progressives
argued that this section of the bill was intended to take the railroads outside
the Sherman Antitrust Act, and thus they demanded a provision by which the
rate agreements between railroads would not go into effect until they had been
approved by the ICC.[22] In short, the clear intention of conservative Republicans
was to reduce the regulation of corporations, an issue of high importance to
progressives, and they seemed to be succeeding.

---

[20] Given progressives' opposition to the railroad regulation that the administration was getting
ready to send to Congress, Taft threatened potentially rebellious progressive Republicans by
stating that he would withhold patronage from congressmen opposing his policies.

[21] In this regard, progressives argued that the railroads would be more interested in the selection
of the attorney general than of the president himself.

[22] Progressives also wanted to include water and electric lines in the scope of the bill, to increase
shippers' powers to select their own route. However, these provisions were not included in
the bill.

At the beginning of 1910, President Taft and Congress were also advancing a federal incorporation bill. Taft argued that this bill would permit combinations of capital that would promote the economy and corporate efficiency. However, progressives feared that the bill would drive large corporations to seek exception from the Sherman Antitrust Act under a federal charter, thereby legalizing industrial monopolies.[23]

Another important event occurred in February 1910, when the president stated that the publishing provision of the Payne-Aldrich Act was a dead letter because funds were not available to pay for the expenses needed to make information about corporations' accounts publicly available.

In terms of conservation, Taft refused to continue supporting the work of the National Conservation Commission and ordered Chief Forester Gifford Pinchot to remove nonforested land from the forest reserves (Carpenter 2001).[24] But what most infuriated progressives was the outcome of a heated dispute between Pinchot and Secretary of Interior Richard A. Ballinger. Pinchot publicly endorsed the allegations made by Louis Glavis, an agent of the Department of the Interior, which charged Ballinger with misconduct in office relating to coal lands in Alaska and accused him of favoring anticonservation interests (Gould 1974; Carpenter 2001). Pinchot made the controversy public in January 1910 by criticizing Ballinger in an open letter to progressive senator Jonathan Dolliver (R-IA). However, President Taft supported Ballinger and dismissed Pinchot. As Carpenter (2001) argues:

> Pinchot's dismissal was the last straw for Insurgents who had grown wary of the president from 1909 onward…. The firing enraged Roosevelt … it started the infamous Cannon revolt of 1910…. House insurgents voted to strip Cannon of his power to name members of the special committee to investigate Ballinger. (Carpenter 2001, 285)

This was a strong signal that conservatives would likely attempt other changes to conservation policies. Progressives were aware that most of such policies had been enacted through executive actions, and thus could be easily annulled by Taft.

All of the policies enacted or being debated in Congress represented substantial shifts away from the progressives' preferences. By the end of February

---

[23] A *Success Magazine* article observed "they charge that the federal incorporation bill would have just one real and obvious effect if passed; it would provide means for the reorganization and perpetuation of the Standard Oil, Tobacco and other trusts which are menaced with dissolution under the Sherman anti-trust law. It would permit them, if dissolved in their present form, to re-incorporate under the new federal act, announce their purpose to be 'good trusts' hereafter, and to continue their concentrated control, their present management, their monopolistic character, their domination of vast industries" ("The Month in America" 1910).

[24] While "to Roosevelt 'conservation' meant government management by experts in the interests of efficient resources development …Taft preferred a freely competitive market and a minimum of governmental interference" (Coletta 1973, 99–100).

1910, the railway bill had been redrafted and reintroduced in the House and the Senate several times to incorporate further amendments supported by the railroad corporations. In the Senate, the bill had even been reported favorably to the floor after more than one hundred amendments proposed by progressives were prevented from consideration in the conservative Republican dominated committee.[25] *Success Magazine* reported that

> the bill, instead of being an advance in the regulation of interstate commerce, is a long step backward, and the effect, if it becomes law would be seriously to impair the efficiency of existing statutes. It furnishes common carriers with new weapons and dulls the edge of those heretofore given to people. (*Success Magazine*, April 1910, 254)

In the House, the Interstate Commerce Committee was preparing to report the bill as originally drafted by the president, without any amendment. At the beginning of March, the *New York Times* stated, "Taft is winning in the fight for the administration bill to amend the Interstate Commerce law" (*NYT*, March 1, 1910).[26] The day before the beginning of the revolt against Cannon, the Senate commenced debate of the railroad bill on the floor. At this time, the *New York Times* reported that

> it seems now unlikely that the insurgents will get the upper hand. The regulars dislike all railroad control … they will do all in their power to prevent the bill from increasing in severity as it passes through Congress. (*NYT*, March 16, 1910)

Thus, days before the revolt, progressives were forlornly contemplating (1) the dismantling of conservation policies as a result of Pinchot's dismissal, (2) the enactment of a railroad regulation bill that would have greatly weakened the ICC, (3) a probusiness federal incorporation bill, (4) the death of a publicity measure that would have allowed greater monitoring of corporations, and (5) the possibility of losing their reelection bids as conservatives were preparing to oppose progressives.

These "highly possible" policy changes were the main impetus for the revolt. While progressives were content to serve under a powerful Speaker who, after implicit or explicit bargaining with their presidential ally, pushed for progressive bills, they were not willing to stand by while a powerful Speaker pushed through only conservative bills. The change in policies during Taft's first year

---

[25] Progressives did write a minority report.

[26] Additionally, to make the "no amendments allowed" threat effective, Taft decided to fight progressive Republicans in their reelection bids. For example, the *Chicago Daily Tribune* reported: "Taft approves campaign to overthrow Insurgents: … the entire campaign plan of the Republican organization … is to be based on regularity and the insurgents will be compelled to fight their battles for election without the aid of the committees on literature or contributions … Regular forces have been urging the President to make a direct attack upon the insurgents in his Chicago speech … this could be done on the basis that the insurgents have been blocking the passage of some of the administration bills" (*Chicago Daily Tribune*, March 7, 1910).

convinced progressives that they needed a new redistribution of power in the House. As Hechler remarked:

> It was "Uncle Joe" Cannon's economic and social philosophy that first aroused the western Congressmen against his autocracy. The question of power in itself did not greatly excite the average Congressmen; but power exercised for reactionary economic and social ends seemed downright pernicious. (Hechler 1940, 31)

Indeed, reading the detailed debate during the actual revolt reveals that policy concerns played a prominent role. Progressives knew that the success of the revolt and the redistribution of power were the keys to influence legislation and to serve their constituency. For example, progressive John Nelson (R-WI) posited,

> If we liberalize these rules now, if we change them by enlarging the Committee on Rules and disqualifying the Speaker from membership upon it, as is proposed by the pending resolution, to that extent we eliminate this issue from the campaign; and what is vastly more important, we make it easier to secure progressive legislation in the House, redeem our platform pledges, and prove our party faithful to its high trust. (*Congressional Record*, March 17, 1910, 3305)

Conservative Republicans objected that if the complaints against the Speaker were related to Cannon's autocratic management of the House, then all the laws enacted during his speakership should be credited to him. Conservative Republican James R. Mann (R-IL) openly wondered why progressives would oppose Cannon and the rules of the House, when those same rules were the ones responsible for many of the progressive policies enacted previously:

> Just what are the objections to Speaker Cannon and what is meant by "Cannonism" or "anti-Cannonism." ... I assume that the main objections to the present Speaker are based on the proposition that, under the rules of the House, he is an autocrat, practically all powerful, and as such is opposed to and prevents consideration of the progressive measures and the enactment into law of the progressive ideas demanded by an enlightened public. The charge is frequently made, and, probably, quite generally believed, that the Speaker controls the consideration of bills in the House of Representatives and largely dominates their form and substance if enacted into law. If this be true, and Mr. Cannon is held personally responsible for the failure to consider measures and to enact proposed and desired legislation, because he is all powerful in the House, then he should by the same reasoning be given credit for the great measures which have been enacted during his speakership.... Among many others may be noted the following: pure-food law; actual governmental control of railroad rates and railroad accounting; providing additional safety and safe-guards for railroad employees; scientific study of means to prevent railway accidents; the employers' liability law ... irrigation and reclamation of arid lands; providing commissions to study river improvement and currency reform; enlarging the power, duties and effectiveness of the Forest Service; (*Congressional Record*, March 17, 1910, 3334).

In response, progressive Henry Allen Cooper (R-WI) stated that

> it is true that some splendid laws were passed. But with the Speaker in the chair and Theodore Roosevelt out of the White House, we would not have had those laws. (*Congressional Record*, 61st Congress, Second Session, 3303).

Thus, while conservative Republicans emphasized that the rules progressives intended to change were the same ones that had allowed the enactment of important progressive legislation, progressives claimed that such laws had been possible only because of the presence of a progressive president. Again, the key to understanding these arguments is the presidential change. A conservative president, holding the autocratic Speaker constant, enabled the passage of conservative legislation and the obstruction of progressive bills.

DIRECTIONALITY OF THE REVOLT

The revolt decentralized power by removing Cannon from the Rules Committee and establishing that the membership of that committee, as well as its chair, would be elected by a majority of House members. After the revolt, Cannon still controlled the floor and could select members and chairs of all committees other than the Rules Committee. Why, if one of the main complaints about Cannon was his discretionary authority over committee assignments, did progressives not remove that power from him? Indeed, during the revolt Cannon offered to resign his Speaker position, only to see that offer rebuffed by a coalition of conservative Republicans and a majority of progressives.

Progressives did not intend to remove all power from Cannon. Removing the Speaker from the Rules Committee was enough to guarantee more policy outcomes that progressives liked.[27] Thus, if the redistribution of power was enough to change the course of policy outcomes, then the content of conservative policies being debated in Congress should have changed radically after the revolt. That is, after the uprising, policies should again have been within the progressives' win set. Because the revolt redistributed power from the Speaker to the non-Speaker faction, the progressives should again have had the capacity to leave their imprint on policy outcomes. The substance of Taft's legislative program that was still in Congress should have changed dramatically toward the progressive direction. Consider, then, what actually happened.

Recall that just before the revolt, the railroad bill that intended to dismantle railroad regulation was about to be enacted into law in almost the same form as it had been introduced. Indeed, this bill, which had strong conservative components, was heavily amended in the progressives' direction. The final version, known as the Mann-Elkins Act, was unanimously supported by progressive and conservative Republicans and passed the House in a party line vote in

---

[27] Indeed, the revolt showed conservatives that if they decided to continue pursuing conservative policies, progressives could again coalesce with Democrats and change the rules more radically.

May 1910. The act was a wholly different measure, now including many of the progressives' policy preferences.[28] As Hechler summarizes,

> all in all, the Progressives were successful in their conduct of the fight on the objectionable provisions of the Mann-Elkins Act ... [they] completely revamped the measure as originally introduced and forced the regulars to modify and abandon whole sections. (1940, 163)

The act included the long- and short-haul clause, as well as interstate telephone and telegraphs lines as common carriers. It provided for the physical valuation of railroads and revoked the attorney general's discretionary power in cases appealed to the Commerce Court from the ICC. It established the Commerce Court to review appeals from ICC decisions, making the United States the defendant in all such appeals. It authorized the ICC to suspend, pending investigation, the rates and classifications believed to be unreasonable, regardless of whether the shipper filed a complaint.[29]

In terms of conservation, Taft urged Congress to enact legislation to legalize the withdrawals of land from entry that Roosevelt had authorized by executive orders. Indeed, more than eight million acres of waterpower, phosphate, and petroleum lands were legally authorized for the first time. Congress also authorized the expenditure of $20 million to complete land reclamation projects already under way.

Another initiative in which progressives were able to exert their influence after the revolt was the Postal Savings Bank Act.[30] Although progressives had been left out of the negotiations before the revolt, the final compromise accommodated both progressives' and conservatives' demands.[31] Progressive representative Victor Murdock (R-KS) gave a rousing speech in favor of the bill, claiming that it would "close the breach of the Republican Party in the House" (Hechler 1940, 161). Furthermore, in June 1910, the Republican Party, in a noncontroversial move, created the discharge process, by which a member of the House could file a motion to discharge a bill from a committee.[32] Both progressives and conservatives supported the measure.

---

[28] The Mann-Elkins Act ranks second in significance among those passed in the 61st Congress. It ranks eleventh in importance among all statutes enacted between 1877 and 1994 (Clinton and Lapinski 2006).

[29] Among other provisions that addressed progressives' preferences were those that accorded to shippers the privilege of designating the route over which their shipments should move, prohibited rates through the medium of false claims, and enlarged the jurisdiction of the ICC over all common carriers and their permits.

[30] The Postal Savings Bank Act ranks seventh in significance among those passed in the 61st Congress. It ranks 357th in importance among all statutes enacted between 1877 and 1994.

[31] Progressives requested as a condition that deposits would be placed in local banks under the supervision of a government board of trustees, while conservatives were pleased because the bill stated that in an emergency, the deposits could be used to purchase government bonds (Carpenter 2001).

[32] The discharge rule stated that on certain days – the first and third Mondays of each month – the motion could be called up after the Unanimous Consent calendar was dealt with and in the

The revolt demonstrated to the conservative wing of the party that progressives were willing to abandon their own party and unite with the opposition to change the institutional prerogatives of the Speaker if their preferences were ignored. The striking change in policy outcomes shows that the revolt was prompted by changes in policies that affected the core of the progressives' ideology. Progressive Miles Poindexter (R-WA) in an interview with K. Hechler on November 1938 reported that

> when asked today whether, in retrospect, his Insurgency was directed against the political autocracy of Cannon, Poindexter replies: "On the surface this was a political battle, the various stages of which seemed purely political at the time. But back of it all were fundamental economic considerations, like adequate conservation of natural resources, and the proper enforcement of the anti-trust laws. Ultimately, Insurgency had an economic basis." (Hechler 1940, 39–40)

Underlying these changes in policies is the change in presidential preferences and the resulting alignment of preferences by which now both the Senate and the president were closer to the Speaker faction. Using roll call data, I compare the voting patterns during Roosevelt's presidency with those during Taft's presidency, before and after the revolt.

PRESIDENTIAL CHANGE, POLICY DIFFERENCES, AND ROLL CALL DATA

Examining roll call votes is one way to ascertain the impact of the presidential turnover on changes in policy outcomes. To be sure, roll call votes do not tell a complete story, because they only assess the issues that received a floor vote, and we know that most of the issues of importance to progressives were still in committees. Nonetheless, they are adequate to reveal the various alignments within the Republican Party. In this case I study the percentage of Republicans and Democrats that supported their respective parties on less than 50 percent of all party votes. Thus, these percentages show the proportion of members who constantly opposed their parties on roll call votes. I show the data for the 57th–61st Congresses. The 61st Congress, when Taft became president, is divided into two periods, before and after the revolt.

Given the constitutional theory, I predict that the level of disagreement within the Republican Party in the House increased after Taft became president. As a new set of presidential preferences made the enactment of conservative policies possible, the level of intraparty disagreement among Republicans should have been significantly higher during the year leading up to the revolt. The disagreement level should have been comparatively lower during Roosevelt's years and after the revolt.

order in which the petitions were entered. If a majority of the House seconded the motion, there could be ten minutes of debate and if a majority of the House discharged, the bill would go to the calendar.

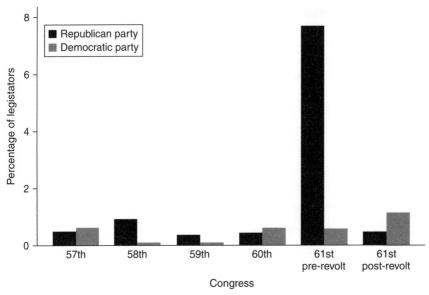

FIGURE 6.3. Percentage of party members who supported their party on less than 50 percent of all party votes.

Figure 6.3 shows the percentage of Republicans and Democrats who supported their respective parties on less than 50 percent of all party votes for the period from the 57th through the 61st Congress (1903–1911).[33] View this figure as capturing the extent of "high conflict" within each party, as the 50-percent threshold ensures that only those representatives who were routinely rebelling are covered. During the half-dozen years of the Roosevelt presidency, no more than 1 percent of the members of either party consistently opposed their parties.

The pattern changes dramatically, but only for Republicans, after Taft's election. Abruptly, almost 8 percent of Republican House members were opposing the majority of their own party, and joining the majority of the other party, more than half the time. This is a remarkable difference when compared to the previous six years and to the tiny defection rates in the year immediately after the revolt. Indeed, after the revolt, the proportion of Republicans who voted against their party returns to the same level as that experienced during Roosevelt's presidency.

The rise in the number of Republicans who voted regularly against their party during the year prior to the revolt attests that the conflict over policy escalated during that period. These trends suggest that the policy content of bills brought

---

[33] Here, party votes are those in which at least 50 percent of Democrats are opposed to at least 50 percent of Republicans.

up for a vote by Speaker Cannon after Taft became president differed from those brought up before or after the revolt. I posit that the progressives' disagreement with these policies, apparent in the high percentage of Republicans who opposed their party for the majority of House votes, accounts for the revolt.

The comparison of the percentages before and after the revolt during the 61st Congress is especially striking, considering that the composition of the House did not change at all between the two periods. The variation in intraparty conflict during this Congress shows that the revolt and the subsequent decentralization of power in the House effectively acted as a mechanism that forced conservatives to moderate policies, that is, to acknowledge progressive preferences. Thus the uprising against Cannon had a strong policy component; the non-Speaker intraparty group, highly discontented with the policies enacted, maneuvered to decentralize power. In this sense, the revolt affected the balance of power of the intraparty groups, empowering the progressives, who after the revolt, and as the roll call data show, were able to steer policy toward their preferences.

ALTERNATIVE EXPLANATION: CANNON WAS MOST AUTOCRATIC DURING THE YEAR PRIOR TO THE REVOLT

One alternative explanation for the timing of the revolt is that the autocratic portrayal of Cannon characterizes only the year before the revolt. Polsby, Gallagher, and Rundquist argue that it is precisely during the 61st Congress that Cannon's indiscriminate use of committee assignments reached its peak, his violations of House members' seniority being minimal before then (Polsby, Gallaher, and Rundquist 1969). The authors argue that progressives did not revolt before 1910 simply because Cannon had not been sufficiently authoritarian previously.

However, recent studies reveal a different situation. First, Krehbiel and Wiseman (Krehbiel and Wiseman 2001) note that the evidence supporting the idea that Cannon was an authoritarian Speaker who demoted progressives from their committee assignments is not compelling, as it "consists predominantly of anecdotes, newspaper editorials, and personal interviews" (2001, 358). Thus, systematic evidence is needed.

In a study of committee assignments, Lawrence, Maltzman, and Wahlbeck (2001) compare written committee requests to the assignments received by freshmen and senior Republicans seeking to transfer to a more desirable committee. They find that Cannon was not vindictive during the 61st Congress, reappointing almost all legislators to their previous committee assignment. However, he granted committee transfers to legislators seeking them, on the basis of legislators' positions on the adoption of rules at the beginning of the 61st Congress. In the end, Lawrence, Maltzman, and Wahlbeck show, legislators returning to the House received at least the committee assignments they had previously held.

In another study, Krehbiel and Wiseman (2005) analyzed legislators' changes in committee portfolio values between the 60th and 61st Congresses.[34] They found that defections from the Speaker's position on the tariff bill and other key votes did not affect Republican legislators' committee portfolio values.[35]

In short, the data on committee portfolio values and the reappointment committee requests of Republicans do not constitute compelling evidence that the revolt occurred in March 1910 because Cannon was particularly manipulative in the committee assignments made in 1909. Cannon's behavior during his last two years does not seem to have differed from his behavior during the 1903–1909 period.

CONCLUSION

My explanation of the revolt against Speaker Cannon does more than simply provide the missing piece of a conceptual and historical puzzle; it also situates the revolt in a wider, constitutionally integral framework that can explain other organizational changes. In this chapter, I argued that the presidential change in 1909 is the key to understanding the revolt against Speaker Cannon and presented evidence supporting my claims. Accounts that focus only on Cannon's alleged dictatorial use of power miss a critical part of the equation. The Cannon case illuminates the linkages between changes in the preferences of the president and subsequent variation in the distribution of power in the House. I have argued that changes in the preferences of outside actors whose approval is necessary to make laws have a profound influence in decisions regarding the distribution of power in the House. Any explanation of House organization must be based on the broader, institutional structure in which the House must operate.

[34] To calculate committee portfolio value, Krehbiel and Wiseman employ a method devised by Groseclose and Stewart (1998), which estimates the average value of a seat in a committee using data on committee transfers. The committee portfolio value for a legislator is the sum of the coefficients for each of the standing committees the legislator sits on. Their estimates covered committee transfer for the period 1887–1911.

[35] It is important to note that even though the 61st Congress met and adopted the rules in March 1909, Cannon delayed decisions on committee assignments until after the Payne-Aldrich Tariff Bill had been approved by the House in April 1909.

7

Conclusion

A goal of this book has been to understand why newly elected members of the U.S. House of Representatives sometimes establish new rules for the upcoming congressional session and sometimes do not. A second, closely related goal has been to understand why, when members of the House do change their rules, they increase the power of some members and reduce the power of others. Other students of Congress have posed the same questions and offered a variety of answers to them. In raising the questions yet again, I did not intend to imply that existing answers are wrong. Rather, I have argued that extant conclusions, which treat the House as an isolated entity that makes laws on its own, are not universal. Rule changes also depend on the preferences of constitutionally established actors who reside outside the House.

Indeed, the Founding Fathers of the United States made sure that it could not be otherwise. In arguably one of the greatest experiments of all time, they established a separation-of-powers system for the United States, built on the idea that no single institution should be able to run roughshod over the others, and thus over the American people. They formulated and wrote into the Constitution a system of checks and balances that has served as the bedrock of American governance and policy making for more than two centuries. Occupants of any one institution know they must bargain with and elicit agreement from occupants of other institutions in order to achieve their policy objectives. Thus, they form expectations of how others will act, given their partisan leanings, and, in turn, formulate behavioral strategies designed to give themselves maximum leverage in policy making. The United States system of checks and balances creates a game of partisan politics that can only be fully understood by outlining the nature of the strategic interactions across institutions.

Moreover, throughout the nation's history, the House majority party has always consisted of at least two distinct factions that differ in their preferences on salient policies. I documented the existence of these factions and showed that scholars have portrayed the policy-making process within Congress as a constant negotiation among factions. More importantly, House rules determine the factions' relative power within the governing coalition. Thus, factions play a key role in the strategic game over power-sharing arrangements.

I used a formal model to generate two sets of predictions, one on the timing of new rule adoption and the other on whether the new rules concentrate power in the House Speaker and his supporters or disperse it among the majority party factions. With respect to the timing of new House rule adoption, my model predicted that, all else constant, there will be more major House rule changes in sessions after a shift in partisan control of one or more of the three key constitutional actors – House, Senate, and/or presidency – than in sessions when no such shift has occurred. With respect to redistribution of power across the two House majority party factions, my model predicted that redistribution depends on the alignment of preferences among the House majority factions, House minority party, Senate, and president.

I tested the predictions with an original data set that covers the period 1879–2013. To build the data set, I studied the positions of factions within the major political parties in depth, including their alignments with the different Speakers, presidents, and Senate pivots. I found that changes in the House majority alone are not sufficient to predict a change in the rules of the House. Rather, changes in the partisanship of the Senate and the president better predict the adoption of new rules. I also found that changes in the alignments among the minority party, Senate, president, and the two majority party factions influence whether new rules centralize power in the hands of the Speaker and his intraparty group or decentralize it across the majority intra party groups. The analysis showed that majority intraparty groups choose rules so as to maximize their gains, given the configuration of preferences among all the constitutional actors.

I also explained one of the most important episodes of rule changes in congressional history: the revolt against Speaker Cannon in 1910. Attributing Cannon's dictatorial use of power as a motivation for the revolt does not credit any of the legislators, or Cannon, for strategic intraparty and interinstitutional bargaining. The Cannon case and the examples from contemporary Congresses noted in Chapter 1 are notable instances of, not notable exceptions to, an empirical regularity: House internal organization responds in predictable ways to changes in the preferences of constitutional actors whose agreement is necessary to make laws.

Looking beyond this study, which focused on House rule making only, where might a constitutional actors' approach be most likely to pay high dividends, given the current state of the literature? Both theoretically and empirically there are two issues that are worth exploring that I did not in this book. First, I treat the Senate as a unitary actor. However, if factions are important within the House, shouldn't we expect them to be significant within parties in the Senate? Looking at factions within the Senate may shed light on the bargaining that occurs not only within the Senate, but also when they need to produce a bicameral agreement with the House. Second, we need to consider that the executive branch is composed of more individuals than just the president and that it may be possible that cabinet members represent distinct factions within the party. Members of the cabinet are important in that they draft many of the bills that become part of the president's legislative agenda, and in that they manage vast sections of the bureaucracy. Understanding the heterogeneity within the executive branch could change our theories regarding presidential coalition building in Congress and how parties interact with the institutional structure to produce certain policy outcomes.

In all, I showed that understanding the redistribution of power within the U.S. House of Representatives requires taking into account the preferences of the Senate and the president. Because the Senate's and the president's approval are necessary to make laws, House members' organizational choices are deeply affected by bicameralism and the separation of powers system within which they act. The incorporation of the preferences of other constitutional actors into an analysis of House rule making is essential.

Appendix A

Constitutional Actors, Partisanship, and House Majority Party Factions

Congress	House Majority	Senate Majority	President's Party	House Majority Party Factions	Speaker Group and Speaker	Faction Closer to President, and President
46th March 18, 1879–March 3, 1881	D	D	R	Conservative Democrats – agrarian Democrats	Conservative Democrat S. Randall (D-PA)	House minority party R Hayes (R-OH)
47th Dec. 5, 1881–March 3, 1883	R	R	R	Stalwarts – half-breeds	Half-breed Republican J. Keifer (R-OH)	Non-Speaker group Stalwart Republicans C. Arthur (R-NY)[1]
48th Dec. 3, 1883–March 3, 1885	D	R	R	Conservative Democrats – agrarian Democrats	Conservative Democrat J Carlisle (D-KY)	House minority party C. Arthur (R-NY)
49th Dec. 7, 1885–March 3, 1887	D	R	D	Conservative Democrats – agrarian Democrats	Conservative Democrat J Carlisle (D-KY)	Speaker group conservative Democrat G. Cleveland (D-NY)
50th Dec. 5, 1887–March 3, 1889	D	R	D	Conservative Democrats – agrarian Democrats	Conservative Democrat J Carlisle (D-KY)	Speaker group conservative Democrat G. Cleveland (D-NY)
51st Dec. 2, 1889–March 3, 1891	R	R	R	Stalwart Republican – half-breed Republican	Stalwart Republican T. Reed (R-ME)	Non-Speaker group B. Harrison (R-OH)
52nd Dec. 7, 1891–March 3, 1893	D	R	R	Conservative Democrats – agrarian Democrats	Conservative Democrat C Crisp (GA)	House minority party B. Harrison (R-OH)

Congress			Factions	Speaker	Speaker group / President
53rd Aug. 7, 1893–March 3, 1895	D	D	Conservative Democrats – agrarian Democrats	Conservative Democrat C Crisp (GA)	Speaker group conservative Democrat; G. Cleveland (D-NY) House minority party; G. Cleveland – conservative Democrat)
54th Dec. 2, 1895–March 3, 1897	R	D	Stalwarts – half-breeds	Stalwart Republican T. Reed (R-ME)	Non-Speaker group half-breed Republican W. McKinley (R-OH)
55th March 15, 1897–March 3, 1899	R	R	Stalwarts – half-breeds	Stalwart Republican T. Reed (R-ME)	Speaker group conservative Republicans W. McKinley (R-OH)
56th Dec. 4, 1899–March 3, 1901	R	R	Conservative Republicans – progressive Republicans	Conservative Republicans D. Henderson (R-IA)	Non-Speaker group progressive Republicans T. Roosevelt (R-NY)
57th Dec. 2, 1901–March 3, 1903	R	R	Conservative Republicans – progressive Republicans	Conservative Republicans D. Henderson (R-IA)	Non-Speaker group progressive Republicans T. Roosevelt (R-NY)
58th Nov. 9, 1903–March 3, 1905	R	R	Conservative Republicans – progressive Republicans	Conservative Republicans Joseph G. Cannon (R-IL)	Non-Speaker group progressive Republicans T. Roosevelt (R-NY)
59th Dec. 4, 1905–March 3, 1907	R	R	Conservative Republicans – progressive Republicans	Conservative Republicans Joseph G. Cannon (R-IL)	Non-Speaker group progressive Republicans T. Roosevelt (R-NY)

(continued)

Congress	House Majority	Senate Majority	President's Party	House Majority Party Factions	Speaker Group and Speaker	Faction Closer to President, and President
60th Dec. 2, 1907– March 3, 1909	R	R	R	Conservative Republicans – progressive Republicans	Conservative Republicans Joseph G. Cannon (R-IL)	Non-Speaker group progressive Republicans T. Roosevelt (R-NY)
61st March 15, 1909–March 3, 1911	R	R	R	Conservative Republicans – progressive Republicans	Conservative Republicans Joseph G. Cannon (R-IL)	Speaker group conservative Republicans W. H. Taft (R-OH)
62nd Apr. 4, 1911– March 3, 1913	D	R	R	Conservative Democrats – reform agrarian Democrats	Reform Agrarian J. B. Clark (D-MO)	House minority party W. H. Taft (R-OH)
63rd Apr. 7, 1913– March 3, 1915	D	D	D	Conservative Democrats – reform agrarian Democrats	Reform agrarian J. B. Clark (D-MO)	Speaker group reform agrarian Democrats W. Wilson (D-NJ)
64th Dec. 6, 1915– March 3, 1917	D	D	D	Conservative Democrats – reform agrarian Democrats	Reform agrarian J. B. Clark (D-MO)	Speaker group reform agrarian Democrats W. Wilson (D-NJ)
65th Apr. 2, 1917– March 3, 1919	D	D	D	Conservative Democrats – reform agrarian Democrats	Reform agrarian J. B. Clark (D-MO)	Speaker group reform agrarian Democrats W. Wilson (D-NJ)

Congress					Speaker	Executive
66th May 19, 1919– March 3, 1921	R	R	D	Conservative Republicans – progressive Republicans	Conservative Republicans F. Gillett (R-MA)	House minority party W. Wilson (D-NJ)
67th Apr. 11, 1921– March 3, 1923	R	R	R	Conservative Republicans – progressive Republicans	Conservative Republicans F. Gillett (R-MA)	Compromise candidate W. Harding (R-OH)[2]
68th Dec. 3, 1923– March 3, 1925	R	R	R	Conservative Republicans – progressive Republicans	Conservative Republicans F. Gillett (R-MA)	Speaker group conservative Republican C. Coolidge (R-MA)
69th Dec. 7, 1925– March 4, 1927	R	R	R	Conservative Republicans – progressive Republicans	Compromise choice between two factions N. Longworth (R-OH)	Speaker group conservative Republican C. Coolidge (R-MA)
70th Dec. 5, 1927– March 3, 1929	R	R	R	Conservative Republicans – progressive Republicans	N. Longworth (R-OH)	Speaker group conservative Republican C. Coolidge (R-MA)
71st Apr. 15, 1929– March 3, 1931	R	R	R	Conservative Republicans – progressive Republicans	N. Longworth (R-OH)	Speaker group conservative Republican H. Hoover (R-CA)
72nd Dec. 7, 1931– March 3, 1933	D	R	R	Conservative/ southern Democrats – liberal/northern Democrats	Conservative/ southern Democrats J N Garner (D-TX)	House minority party H. Hoover (R-CA)

(continued)

Congress	House Majority	Senate Majority	President's Party	House Majority Party Factions	Speaker Group and Speaker	Faction Closer to President, and President
73rd March 9, 1933–June 18, 1934	D	D	D	Conservative/Southern democrats – liberal/northern Democrats	Liberal/northern Democrats H. T. Rainey (D-IL)[3]	Speaker group liberal/northern Democrat F. D. Roosevelt (D-NY)
74th Jan. 3, 1935–June 20, 1936	D	D	D	Conservative/southern Democrats – liberal/northern Democrats	Conservative/southern Democrat J. W. Byrns (D-TN)[4]	Non-Speaker group liberal/northern Democrat F. D. Roosevelt (D-NY)
75th Jan. 5, 1937–June 16, 1938	D	D	D	Conservative/southern Democrats – liberal/northern Democrats	Conservative/southern Democrat W. Bankhead (D-AL)	Non-Speaker group liberal/northern Democrat F. D. Roosevelt (D-NY)
76th Jan. 3, 1939–Jan. 3, 1941	D	D	D	Conservative/southern Democrats – liberal/northern Democrats	Conservative/southern Democrat W. Bankhead (D-AL)[5]	Non-Speaker group liberal/northern Democrat F. D. Roosevelt (D-NY)
77th Jan. 3, 1941–Dec. 16, 1942	D	D	D	Conservative/southern Democrats – liberal/northern Democrats	Conservative/southern Democrat S. Rayburn (D-TX)	Non-Speaker group liberal/northern Democrat F. D. Roosevelt (D-NY)

78th Jan. 6, 1943–Dec. 19, 1944	D	D	Conservative/ southern Democrats – liberal/northern Democrats	Conservative/ southern Democrat S. Rayburn (D-TX)	Non-Speaker group liberal/northern Democrat F. D. Roosevelt (D-NY)
79th Jan. 3, 1945–Aug. 2, 1946	D	D	Conservative/ southern Democrats – liberal/northern Democrats	Conservative/ southern Democrat S. Rayburn (D-TX)	Non-Speaker group liberal/northern Democrat H. Truman (D-MO)[6]
80th Jan. 3, 1947–Dec. 31, 1948	R	R	Conservative Republicans – liberal Republicans	Liberal Republicans J. Martin Jr. (R-MA)	House minority party H. Truman (D-MO)
81st Jan. 3, 1949–Jan. 2, 1951	D	D	Conservative/ southern Democrats – liberal/northern Democrats	Conservative/ southern Democrat S. Rayburn (D-TX)	Non-Speaker group liberal/northern Democrat H. Truman (D-MO)
82nd Jan. 3, 1951–July 2, 1952	D	D	Conservative/ southern Democrats – liberal/northern Democrats	Conservative/ southern Democrat S. Rayburn (D-TX)	Non-Speaker group liberal/northern Democrat H. Truman (D-MO)
83rd Jan. 3, 1953–Dec. 2, 1954	R	R	Conservative Republicans – liberal Republicans	Liberal republicans J. Martin Jr. (R-MA)	Speaker group liberal Republicans D. Eisenhower (R-NY)

(continued)

Congress	House Majority	Senate Majority	President's Party	House Majority Party Factions	Speaker Group and Speaker	Faction Closer to President, and President
84th Jan. 5, 1955–July 27, 1956	D	D	R	Conservative/ southern Democrats – liberal/northern Democrats	Conservative/ southern Democrat S. Rayburn (D-TX)	House minority party D. Eisenhower (R-NY)
85th Jan. 3, 1957–Aug. 24, 1958	D	D	R	Conservative/ southern Democrats – liberal/northern Democrats	Conservative/ southern Democrat S. Rayburn (D-TX)	House minority party D. Eisenhower (R-NY)
86th Jan. 7, 1959–Sept. 1, 1960	D	D	R	Conservative/ southern Democrats – liberal/northern Democrats	Conservative/ southern Democrat S. Rayburn (D-TX)	House minority party D. Eisenhower (R-NY)
87th Jan. 3, 1961–Oct. 13, 1962	D	D	D	Conservative/ southern Democrats – liberal/northern Democrats	Conservative/ southern Democrat S. Rayburn (D-TX)[7]	Non-Speaker group liberal/northern Democrat J. F. Kennedy (D-MA)
88th Jan. 9, 1963–Oct. 3, 1964	D	D	D	Conservative/ southern Democrats – liberal/northern Democrats	Liberal/northern Democrat J. McCormack (D-MA)	Speaker group liberal/northern Democrat J. F. Kennedy (D-MA)[8]

89th Jan. 4, 1965–Oct. 22, 1966	D	D	D	Conservative/ southern Democrats – liberal/northern Democrats	Liberal/northern Democrat J. McCormack (D-MA)	Speaker group liberal/northern Democrat L. B. Johnson (D-TX)
90th Jan. 10, 1967–Oct. 14, 1968	D	D	D	Conservative/ southern Democrats – liberal/northern Democrats	Liberal/northern Democrat J. McCormack (D-MA)	Speaker group liberal/northern Democrat L. B. Johnson (D-TX)
91st Jan. 3, 1969–Jan. 2, 1971	D	D	R	Conservative/ southern Democrats – liberal/northern Democrats	Liberal/northern Democrat J. McCormack (D-MA)	House minority party R. Nixon (R-CA)
92nd Jan. 21, 1971–Oct. 18, 1972	D	D	R	New Democrats – New Left Democrats	New Left Democrats C. Albert (D-OK)	House minority party R. Nixon (R-CA)
93rd Jan. 3, 1973–Dec. 20, 1974	D	D	R	New Democrats – New Left Democrats	New Left Democrats C. Albert (D-OK)	House minority party R. Nixon (R-CA)
94th Jan. 14, 1975–Oct. 1, 1976	D	D	R	New Democrats – New Left Democrats	New Left Democrats C. Albert (D-OK)	House minority party G. Ford (R-MI)
95th Jan. 4, 1977–Oct. 15, 1978	D	D	D	New Democrats – New Left Democrats	New Left Democrats T. O'Neill (D-MA)	New Left Democrats Carter (D-GA)
96th Jan. 15, 1979–Dec. 16, 1980	D	D	D	New Democrats – New Left Democrats	New Left Democrats T. O'Neill (D-MA)	New Left Democrats Carter (D-GA)

(continued)

Congress	House Majority	Senate Majority	President's Party	House Majority Party Factions	Speaker Group and Speaker	Faction Closer to President, and President
97th Jan. 5, 1981–Dec. 23, 1982	D	R	R	New Democrats – New Left Democrats	New Left Democrats T. O'Neill (D-MA)	House minority party R. Reagan (R-CA)
98th Jan. 3, 1983–Oct. 12, 1984	D	R	R	New Democrats – New Left Democrats	New Left Democrats T. O'Neill (D-MA)	House minority party R. Reagan (R-CA)
99th Jan. 3, 1985–Oct. 18, 1986	D	R	R	New Democrats – New Left Democrats	New Left Democrats T. O'Neill (D-MA).	House minority party R. Reagan (R-CA)
100th Jan. 6, 1987–Oct. 22, 1988	D	D	R	New Democrats – New Left Democrats	New Democrats J. Wright (D-TX).	House minority party R. Reagan (R-CA)
101st Jan. 3, 1989–Oct. 28, 1990	D	D	R	New Democrats – New Left Democrats	New Democrats J. Wright (D-TX)[9]	House minority party G. H. W. Bush (R-TX)
102nd Jan. 3, 1991–Oct. 9, 1992	D	D	R	New Democrats – New Left Democrats	New Left Democrats T. Foley (D-WA)	House minority party G. H. W. Bush (R-TX)
103rd Jan. 5, 1993–Dec. 1, 1994	D	D	D	New Democrats – New Left Democrats	New Left Democrats T. Foley (D-WA)	Non-Speaker group New Democrats W. Clinton (D-AR)
104th Jan. 4, 1995–Oct. 4, 1996	R	R	D	New Right – moderate Republicans	New Right N. Gingrich (R-GA)	House minority party W. Clinton (D-AR)
105th Jan. 7, 1997–Dec. 19, 1998	R	R	D	New Right – moderate Republicans	New Right N. Gingrich (R-GA)	House minority party W. Clinton (D-AR)

						House minority party
106th Jan. 6, 1999–Dec. 15, 2000	R	R	D	New Right – moderate Republicans	New Right J. D. Hastert (R-IL)	W. Clinton (D-AR)
107th Jan. 3, 2001–Nov. 22, 2002	R	D[10]	R	New Right – moderate Republicans	New Right J. D. Hastert (R-IL)	New Right G. W. Bush (R-TX)
108th Jan. 7, 2003–Dec. 9, 2004	R	R	R	New Right – moderate Republicans	New Right J. D. Hastert (R-IL)	New Right G. W. Bush (R-TX)
109th Jan. 4, 2005–Dec. 8, 2006	R	R	R	New Right – moderate Republicans	New Right J. D. Hastert (R-IL)	New Right G. W. Bush (R-TX)
110th Jan. 4, 2007–Jan 3, 2009	D	D	R	New Democrats/ Blue Dogs – New Left Democrats	New Left Democrats N. Pelosi (D-CA)	New Right G. W. Bush (R-TX)
111th Jan. 6, 2009–Dec 22, 2010	D	D	D	New Democrats/ Blue Dogs – New Left Democrats	New Left Democrats N. Pelosi (D-CA)	New Left Democrats B. Obama (D-IL)

[1] President Garfield was assassinated on September 1881, before the congressional session began.

[2] Harding died in office, August 2, 1923. Replaced by Vice President C. Coolidge.

[3] Rainey died in office on August 19, 1934. and Byrns was backed by a coalition of northeastern, border and Midwestern democrats (Peters 1990)

[4] Byrns died in office on June 4th, 1936.

[5] Bankhead died while in office, on September 15th, 1940. Replaced by S. Rayburn (D-TX) on September 16th, 1940.

[6] He became President on April 12th, 1945, after Roosevelt's death.

[7] Rayburn died in office, on November 16th, 1961. Replaced by J. McCormack (D-MA)

[8] Replaced by L.B. Johnson (D-TX) on 11–22–1963.

[9] Replaced by T. Foley (D-WA) on June 6th, 1989.

[10] In this Congress, Republicans and Democrats had the same number of Senators. Thus, Democrats constituted the majority between Jan 3 and Jan 20 2001, when President Clinton was still in office and the tie-breaking vote in the Senate belonged to Democratic vice-president Al Gore. When Republican President George Bush and Vice President Cheney were sworn into office on Jan 20, Republicans became the majority in the Senate. On June 5 2001, Vermont Republican James J. Jeffords became an independent and began caucusing with Democrats, putting them in charge of the Senate and throwing the GOP into the minority.

Appendix B

Theoretical Proof

Lemma 1. The outcome of the override subgame is $L = r \Leftrightarrow s \neq p$ and $\%P \leq 1/3$ and $min(|s - q| - |s - r| - v, |z - q| - |z - r|) > 0$. Otherwise, $L = q$.

Proof. Supermajorities in the House and Senate must agree to override a rejection. In the House, $2/3$ of the membership must support an override. In the Senate, we represent supermajority support for an override as the requirement that the reconciliation, r, be at least distance v closer to s than the status quo q is to s.

Reaching the override subgame implies that the president previously rejected r. This fact has an implication for the feasibility of an override. Let $p \in \{F_1, F_2, F_3\}$ be the president's ideal point and $\%P$ be the percentage of House members who are from the president's faction. Since no group has a majority of House seats, $\%P \in [0, .5]$. Since the president preferred q to r, this faction has the same preference by definition. Therefore, if $\%P > 1/3$, the House will not override the rejection and the legislative outcome is $L = q$.

Now suppose $s = p$ – the Senate and the president are from the same faction. Since getting to the override stage implies that the president preferred q to r, the Senate must have the same preference. Therefore, the Senate will not override the rejection and the legislative outcome is $L = q$.

The remaining case is $s \neq p$ and $|s - q| - |s - r| - v > 0$ and $\%P \leq 1/3$. Here, the Senate votes to override the rejection. Let $\%S$ denote the percentage of House members who are from the same faction as the Senate, where $\%S \in [0, .5]$. Since the Senate previously approved r, as a necessary condition for reaching the constitutional stage, it must be that $|s - q| - |s - r| > 0$. Therefore, $\%S$ of the House also prefers r to q. Since $\%P \leq 1/3$ of House members will not support an override and $\%S \leq .5$ will support it, the remaining faction is pivotal with respect to an override. As in the text's presentation of Proposition 1, let $F_i \neq s \neq p \in \{F_1, F_2, F_3\}$ denote that faction (i.e., House members who are from a different faction than either the Senate or the president), where %*Fi* refers to the size of that faction in the House and %*P* + %*S* + %*Fi* = 1. Then, if this faction prefers *r* to *q* (i.e., |*Fi* − *q*| − |*Fi* − *r*| > 0), then the rejection is overridden. *QED.*

Lemma 2. The outcome of the presidential subgame is *L* = *r* ⇔ |*p* − *q*| − |*p* − *r*| > 0 OR [|*p* − *q*| − |*p* − *r*| ≤ 0 and %*P* ≤ 1/3 and |*s* − *q*| − |*s* − *r*| − *v* > 0 *and* |*Fi* − *q*| − |*Fi* − *r*| > 0]. Otherwise, *L* = *q.*

Proof. First, we need a way of describing what the president will do when the House and Senate will override a rejection. In such cases, the president's choice is inconsequential to the game's legislative outcome, *L* = *r*. For this purpose, let $\pi_p \in (-\infty, \infty)$ represent the president's public stance in conditions where he anticipates an override. $\pi_p > 0$ represents cases where even though the president cannot affect the legislative outcome in the game's constitutional stage, s/he wants to be seen approving *r*. $\pi_p < 0$ represents cases when s/he prefers to be seen opposing *r*. This term does not affect the results but does allow behavioral predictions when the president's choice does not affect the final outcome.

If the president anticipates an override, then the relevant utilities are $U_p(q, \pi_p) = -|p - r|$ and $U_p(r, \pi_p) = -|p - r| + \pi_p$. If $\pi_p > 0$, then the president chooses *r*. If $\pi_p \leq 0$, then the president chooses *q*. If a rejection will not be overridden, then the relevant utilities are $U_p(q) = -|p - q|$ and $U_p(r) = -|p - r|$. If |*p* − *q*| − |*p* − *r*| > 0, then the president chooses *r*. If |*p* − *q*| − |*p* − *r*| ≤ 0, then he or she chooses *q*. By implication,

- If *s* ≠ *p* and %*P* ≤ 1/3 and *min*(|*s* − *q*| − |*s* − *r*|−*v*, |*Fi* − *q*| − |*Fi* − *r*|) > 0 and $\pi_p > 0$, then the president approves *r* under threat of override and the game ends with *L* = *r*.
- If *s* ≠ *p* and %*P* ≤ 1/3 and *min*(|*s* − *q*| − |*s* − *r*|−*v*, |*Fi* − *q*| − |*Fi* − *r*|) > 0 and $\pi_p \leq 0$, then the president rejects *r* under threat of override and the game goes to the override stage (when the rejection is overridden).
- If [*s* = *p* or %*P* > 1/3 or *max*(|*s* − *q*| − |*s* − *r*|−*v*, |*Fi* − *q*| − |*Fi* − *r*|) ≤ 0] and |*p* − *q*| − |*p* − *r*| > 0, then the president approves *r* with no override threat and the game ends with *L* = *r*.
- If [[*s* = *p* or %*P* > 1/3 or *max*(|*s* − *q*| − |*s* − *r*|−*v*, |*Fi* − *q*| − |*Fi* − *r*|) ≤ 0] and |*p* − *q*| − |*p* − *r*| ≤ 0], then the president rejects *r* and the game goes to the override stage (when the rejection survives). *QED.*

Lemma 3. The outcome of the Senate subgame is *L* = *r* ⇔ [|*s* − *q*| − |*s* − *r*| > 0 and |*p* − *q*| − |*p* − *r*| > 0] OR [|*p* − *q*| − |*p* − *r*| ≤ 0 and %*P* ≤ 1/3 and |*s* − *q*| − |*s* − *r*| −*v* > 0 and |*Fi* − *q*| − |*Fi* − *r*| > 0]. Otherwise, *L* = *q.*

Proof. Let $\pi_s \in \{-\infty, \infty\}$ represent the Senate's public stance in conditions when it anticipates that the president will reject *r* and it will stand. For the Senate, the relevant utilities are $U_s(q) = -|s - q|$, $U_s(r) = -|s - r|$ if *L* = *r* is the outcome of the presidential subgame just described, and $U_s(r) = -|s - q| + \pi_s$ if *L* = *q* is the outcome of the subgame.

If $L = q$ is the outcome of the presidential subgame and $\pi_S > 0$, the Senate approves r. If $\pi_S \leq 0$, the Senate defeats r. If $L = r$ is the outcome of the presidential subgame and $|s - q| - |s - r| > 0$, then the Senate approves r. But if $|s - q| - |s - r| \leq 0$, then the Senate defeats r. QED.

We complete the proof of Proposition 1 by examining House factions' constitutional stage decisions. Let $\pi_i \in (-\infty, \infty)$ represent Fi's ($i \in \{1, 2, 3\}$) public stance in conditions when it anticipates a rejection that will stand. For Fi, the relevant utilities are $U_i(q) = -|Fi - q|$, $U_i(r) = -|Fi - r|$ if $L = r$ is the outcome of the Senate subgame, and $U_i(r) = -|Fi - q| + \pi_i$ if $L = q$ is the outcome of the Senate subgame. If $L = q$ is the outcome of the Senate subgame, or if $|Fj - q| - |Fj - r| > 0$ for House factions $Fj \neq Fi$ ($j \in \{1, 2, 3\}\backslash i$), then if $\pi_i > 0$, then Fi votes for r. If $\pi_i \leq 0$, Fi votes against r. If $L = r$ is the outcome of the Senate subgame, then if $|Fi - q| - |Fi - r| > 0$, then Fi approves r and if $|Fi - q| - |Fi - r| \leq 0$, then Fi votes against r.

Two of the three factions must approve r for the game to proceed to the Senate subgame. A necessary condition for $L = r$ in Lemma 3 is $|s - q| - |s - r| > 0$. If this condition is satisfied, then the House faction whose members are from the same ideological group as the Senate also support r by definition – therefore, only one other group's support is needed. Let $Fi \neq s$ be such a faction. Then, the House supports r if $[s \neq p$ and $\%P \leq 1/3$ and $min(|s - q| - |s - r|-v, |Fi - q| - |Fi - r|) > 0]$. In the case $s = p$, let $Fj \neq Fi \neq s = p \in \{F1, F2, F3\}$ denote the set of House members who are not in faction Fi and not in the faction that shares the Senate and the President's ideal point. Fj is pivotal in the case $[s = p$ and $|s - q| - |s - r| > 0$ and $|Fi - q| - |Fi - r| \leq 0]$, which completes all contingencies described in the proposition. QED.

RECONCILIATION STAGE

For any set of ideal points, the reconciliation algorithm yields the following r:

- $r_i = mid_i \Leftrightarrow [|s - q| - |s - mid_i| > 0$ and $|p - q| - |p - mid_i| > 0$ and $s \neq p]$ OR $[s = p$ and $|s - q| - |s - mid_i| > 0$ and $(|Fj - q| - |Fj - mid_i| > 0$ or $|Fi - q| - |Fi - mid_i| > 0)]$ OR $[|p - q| - |p - mid_i| \leq 0$ and $\%P \leq 1/3$ and $|s - q| - |s - mid_i|-v > 0$ and $|Fi - q| - |Fi - mid_i| > 0]$
- $r_i = sec_i \Leftrightarrow [|s - q| - |s - mid_i| \leq 0$ OR $[s = p$ and $|s - q| - |s - mid_i| > 0$ and $|Fj - q| - |Fj - mid_i| \leq 0$ and $|Fi - q| - |Fi - mid_i| \leq 0]$ OR $[|s - q| - |s - mid_i| > 0$ and $|p - q| - |p - mid_i| \leq 0$ and $(\%P > 1/3$ or $|s - q| - |s - mid_i|-v \leq 0$ or $|Fi - q| - |Fi - mid_i|) \leq 0)]$ AND $[[|s - q| - |s - sec_i| > 0$ and $|p - q| - |p - sec_i| > 0$ and $s \neq p]$ OR $[s = p$ and $|s - q| - |s - sec_i| > 0$ and $(|Fj - q| - |Fj - sec_i| > 0$ or $|Fi - q| - |Fi - sec_i| > 0)]$ OR $[|p - q| - |p - sec_i| \leq 0$ and $\%P \leq 1/3$ and $|s - q| - |s - sec_i|-v > 0$ and $|Fi - q| - |Fi - sec_i| > 0]]$.
- $r_i = q \Leftrightarrow |s - q| - |s - sec_i| \leq 0$ OR $[s = p$ and $|s - q| - |s - sec_i| > 0$ and $|Fj - q| - |Fj - sec_i| \leq 0$ and $|Fi - q| - |Fi - sec_i| \leq 0]$ OR $[|s - q| - |s - sec_i| > 0$ and $|p - q| - |p - sec_i| \leq 0$ and $(\%P > 1/3$ or $|s - q| - |s - sec_i|-v \leq 0$ or $|Fi - q| - |Fi - sec_i|) \leq 0.)]$

POWER − SHARING STAGE

Again, we proceed by backward induction.

F_3's Reaction to F_2's Offer

At this decision node, the consequence of F_2's failing to make an acceptable offer is $L = q$. F_3 will accept offer c_2^3 if and only if $-c_2^3|F_3 - r_2| - (1 - c_2^3)|F_3 - r_3| \geq -|F_3 - q|$. This means that if F_2 wants to coalesce with F_3, it must offer

- $c_2^3 \geq [|F_3 - r_3| - |F_3 - q|]/[(|F_3 - r_3| - |F_3 - r_2|)]$ if $|F_3 - r_3| > |F_3 - r_2|$
- $c_2^3 \leq [|F_3 - r_3| - |F_3 - q|]/[(|F_3 - r_3| - |F_3 - r_2|)]$ if $|F_3 - r_3| < |F_3 - r_2|$
- If $|F_3 - r_3| = |F_3 - r_2|$, F_3 will accept any offer by the tie − breaking rule and the fact that r_3 is at least as close to F_3 as is q (by definition of the reconciliation algorithm).

Two lemmas simplify the specification of further steps in the backward induction process.

Lemma 4. If $|F_3 - r_3| \geq |F_3 - r_2|$, then F_3 will accept any offer from F_2.

Proof. Since r_3 is at least as close to F_3 as is q (by the reconciliation definition), $|F_3 - r_3| - |F_3 - q| \leq 0$, $(|F_3 - r_3| - |F_3 - q|)/(|F_3 - r_3| - |F_3 - r_2|)$ is nonpositive. Since, $c_2^3 \in [0, 1]$ the condition is satisfied for any c_2^3. QED.

Lemma 5. Two factions cannot strictly prefer one another's reconciliations simultaneously.

Proof. Consider two factions A, $B \in \{F_1, F_2, F_3\}$. r_A and r_B are the points in CS that are closest to the midpoint of the line connecting A and s and B and s, respectively. Either $A = s$ or $B = s$ or neither A nor B equal s. Let $A = s$. By the definition of a reconciliation, the midpoint of the line connecting A and s is s. Therefore, r_A is the point in CS that is closest to A. Hence A prefers r_A to any other reconciliation. By identical logic, B prefers r_B to any other reconciliation when $B = s$. Now suppose that neither A nor B equals s. Then, if r_A is closer to B than is r_B and if r_A is the closest point in CS to the midpoint of s and A, then A must be further from s than B. If A is further from s than B, and r_B is closer to s than r_A, then r_B cannot be closer to A than is r_A. Therefore, B cannot prefer r_A when A strongly prefers r_B. QED.

F_2's Offer

F_2's chooses a value of c_2^3 that maximizes its utility subject to three constraints. One constraint is $c_2^3 \in [0, 1]$. The second (acceptability) constraint is that F_3 will accept it. The parameters of this constraint are listed under "F_3's reaction to F_2's offer" and Lemma 4. The third constraint pertains to incentive compatibility. Since F_2 can prefer q to r_3, there exist values of c_2^3 that, if accepted, will make

$F2$ worse off than if $F3$ rejects. Therefore, $F2$'s incentive constraint is $U_2(c_2{}^3, F3$ *accepts*$) = -c_2{}^3|F2 - r_2| - (1 - c_2{}^3)|F2 - r_3| \geq U_2(c_2{}^3, F3$ *rejects*$) = -|F2 - q|$.

No acceptable offer assumption (NAO). We assume, without loss of generality, that if no offer in $c_x{}^y \in [0, 1]$ satisfies the acceptability constraint for any relevant Fy, then Fx offers $c_x{}^y = 1$ if $|Fx - r(Fy, s)| \geq |Fx - r(Fx, s)|$ and offers $c_x{}^y = 0$, otherwise.

Lemma 6. $F2$'s offer and $F3$'s response are as follows:

- If $min(|F3 - r_3| - |F3 - r_2|, |F2 - r_3| - |F2 - r_2|) \geq 0$, then $c_2{}^3 = 1$ and $F3$ accepts.
- If $|F2 - r_3| \leq |F2 - r_2|$, then $c_2{}^3 = 0$ and $F3$ accepts.
- If $|F2 - r_3| - |F2 - r_2| > 0 > |F3 - r_3| - |F3 - r_2|$ and $min([|F3 - r_3| - |F3 - q|]/ [|F3 - r_3| - |F3 - r_2|], 1) \geq (|F2 - q| - |F2 - r_3|)/(|F2 - r_2| - |F2 - r_3|)$, then $c_2{}^3 = min([|F3 - r_3| - |F3 - q|]/[|F3 - r_3| - |F3 - r_2|], 1)$ and $F3$ accepts.
- If $|F2 - r_3| - |F2 - r_2| > 0 > |F3 - r_3| - |F3 - r_2|$ and $min([|F3 - r_3| - |F3 - q|]/ [|F3 - r_3| - |F3 - r_2|], 1) < (|F2 - q| - |F2 - r_3|)/(|F2 - r_2| - |F2 - r_3|)$, then $c_2{}^3 = 1$ and $F3$ rejects.

Proof. In the first bulleted case, $F3$ prefers r_2 to r_3, so the acceptability constraint is not binding. Since $|F2 - r_3| > |F2 - r_2|$, $max\ U_2(c_2{}^3) = 1$. In the second bulleted case, $F2$ prefers r_3 to r_2. Since $|F2 - r_3| - |F2 - r_2| < 0$, $max\ U_2(c_2{}^3) = 0$. If $|F3 - r_3| < |F3 - r_2|$, $F3$ accepts the offer because it shares $F2$'s preferences over other reconciliations. Since $|F2 - r_3| \leq |F2 - r_2|$, Lemma 5 renders $|F3 - r_3| > |F3 - r_2|$ impossible. In the third and fourth bullets, each faction prefers its own reconciliation. Since $|F2 - r_3| - |F2 - r_2| > 0$, $max\ U_2(c_2{}^3) = 1$. However, $F3$'s acceptability constraint is binding. In the third bullet, $\exists\ c_2{}^3 \in [0, 1]$ that satisfies the acceptability and incentive compatibility constraints, so $F2$ offers the largest value of $c_2{}^3$ that $F3$ will accept. In the fourth bullet, there exists no such offer, so $c_2{}^3 = 1$ by the NAO assumption. QED.

$F2$'s and $F3$'s Response to $F1$'s Offer

There are four cases to consider. Note that with respect to acceptability constraints, the cases $c_2{}^3 = 0$ and $c_2{}^3 = 1$ are mirror images of one another.

- If $|F2 - r_3| - |F2 - r_2| > 0 > |F3 - r_3| - |F3 - r_2|$, and $min([|F3 - r_3| - |F3 - q|]/ [|F3 - r_3| - |F3 - r_2|], 1) \geq (|F2 - q| - |F2 - r_3|)/(|F2 - r_2| - |F2 - r_3|)$ then the policy consequence of rejecting $F1$'s offer stems from $c_2{}^3 = min([|F3 - r_3| - |F3 - q|]/[|F3 - r_3| - |F3 - r_2|], 1)$.
  - $F2$ acceptability constraint: If $|F2 - r_2| \geq |F2 - r_1|$, accept any offer. If $|F2 - r_2| < |F2 - r_1|$ then $F1$ must offer $c_1{}^2 \leq [(1 - c_2{}^3)(|F2 - r_2| - |F2 - r_3|)] / (|F2 - r_2| - |F2 - r_1|)$.
  - $F3$ acceptability constraint: If $|F3 - r_3| \geq |F3 - r_1|$, accept any offer. If $|F3 - r_3| < |F3 - r_1|$, then $F1$ must offer $c_1{}^3 \leq c_2{}^3(|F3 - r_3| - |F3 - r_2|)/(|F3 - r_3| - |F3 - r_1|)$.

- If $|F_2 - r_3| - |F_2 - r_2| > 0 > |F_3 - r_3| - |F_3 - r_2|$, and $min([|F_3 - r_3| - |F_3 - q|]/[|F_3 - r_3| - |F_3 - r_2|], 1) < (|F_2 - q| - |F_2 - r_3|)/ (|F_2 - r_2| - |F_2 - r_3|)$ then the policy consequence of rejecting F_1's offer is $L = q$ (i.e., $c_2^3 = 1$ *and F_3 rejects*).
  - F_2 acceptability constraint: If $|F_2 - r_2| \geq |F_2 - r_1|$, accept any offer. If $|F_2 - r_2| < |F_2 - r_1|$, then F_1 must offer $c_1^2 \leq [|F_2 - r_2| - |F_2 - q|]/[|F_2 - r_2| - |F_2 - r_1|]$
  - F_3 acceptability constraint: If $|F_3 - r_3| \geq |F_3 - r_1|$, accept any offer. If $|F_3 - r_3| < |F_3 - r_1|$, then F_1 must offer $c_1^3 \leq [|F_3 - r_3| - |F_3 - q|]/[|F_3 - r_3| - |F_3 - r_1|]$
- If $min(|F_3 - r_3| - |F_3 - r_2|, |F_2 - r_3| - |F_2 - r_2|) \geq 0$, then the policy consequence of rejecting F_1's offer is $L = r_2$ (i.e., $c_2^3 = 1$ *and F_3 accepts*).
  - F_2 acceptability constraint: If $|F_2 - r_2| \geq |F_2 - r_1|$, accept any offer. If $|F_2 - r_2| < |F_2 - r_1|$, reject any offer $c_1^2 > 0$.
  - F_3 acceptability constraint: If $|F_3 - r_3| > |F_3 - r_1|$, then F_1 must offer $c_1^3 \geq (|F_3 - r_3| - |F_3 - r_2|)/ (|F_3 - r_3| - |F_3 - r_1|)$. If $|F_3 - r_1| \geq |F_3 - r_3| \geq |F_3 - r_2|$, then reject any offer. If $|F_3 - r_3| = |F_3 - r_1| = |F_3 - r_2|$, then accept any offer.
- If $|F_2 - r_3| \leq |F_2 - r_2|$, then the policy consequence of rejecting F_1's offer is $L = r_3$ (i.e., $c_2^3 = 0$ *and F_3 accepts*).
  - F_2 acceptability constraint: If $|F_2 - r_2| > |F_2 - r_1|$, then F_1 must offer $c_1^2 \geq (|F_2 - r_2| - |F_2 - r_3|)/ (|F_2 - r_2| - |F_2 - r_1|)$. If $|F_2 - r_1| \geq |F_2 - r_2| > |F_2 - r_3|$, then reject any offer. If $|F_2 - r_2| = |F_2 - r_1| = |F_2 - r_3|$, then accept any offer.
  - F_3 acceptability constraint: If $|F_3 - r_3| \geq |F_3 - r_1|$, accept any offer. If $|F_3 - r_3| < |F_3 - r_1|$, reject any offer $c_1^3 > 0$.

F_1's Offer

F_1's chooses to make an offer that maximizes its utility subject to three constraints. One constraint is $\{c_1^2, c_1^3\} \in [0, 1]$. The second (acceptability) constraint is that F_2 or F_3 will accept it. A third constraint is incentive compatibility. This constraint is $min (U_1(c_1^2, F_2 \text{ accepts}), U_1(c_1^3, F_3 \text{ accepts})) \geq U_1(\text{offer rejected})$, when $U_1(c_1^2, F_2 \text{ accepts}) = -c_1^2|F_1 - r_1| - (1 - c_1^2)|F_1 - r_2|$, $U_1(c_1^3, F_3 \text{ accepts}) = -c_1^3|F_1 - r_1| - (1 - c_1^3)|F_1 - r_3|$ and then $U_1(\text{offer rejected})$ depends on the consequence of F_2's offer to F_3. In the following, we determine F_1's offer with respect to the four mutually exclusive and collectively exhaustive consequences listed in Lemma 6.

<u>Case 1.</u> If $|F_2 - r_3| - |F_2 - r_2| > 0 > |F_3-r_3| - |F_3 - r_2|$ and $min([|F_3 - r_3| - |F_3 - q|]/[|F_3 - r_3| - |F_3 - r_2|], 1) \geq (|F_2 - q| - |F_2 - r_3|)/ (|F_2 - r_2| - |F_2 - r_3|)$, then the consequence of a failed offer from F_1 is $c_2^3 = min([|F_3 - r_3| - |F_3 - q|]/[|F_3 - r_3| - |F_3 - r_2|], 1)$ and F_3 accepts.

This case has four collectively exhaustive subcases, A–D.

A. If $|F2 - r_2| \geq |F2 - r_1|$ and $|F3 - r_3| \geq |F3 - r_1|$, F2 and F3 will accept any offer.

So, if $|F2 - r_2| \geq |F2 - r_1|$ and $|F3 - r_3| \geq |F3 - r_1|$ and $|F1 - r_1| \leq min(|F1 - r_2|, |F1 - r_3|)$, then $c_1^2 = 1$ and F2 *accepts*. If $|F2 - r_2| > |F2 - r_1|$, Lemma 5 renders $|F1 - r_2| < |F1 - r_1|$ impossible. If $|F2 - r_2| = |F2 - r_1|$ and $|F3 - r_3| \geq |F3 - r_1|$ and $|F1 - r_2| < |F1 - r_1|$ and $|F1 - r_2| \leq |F1 - r_3|$, then $c_1^2 = 0$ and F2 *accepts*. If $|F3 - r_3| > |F3 - r_1|$, Lemma 5 renders $|F1 - r_3| < |F1 - r_1|$ impossible. And if $|F2 - r_2| \geq |F2 - r_1|$ and $|F3 - r_3| = |F3 - r_1|$ and $|F1 - r_3| < min(|F1 - r_1|, |F1 - r_2|)$, then $c_1^3 = 0$ and F3 *accepts*.

B. If $|F2 - r_2| \geq |F2 - r_1|$ and $|F3 - r_3| < |F3 - r_1|$, F2 will accept any offer.

So, if $|F2 - r_2| \geq |F2 - r_1|$ and $|F3 - r_3| < |F3 - r_1|$ and $|F1 - r_1| \leq min(|F1 - r_2|, |F1 - r_3|)$, then $c_1^2 = 1$ and F2 *accepts*. If $|F2 - r_2| > |F2 - r_1|$, Lemma 5 renders $|F1 - r_2| < |F1 - r_1|$ impossible. If $|F2 - r_2| = |F2 - r_1|$ and $|F3 - r_3| < |F3 - r_1|$ and $|F1 - r_2| < |F1 - r_1|$ and $|F1 - r_2| \leq |F1 - r_3|$, then $c_1^2 = 0$ and F2 *accepts*. If $|F2 - r_2| \geq |F2 - r_1|$ and $|F3 - r_3| < |F3 - r_1|$ and $|F1 - r_3| < min(|F1 - r_1|, |F1 - r_2|)$, then $c_1^3 = 0$ and F3 *accepts*.

C. If $|F2 - r_2| < |F2 - r_1|$ and $|F3 - r_3| \geq |F3 - r_1|$, F3 will accept any offer.

So, if $|F2 - r_2| < |F2 - r_1|$ and $|F3 - r_3| \geq |F3 - r_1|$ and $|F1 - r_1| \leq min(|F1 - r_2|, |F1 - r_3|)$, then $c_1^3 = 1$ and F3 *accepts*. If $|F2 - r_2| < |F2 - r_1|$ and $|F3 - r_3| \geq |F3 - r_1|$ and $|F1 - r_2| < min(|F1 - r_1|, |F1 - r_3|)$, then $c_1^2 = 0$ and F2 *accepts*. If $|F3 - r_3| > |F3 - r_1|$, Lemma 5 renders $|F1 - r_3| < |F1 - r_1|$ impossible. If $|F2 - r_2| < |F2 - r_1|$ and $|F3 - r_3| = |F3 - r_1|$ and $|F1 - r_3| < min(|F1 - r_1|, |F1 - r_2|)$, then $c_1^3 = 0$ and F3 *accepts*.

D. If $|F2 - r_2| < |F2 - r_1|$ and $|F3 - r_3| < |F3 - r_1|$, F2 and F3 require minimum power shares to enter agreements. For notational simplicity, let $c_2^{*3} = min\{[|F3 - r_3| - |F3 - q|]/[|F3 - r_3| - |F3 - r_2|], 1\}$, $M_1^2(c_2^{*3}) = min\{(1 - c_2^{*3})((|F2 - r_3| - |F2 - r_2|)/(|F2 - r_1| - |F2 - r_2|)), 1\}$ and $M_1^3(c_2^{*3}) = min\{c_2^{*3}((|F3 - r_2| - |F3 - r_3|)/(|F3 - r_1| - |F3 - r_3|)), 1\}$. The last two terms are the minimal acceptable offer for the case when all three factions most prefer their own faction's reconciliation, r.

So, if $|F2 - r_2| < |F2 - r_1|$ and $|F3 - r_3| < |F3 - r_1|$ and $|F1 - r_1| < min(|F1 - r_2|, |F1 - r_3|)$, and

- $M_1^2(c_2^{*3})|F1 - r_1| + (1 - M_1^2(c_2^{*3}))|F1 - r_2| \leq min(c_2^{*3}|F1 - r_2| + (1 - c_2^{*3})|F1 - r_3|, M_1^3(c_2^{*3})|F1 - r_1| + (1 - M_1^3(c_2^{*3}))|F1 - r_3|)$, then $c_1^2 = M_1^2(c_2^{*3})$ and F2 *accepts*.
- $M_1^3(c_2^{*3})|F1 - r_1| + (1 - M_1^3(c_2^{*3}))|F1 - r_3| < M_1^2(c_2^{*3})|F1 - r_1| + (1 - M_1^2(c_2^{*3}))|F1 - r_2|$ and $M_1^3(c_2^{*3})|F1 - r_1| + (1 - M_1^3(c_2^{*3}))|F1 - r_3| \leq c_2^{*3}|F1 - r_2| + (1 - c_2^{*3})|F1 - r_3|$, then $c_1^3 = M_1^3(c_2^{*3})$ and F3 *accepts*.

Appendix B 149

- $c_{23}^{*}|F1 - r_2| + (1 - c_{23}^{*})|F1 - r_3| < min([M_1^2(c_{23}^{*})|F1 - r_1|] + [(1 - M_1^2(c_{23}^{*}))|F1 - r_2|], [M_1^3(c_{23}^{*})|F1 - r_1|] + [(1 - M_1^3(c_{23}^{*}))|F1 - r_3|])$, then $c_1^2 = 0$ and $F2$ rejects.

If $|F2 - r_2| < |F2 - r_1|$ and $|F3 - r_3| < |F3 - r_1|$ and $|F1 - r_2| < |F1 - r_1|$ and $|F1 - r_2| \leq |F1 - r_3|$, then $c_1^2 = 0$ and $F2$ *accepts*. And If $|F2 - r_2| < |F2 - r_1|$ and $|F3 - r_3| < |F3 - r_1|$ and $|F1 - r_3| < min(|F1 - r_1|, |F1 - r_2|)$, then $c_1^3 = 0$ and $F3$ *accepts*.

<u>Case 2</u>: If $|F2 - r_3| - |F2 - r_2| > 0 > |F3 - r_3| - |F3 - r_2|$ and $min([|F3 - r_3| - |F3 - q|]/[|F3 - r_3| - |F3 - r_2|], 1) < (|F2 - q| - |F2 - r_3|)/(|F2 - r_2| - |F2 - r_3|)$, then the consequence of a failed offer from $F1$ is $L = q$ (i.e., $c_2^3 = 1$ and $F3$ rejects).

This case has the same four subcases as case 1. The first three subcases of case 2 are identical to subcases A, B, and C of case 1. Let $M_1^2(q) = min((|F2 - r_2| - |F2 - q|)/(|F2 - r_2| - |F2 - r_1|), 1)$ and let $M_1^3(q)$ be defined analogously. These terms are the minimal acceptable offer for the case when all three factions most prefer their own faction's reconciliation, r.

D'. If $|F2 - r_2| < |F2 - r_1|$ and $|F3 - r_3| < |F3 - r_1|$, $F2$ and $F3$ require minimum power shares to enter agreements.

So if $|F2 - r_2| < |F2 - r_1|$ and $|F3 - r_3| < |F3 - r_1|$ and $|F1 - r_1| < min(|F1 - r_2|, |F1 - r_3|)$, and

- $M_1^2(q)|F1 - r_1| + (1 - M_1^2(q))|F1 - r_2| \leq min(|F1 - q|, M_1^3(q)|F1 - r_1| + (1 - M_1^3(q))|F1 - r_3|)$, then $c_1^2 = M_1^2(q)$ and $F2$ *accepts*.
- $M_1^3(q)|F1 - r_1| + (1 - M_1^3(q))|F1 - r_3| < M_1^2(q)|F1 - r_1| + (1 - M_1^2(q))|F1 - r_2|$ and
- $M_1^3(q)|F1 - r_1| + (1 - M_1^3(q))|F1 - r_3| \leq |F1 - q|$, then $c_1^3 = M_1^3(q)$ and $F3$ *accepts*.
- $|F1 - q| < min([M_1^2(q)|F1 - r_1|] + [(1 - M_1^2(q))|F1 - r_2|], [M_1^3(q)|F1 - r_1|] + [(1 - M_1^3(q))|F1 - r_3|])$, then $c_1^2 = 0$ and $F2$ *rejects*.

If $|F2 - r_2| < |F2 - r_1|$ and $|F3 - r_3| < |F3 - r_1|$ and $|F1 - r_2| < |F1 - r_1|$ and $|F1 - r_2| \leq |F1 - r_3|$, then $c_1^2 = 0$ and $F2$ *accepts*. And if $|F2 - r_2| < |F2 - r_1|$ and $|F3 - r_3| < |F3 - r_1|$ and $|F1 - r_3| < min(|F1 - r_1|, |F1 - r_2|)$, then $c_1^3 = 0$ and $F3$ *accepts*.

<u>Case 3</u>: If $min(|F3 - r_3| - |F3 - r_2|, |F2 - r_3| - |F2 - r_2|) \geq 0$, then $c_2^3 = 1$ and $F3$ accepts.

Since, $c_2^3 = 0$ and $c_2^3 = 1$ are mirror images with respect to acceptability constraints, we can characterize the dynamics of both using a single case.

A. If $|F2 - r_2 \geq |F2 - r_1|$ and $|F3 - r_3| = |F3 - r_1| = |F3 - r_2|$, $F2$ and $F3$ will accept any offer.

So, if $|F2 - r_2| \geq |F2 - r_1|$ and $|F3 - r_3| = |F3 - r_1| = |F3 - r_2|$ and $|F1 - r_1| \leq min(|F1 - r_2|, |F1 - r_3|)$, then $c_1^2 = 1$ and $F2$ *accepts*. If $|F2 - r_2| > |F2 - r_1|$, Lemma 5 renders $|F1 - r_2| < |F1 - r_1|$ impossible. If $|F2 - r_2| = |F2 - r_1|$ and $|F3 - r_3| = |F3 - r_1| =$

$|F_3 - r_2|$ and $|F_1 - r_2| < min(|F_1 - r_1|, |F_1 - r_3|)$, then $c_1^2 = 0$ and F_2 *accepts*. And if $|F_2 - r_2| \geq |F_2 - r_1|$ and $|F_3 - r_3| = |F_3 - r_1| = |F_3 - r_2|$ and $|F_1 - r_3| < min(|F_1 - r_1|, |F_1 - r_2|)$, then $c_1^3 = 0$ and F_3 *accepts*.

B. If $|F_2 - r_2| < |F_2 - r_1|$ and either $|F_3 - r_3| < |F_3 - r_1|$ or $|F_3 - r_3| = |F_3 - r_1| > |F_3 - r_2|$, all offers > 0 will be rejected (since the consequence of rejection is r_2). Therefore, $c_1^2 = 0$, F_2 *rejects* and $L = r_2$.

C. If $|F_2 - r_2| \geq |F_2 - r_1|$ and $|F_3 - r_3| < |F_3 - r_1|$ or $|F_3 - r_3| = |F_3 - r_1| > |F_3 - r_2|$, only F_2 will accept an offer.

So, if $|F_2 - r_2| \geq |F_2 - r_1|$ and $|F_3 - r_3| < |F_3 - r_1|$ or $|F_3 - r_3| = |F_3 - r_1| > |F_3 - r_2|$ and $|F_1 - r_1| \leq |F_1 - r_2|$, then $c_1^2 = 1$ and F_2 *accepts*. If $|F_2 - r_2| = |F_2 - r_1|$ and $|F_3 - r_3| < |F_3 - r_1|$ or $|F_3 - r_3| = |F_3 - r_1| > |F_3 - r_2|$ and $|F_1 - r_2| < |F_1 - r_1|$, then $c_1^2 = 0$ and F_2 *accepts*. And if $|F_2 - r_2| > |F_2 - r_1|$, Lemma 5 renders $|F_1 - r_2| < |F_1 - r_1|$ impossible.

D. If $|F_2 - r_2| < |F_2 - r_1|$ and $|F_3 - r_3| = |F_3 - r_1| = |F_3 - r_2|$, only F_3 will accept a nonzero offer. F_1 coalesces with F_3 unless it strictly prefers r_2 to any other r.

So, if $|F_2 - r_2| < |F_2 - r_1|$ and $|F_3 - r_3| = |F_3 - r_1| = |F_3 - r_2|$ and $|F_1 - r_1| \leq min(|F_1 - r_2|, |F_1 - r_3|)$, then $c_1^3 = 1$ and F_3 *accepts*. If $|F_2 - r_2| < |F_2 - r_1|$ and $|F_3 - r_3| = |F_3 - r_1| = |F_3 - r_2|$ and $|F_1 - r_2| < |F_1 - r_1|$ and $|F_1 - r_1| \leq |F_1 - r_3|$, then $c_1^2 = 0$. And if $|F_2 - r_2| < |F_2 - r_1|$ and $|F_3 - r_3| = |F_3 - r_1| = |F_3 - r_2|$ and $|F_1 - r_3| < min(|F_1 - r_1|, |F_1 - r_2|)$, then $c_1^3 = 0$ and F_3 *accepts*.

E. If $|F_2 - r_2| \geq |F_2 - r_1|$ and $|F_3 - r_3| > |F_3 - r_1|$, then F_2 will accept any offer. F_1 coalesces with F_2 unless it strictly prefers r_3 to any other r.

So if $|F_2 - r_2| \geq |F_2 - r_1|$ and $|F_3 - r_3| > |F_3 - r_1|$ *and* $|F_1 - r_1| \leq min(|F_1 - r_2|, |F_1 - r_3|)$, then $c_1^2 = 1$ *and F_2 accepts*. If $|F_3 - r_3| > |F_3 - r_1|$, Lemma 5 renders $|F_1 - r_3| < |F_1 - r_1|$ impossible. If $|F_2 - r_2| > |F_2 - r_1|$, Lemma 5 renders $|F_1 - r_2| < |F_1 - r_1|$ impossible. If $|F_2 - r_2| = |F_2 - r_1|$ and $|F_3 - r_3| > |F_3 - r_1|$ and $|F_1 - r_2| < |F_1 - r_1|$ and $|F_1 - r_1| \leq |F_1 - r_3|$, then $c_1^2 = 0$ *and F_2 accepts*.

F. If $|F_2 - r_2| < |F_2 - r_1|$ and $|F_3 - r_3| > |F_3 - r_1|$, then F_2 will reject any nonzero offer.

So, if $|F_2 - r_2| < |F_2 - r_1|$ and $|F_3 - r_3| > |F_3 - r_1|$ and $|F_1 - r_1| \leq min(|F_1 - r_2|, |F_1 - r_3|)$, then $c_1^3 = 1$ *and F_3 accepts*.

If $|F_2 - r_2| < |F_2 - r_1|$ and $|F_3 - r_3| > |F_3 - r_1|$ and $|F_1 - r_2| < |F_1 - r_1|$ and $|F_1 - r_2| \leq |F_1 - r_3|$, then $c_1^2 = 0$ *and F_2 accepts*. And if $|F_3 - r_3| > |F_3 - r_1|$, then Lemma 5 renders $|F_1 - r_1| > |F_1 - r_3|$ impossible.

Proof of Proposition 2. The equilibrium described earlier is unique. From the equilibrium, it follows that if all of the game's parameters remain constant at any set of initial values, there can be no change in the offers or the outcome.

As the examples in the text indicate, there exist changes in the ideal point of the president or the Senate that are sufficient to change the reconciliation that at least one potential coalition would produce. Some of these changes are sufficient to change at least one House faction's preferences over the three reconciliations that can emerge and to change the offer that factions will make and accept in equilibrium. Therefore, changes in s or p can change the balance of power in the House.

Appendix C

List of Changes in the Rules and Procedures of the House

Congress	Effect[1]	Rule Change
46th (1879–1881)	2	Required debate on suspension of the rules and previous question; reinstated seconding of suspension motions. First definite rule (as opposed to precedent) establishing the priority of conference reports over other House business.
47th (1881–1883)	2	Limited dilatory motions in contested election cases; suspension votes reduced from two-thirds to a simple majority for some bills; Rules Committee granted power to report bill-specific rules.
49th (1885–1887)	2	Removal of the Holman Rule.
51st (1889–1891)	2	Reed's rules adopted: abolished disappearing quorum; restricted dilatory motions.
52nd (1891–1893)	1	Reed's rules repealed; increased Rules Committee prerogatives (reports privileged, although not protected from disappearing quorum); restored Holman rule.
53rd (1893–1895)	2	Readopted Reed's disappearing quorum rule, increased prerogatives of the Rules Committee (allow the committee to sit while the House was in session); rule of 100 members as a requisite for quorum in the Committee of the Whole. By the end of the session all the remainder of Reed's rules had been readopted.
54th (1895–1897)	2	Readopted remainder of Reed's rules; removal of the Holman rule.
61st (1909–1911)	1	Strengthened Calendar Wednesday; created discharge process; motion to recommit guarantee for minority; enlarged Rules Committee and removed Speaker from chairmanship of Rules Committee.

Congress	Effect[1]	Rule Change
62nd (1911–1913)	1	Remove Speaker power to appoint chair and committee members and transfer of that power to a majority of the House; tightened germaneness requirement on revenue bills; restoration of the Holman rule; strengthened Calendar Wednesday.
64th (1915–1917)	1	Made Calendar Wednesday process more workable; House adopted a resolution revising the Calendar Wednesday rule to speed up its work: debate on bills considered on Calendar Wednesday limited to two hours, and no committee permitted to occupy more than two Wednesdays with its business.
66th (1919–1921)	2	Appropriation Committee gained exclusive jurisdiction over appropriation matters; previously control over appropriations distributed among seven committees.
67th (1921–1923)	2	Gave the chair of Rules Committee more discretion over when to report bills.
68th (1923–1925)	1	Liberalized discharge rule, loosened germaneness rule on revenue bills; rule pocket veto banned; two-thirds vote required to waive layover rules.
69th (1925–1927)	2	Discharge petition rule tightened.
72nd (1931–1933)	1	Liberalized discharge rule; loosened Speaker control over discharging conferees; limited number of days a committee can occupy on Calendar Wednesday to one.
73rd (1933–1935)	2	Special orders reported by Rules Committee made nondivisible.
74th (1935–1937)	2	Discharge petition signatures increased from 145 to 218
79th (1945–1947)	2	House Un-American Activities Committee granted standing committee status; Legislative Reorganization Act of 1946 reduced the number of committees, limited committee assignment of representatives, increased committee staff, and provided for committee oversight.
80th (1947–1949)	2	Reduction in number of committees from forty-three to nineteen.
81st (1949–1951)	1	Twenty-one-day rule adopted, making bypassing Rules Committee easier.
82nd (1951–1953)	2	Twenty-one-day rule repealed.
87th (1961–1963)	2	Rules Committee expanded from twelve to fifteen (added two Democrats and one Republican).

(continued)

Congress	Effect[1]	Rule Change
89th (1965–1967)	2	Twenty-one-day rule adopted, making bypassing Rules Committee easier – in this version the Speaker had complete discretion in recognizing members seeking to make motions under this rule, and any member of a committee designated by that committee might make the motion; limited obstruction tactics; House rules amended to make it possible for the House to send bills to conference by majority rule.
91st (1969–1971)	2	Legislative Reorganization Act of 1970.
92nd (1971–1973)	2	Minority party guarantee of committee investigatory staff funding eliminated; Amended Rules XX and XXVIII as they pertained to nongermane Senate amendments.[2]
		First round of Democratic Caucus reform: (1) upon the demand of 10 members, a separate vote could be held on any committee chair; (2) limit on the number of subcommittee chairmanships a member could hold (no more than one).
93rd (1973–1975)	2	Second round of Democratic Caucus reform: (1) automatic votes on all chairmen and secret ballot on them if 20 percent of the caucus demanded it; (2) Subcommittee Bill of Rights: (i) each committee would caucus and adopt rules that fixed jurisdictions of subcommittees and matters submitted to the appropriate jurisdiction within two weeks (before subcommittees were numbered so chairman could send a bill to any subcommittee he chose); (ii) provided staff and resources; (iii) ratio of Democrats to Republicans similar to the ratio in full committees. Created Steering and Policy Committee chaired by the Speaker that would make recommendations on legislative priorities and party policy; committee would also recommend to the Committee on Committees nominees for chairman of House standing committees.
		Limits on minority obstruction; various devices adopted to expedite business (for example, made workable the rule to cut time spent in quorum calls); Guarantee of 1/3 fund for minority for temporary staff; amended Rules XX and XXVIII as they pertained to nongermane Senate amendments.

Congress	Effect[1]	Rule Change
94th (1975–1977)	2	Proxy voting ban in committee eliminated; eliminated 1974 guarantee of one-third of funds for minority investigatory staffing; Rules Committee can waive requirement for two-hour availability of conference reports; referral of legislation to more than one committee allowed; abolished House Un-American Activities Committee.
95th (1977–1979)	2	Increased number of days for suspensions; Speaker given authority to set time limits on each committee's consideration of a bill; limited obstruction tactics; abolished Joint Committee on Atomic Energy.
96th (1979–1981)	2	Increased threshold for demanding a recorded vote; limited obstruction tactics.
98th (1983–1985)	2	Limited riders to appropriation bills; restored Holman rule.
100th (1987–1989)	2	Waived two-thirds rule for consideration of rules reports.
102nd (1991–1993)	2	Series of changes, including requirement that any legislation with direct spending or revenues include a binding Congressional Budget Office estimate for "pay as you go" sequestration.
103rd (1993–1995)	2	Package of changes allowing delegates to vote in Committee of the Whole and committee chairs to declare a quorum once a majority of members had been present for some part of the session; eliminated three select committees, made public the names of members who sign discharge petitions.
104th (1995–1997)	2	Eliminated three committees (DC, Merchant Marine, and Post Office; jurisdiction given to extant committees); several issues in the Commerce Committee's turf divided among other committees; proxy voting banned; required supermajority for tax increases; term limits on committee and subcommittee chairs (three terms) and Speaker (four terms), committee staff cut by 1/3 compared to 103rd, members allowed to serve in no more than two standing committees and four subcommittees; Speaker no longer allowed to send a bill to more than one committee simultaneously; committee chairs given more authority over hiring subcommittee staff.
107th (2001–2003)	2	Elimination of Banking Committee, creation of Financial Services Committee; large part of Banking Committee's jurisdiction to Commerce Committee.

(*continued*)

Congress	Effect[1]	Rule Change
108th (2003–2005)	2	Repealed six-year term limit for Speaker; change in rules to curtail minority dissent: more time required to get consideration of nonbinding floor motions to instruct conferees, which are often used by the minority to advance their arguments on legislation; under the new rules, chairman may postpone committee votes (can postpone balloting until they have the votes to win). Also eased the stringent gift ban that the GOP had adopted after ten months of control in 1995.
110th (2007–2008)	2	Pay-go rules: new lobbying rules: members and staff cannot accept gifts or meals from lobbyists, who also cannot pay for trips; vote cannot be held open longer than fifteen-minute minimum just to reverse an outcome (highly criticized practice employed by Republicans); conference committees also required to be open to all conferees.
111th (2009–2010)	2	New rules relaxed pay-go requirements: House members could attach an emergency designation to a spending bill in response to an act of war, terrorism, or natural disaster or a prolonged period of low economic growth, exempting the bill from the "pay-go" requirements; in addition, legislators could also link bills that did not meet the waiver requirements with those exempted ones New rules package also severely restricted the minority party's right to offer a motion to recommit, requiring that any vote to recommit an amended bill should include instructions that it be returned to the floor "forthwith" (i.e., House must vote on the amended bill within minutes).
112th (2011–2013)	1	New rules repeal the so-called Gephardt rule, which had allowed the House automatically to send the Senate a separate debt ceiling measure, deemed to have passed after the House had adopted a budget resolution; new rules also substituted the previous "pay-go" rule with a new "cut-go" rule so that any new spending programs could only be accompanied by equal spending cuts, not tax increases.

[1] Decentralization of rules is coded as 1. Centralization of rules is coded as 2.

[2] The subsequent actions taken in 1972 and 1974 remedied unanticipated problems with the 1970 provisions and extended the newly established procedures to cover other parliamentary contingencies.

Appendix D

Universe of Rules and Procedures

In what follows I explain in more detail the rules and procedures adopted in three Congresses, that I coded as significant changes, but that Schickler does not include in his list of rules and procedures.

1. 49TH CONGRESS (1885–1887): THE HOLMAN RULE

The Holman rule, first adopted in the House in 1876 by a new Democratic majority, allowed members of the Appropriations Committee to add riders to appropriation bills. As Hasbrouck explains, the Holman rule

> allows amendments to be made to an appropriation bill even though they change existing law and are germane only in a general way to the subject-matter of the bill, provided the presiding officer can be persuaded their general effect is to reduce expenditures, and provided they are authorized by the House committee having jurisdiction over such legislation. (1927, 115)

The Holman rule is important because it functioned as an instrument of the House majority to further their own legislative interests, given a president and a Senate of the opposition party. By allowing the majority to insert their preferences in a general appropriation bill that the president would likely sign, this rule made those issues veto-proof (i.e., the president would veto them if they were a single bill). For instance, referring to the Holman rule, Cox and McCubbins argue that

> the majority party can insert some of its legislative priorities –those the President would veto if submitted separately – in the safe confines of a general appropriations bills that must be passed. (Cox and McCubbins 2005, 82)

In this sense, the adoption of this rule strengthened the House majority party when it had to negotiate with a president of the opposition party; thus the enactment of the Holman rule has always coincided with the election of an opposition president. While I follow Schickler and Cox and McCubbins in designating the adoption of the Holman rule as a majority win and incorporate it into their lists, I disagree with their claim that the removal of the Holman rule is neither a "minority victory nor a majority loss."

For this study, I include the abolishment of the Holman rule in the list of rules and procedures because the elimination of the rule indicates the inability of members of the Appropriations Committee to include some of their preferences in a general appropriations bill, even when they enjoy an allied president. The dismissal of the rule transferred power from members of the Appropriations Committee, who could have attached legislative raiders to appropriation bills, to the party leadership, who controlled the agenda and the introduction of amendments. Furthermore, and as will be clear in the next chapter, the decision by the majority party to remove the Holman rule further elucidates the role of the Senate's and president's preferences in House rules decisions.

In practical terms, including the elimination of the Holman rule in the list of rules and procedures changes the coding for only one Congress, the 49th Congress (1885–1887). In 1885 the majority party, the Democrats, abolished the Holman rule when the Democratic president, Grover Cleveland, occupied the White House. The House majority party no longer needed to add riders to bills in order to get legislative benefits.

2. 67TH CONGRESS (*1921–1923*): MORE POWER TO RULES COMMITTEE

In this Congress, the Republican majority adopted new rules and procedures that gave the chair of the Rules Committee more discretion over the management of bills, concentrating power in the conservative Republican leadership that controlled the committee. Cox and McCubbins (2005) note this rule change; they argue that it substantially altered the distribution of power within the House.

3. 100TH CONGRESS (*1987–1988*): CHANGES FOR THE CONSIDERATION OF RULES COMMITTEE REPORTS

In the 100th Congress, the Democratic majority waived the two-thirds majority required by the normal rules of the House for consideration of the Rules Committee's reports. With this change, only a majority was needed to waive the two-thirds requisite. Cox and McCubbins (2005) also note this rule change.

Appendix E

Coding of William H. Taft and Calvin Coolidge Presidencies

As mentioned in the chapter, although the president's partisanship did not change when William Howard Taft replaced Theodore Roosevelt, or when Calvin Coolidge replaced Warren Harding, I code these two presidential transitions as if the partisanship had changed. Chapter 7 focuses on the Roosevelt-Taft transition and explains in detail my decision. Here I will focus on the Harding-Coolidge presidential change.

Calvin Coolidge became president in August 1923, after the sudden death of President Warren Harding. Both Harding and Coolidge, his vice president, were Republicans, but they were dramatically different in policy preferences.

First, progressives had supported Harding's campaign for president. He was the compromise choice between progressive and conservative Republicans. Important progressive figures like Wisconsin senator Robert LaFollette strongly campaigned for Harding (Trani and Wilson 1977). His cabinet included progressive figures not popular in the conservative wing of the party, prominently Charles Evans Hughes as secretary of state and Henry C. Wallace as secretary of agriculture. Wallace was an "outspoken editor of an Iowa farm journal, [whose] politics were moderately progressive ... [and] his liberal tendencies were obnoxious to the conservative wing" (Trani and Wilson 1977, 39).

Furthermore, Harding pushed for policies favored by progressives. In 1921 he signed the Sheppard Towner Maternity and Infancy Protection Act, which allocated federal money to states for rural prenatal and baby care centers, supplied for medical care for women and children, as well as pre- and postnatal instruction. The Veteran Bureau was established as an independent agency directly responsible to the president for administering all forms of veteran relief. With respect to regulation, in 1921 Congress passed the Packers and Stockyard Acts, which enabled the secretary of agriculture to provide modest supervision over packers and to regulate and preserve competition among producers of livestock, poultry, and dairy products. This law made it more difficult for packers to control prices paid to farmers: "Rural America viewed it as a step in the right direction." In 1922 the president signed the Grain Futures Act, which established government regulation of the commodity exchanges based on the Interstate Commerce clause. In the same year the Capper-Volstead Act, which provided legal protection for cooperatives, became law. The act exempted farm cooperatives from antitrust laws by allowing farmers to engage in cooperative buying and selling.

To aid farmers, a key constituency of progressives, Harding signed the Farm Loan Act, which provided for further capital for federal land banks.[1] The act was strongly opposed by Secretary of the Treasury Andrew W. Mellon, a procorporation conservative Republican. A month later, in August 1921, Congress passed the Emergency Agricultural Credit Act, which provided short-term loan assistance to farmers. Furthermore, the president supported the extension for an additional year of the War Finance Corporation, which could underwrite farm credit and could make money available for farmers to buy seed in areas suffering from crop failures. All of these measures aimed to solve the farm problem and were welcomed by progressives, a majority of whom represented rural areas. Controversy over these measures "extended into Harding's cabinet and became the basis of a prolonged struggle between Wallace and Mellon" (Trani and Wilson 1977, 69). Progressives also achieved some victories on tax reform. Although Secretary of Treasury Mellon pushed to decrease the existent corporate tax of 10 percent and to reduce the maximum surtax from 65 percent to 32 percent, Congress instead increased the corporate tax to 12.5 percent and reduced the surtax tax only to 50 percent. Although this tax reform, part of the Revenue Act of 1921, provided substantial tax savings for the rich, it provided much less than had originally been proposed.

However, in August 1923 Harding died unexpectedly and Coolidge became president. Congress was not in session at the time and did not reconvene until December 1923. This presidential change really meant a change in the CS for the Republicans, especially progressives.

First, progressive Republicans were not expecting Coolidge to become president. As the *New York Times* remarked,

> By no stretch of fancy could it be said that the Republican leaders ever considered the possibility of Mr. Coolidge being in the running for the party nomination for President....The passing of Mr. Harding ... has thrown party affairs into a turmoil ... the party faces an internal struggle between the various divergent groups which compose it.... The great bulk of party men were able to rally around President Harding. (Oulahan 1923)

---

[1]   This legislation modified the Farm Loan Act, so that long-term credit became easily available.

When Congress met for the first time after Harding's death, progressives identified Calvin Coolidge with the conservative intraparty group in the Republican Party (Ripley 1967); Coolidge's positions on issues of extreme importance to progressives (e.g., reduction of railroad rates, aid for wheat farmers, relief from taxation) were unknown. The *New York Times* mentioned:

> The Republican leaders today, two weeks before the assembling of Congress, are without a program. They say privately they do not know what tack will be assumed on bonus, taxation, and the questions uppermost in the public mind.[2]("Urging Coolidge to Lead Tax Fight; Republicans Want the President to Take Charge of Revision Movement" 1923)

What mattered at the beginning of the 68th Congress was the perception that intraparty groups had about the preferences of the president. In this case, the conservatism of Coolidge was the main information that progressives took into account when deciding about the distribution of power in 1923.

---

[2] The only plan progressives had seen before the opening of the 68th Congress was the taxation revision program (Mellon plan), which in many issues was opposed to progressives' ideas.

Appendix F

Directionality of Rules and Procedures

Table F.1 presents a crosstab of Schickler's and my classification.[1] It assigns each Congress from the 46th through the 105th to one cell. There are thirty-three Congresses for which Schickler and I both record changes in the rules of the House.

There are twenty-one cases where Schickler argues that the rules enhanced the power of the majority party. For nineteen of those cases, I conclude that the rules centralized power in the Speaker and his intraparty group. In essence, the interpretation for these nineteen cases is similar because we both note that the new rules empowered the Speaker. In the two other cases, the 62nd and 81st Congresses, I claim the new rules decentralized power within the majority party. For these two cases, the inclusion of intraparty groups in the analysis changes the understanding of the effect of new rules; I explain these two cases in detail in the next section.

There are eight cases that Schickler argues undermine the power of the majority party. I conclude that rules decentralized power in the majority party in the 61st, 64th, 68th, and 72nd Congresses; centralized it in the 79th and 82nd Congresses; and did not affect the distribution of power within the House in the 60th and 90th Congresses.

Schickler argues there were no changes in the distribution of power in the 46th, 52nd, 91st, and 103rd Congresses because the effects of the new rules canceled each other out; some of the rules enhanced the power of the majority party, while others undermined it. I concluded that the new rules concentrated power in the Speaker in the 46th, 91st, and 103rd Congresses and increased the power of the non-Speaker group in the 52nd Congress. I also explain these cases in detail in the next section.

---

[1]   As mentioned in Chapter 5, Schickler classifies Congresses depending on whether new rules enhanced, reduced, or had no effect on the power of the majority party.

TABLE F.1. *Effect of new rules in the House: Schickler and Sin's classification*

	Sin – Centralization of power in the Speaker	Sin – Decentralization of power within the majority party	Sin – No effect of new rules on distribution of power in the Congress
Schickler – Enhancement of majority party power	Nineteen Congresses (47th, 51st, 53rd, 54th, 66th, 69th, 73rd, 74th, 80th, 87th, 89th, 92nd, 93rd, 94th, 95th, 96th, 98th, 102nd, and 104th)	Two Congresses (62nd, 81st)	
Schickler – Reduction of majority party power	Two Congresses (79th, 82nd)	Four Congresses (61st, 64th, 68th, and 72nd)	Two Congresses (60th, 90th)
Schickler – Changes in rules in opposite directions that cancel each other	Three Congresses (46th, 91st, and 103rd)	One Congress (52nd)	

CENTRALIZATION, DECENTRALIZATION, AND NO EFFECT OF NEW RULES

The Adoption and Dismissal of the Twenty-One-Day Rule, 81st (1949–1950), 82nd (1951–1952), and 90th (1967–1968) Congresses

At the beginning of the 81st Congress, the House adopted what became known as the "twenty-one-day rule," by which committee chairs gained the authority to bring bills to the floor that had not been granted a rule by the Rules Committee within twenty-one days of its submission. The adoption of the twenty-one-day rule made it easier to bypass the Rules Committee. At the beginning of the 82nd Congress, however, a coalition of southern Democrats and Republicans repealed the rule, shifting power back to the Rules Committee.

At the time of the twenty-one-day rule adoption, the House was in the hands of the Democratic Party (263 legislators), although the party was deeply divided between the non-Speaker group of northern liberal Democrats (about 148 legislators) and the Speaker group of southern conservative Democrats (about 115 legislators), who were closer ideologically to Speaker Sam Rayburn (D-TX). The Rules Committee was a stronghold of southern Democrats, who were able to restrict the flow of legislation in the committee through an alliance with conservative Republicans.

Schickler argues that adoption of the twenty-one-day rule represents a majority party gain, because it increased the power of the "Democratic majority party" to bypass the Rules Committee. With the rule in place, the "Democratic Party" could bring issues to the floor that had been blocked in the committee. Consistent with the argument, he interprets the repeal of the twenty-one-day rule in the 82nd Congress as undermining the power of the "Democratic majority party" to set the agenda by favoring the Republican Party, which, together with southern Democrats, controlled the Rules Committee.

However, who is the "Democratic majority party"? Is it the southern conservative Democrats, who controlled the speakership and about 115 seats (44 percent of the Democratic delegation) in both Congresses? Or is it the northern liberal Democrats, who controlled about 145 seats (56 percent of the party) in the 81st Congress and 120 seats in 82nd Congress? Schickler clearly associates the majority party with northern Democrats. However, northern Democrats did not control the Democratic Party; the speakership, the Rules Committee, and many of the other powerful House committees were in the hands of southern Democrats.

In contrast to Schickler, I claim that the adoption of the rule in the 81st Congress decentralized power within the House majority party by shifting prerogatives from the Speaker group, the southern Democrats who controlled the Rules Committee and the speakership, to the non-Speaker group, the northern liberal Democrats. When the rule was adopted, it gave northern Democrats the power to push liberal legislation through the House, actions that were once again hindered after its later repeal.

For instance, the twenty-one-day rule effectively helped northern Democrats in their bargaining with southern Democrats, as they were able to advocate successfully many of the "Fair Deal" policies promoted by President Truman. For instance, the *New York Times* indicated that the twenty-one-day rule

> was adopted at the outset of the 81st Congress to prevent pioneering features of the Fair Deal from being pigeonholed in the Rules Committee, then, as now, in control of the conservative Republican-southern Democrat coalition. (*NYT*, January 4, 1951)

Indeed, the rule was important in forcing liberal bills, like the creation of the National Science Foundation and statehood for Hawaii and Alaska (Polsby 2004), to the floor. In its evaluation of the 81st Congress, *Congressional Quarterly* observes:

> The 21-day rule was helpful in negotiating other legislation in the floor even when it was not invoked. In the 81st congress the rule was invoked for the antipoll tax bill and the rivers and harbors bill. The threat of its use forced action on the minimum wage, social security and housing bills. (*CQ Press*, 1950, 577)

The twenty-one-day rule was again adopted at the beginning of the 89th Congress (1965–1966). This time the twenty-one-day rule was different from the earlier version because the Speaker, now northern Democrat John McCormack (D-MA), had complete power to recognize the legislators who wanted to make a motion under the rule. Schickler posits that the effect of the rule was to enhance the power of the majority party, whereas I argue that it centralized power in the Speaker and his intraparty group, the northern Democrats. Indeed, the twenty-one-day rule gave northern Democrats a bargaining tool against the very conservative southern Democrat Rules Committee chair Howard Smith (D-VA), who kept tight control of the committee. As Sheppard (1985) claims:

> The most significant procedural reform passed during the 1964–1966 period of liberal ascendancy further tinkered with House procedures to side-step the Rules Committee, this time by means of the 21-day Rule. This was another attempt to undermine the Rules Committee's capacity to act as a legislative roadblock. (Sheppard 1985, 15)

The argument is corroborated by a *Washington Post* editorial on the twenty-one-day rule that observes:

> The big news is that the House Rules Committee is no longer an inviolable fortress in which legislation can be stifled by a Republican-Dixiecrat coalition. (*Washington Post*, January 5, 1965, A12)

In tandem with the twenty-one-day rule, northern Democrats, with the crucial support of twenty-five pivotal liberal Republicans, adopted additional rules in 1965 that further enhanced the power of the Speaker and limited that of the Rules Committee. The new rules gave the Speaker discretionary authority to entertain motions to send legislation already approved by the Senate and the House to conference. Previously, a bill could be sent to conference only by the unanimous consent of the House or after clearance by the Rules Committee.[2] Together with the twenty-one-day rule, the new rules curbed the power of the Rules Committee and were very important for the enactment of L. B. Johnson's presidential agenda.[3] For instance, as a *New York Times* editorial observed,

> The Democrats, in party caucus, also approved proposals for major changes in House rules to curtail the power of conservatives to obstruct Johnson's legislative program ... the new procedure makes impossible for the House Rules Committee to obstruct legislation against the Speaker wishes. (*NYT*, January 3, 1965)

---

[2] This procedure had allowed the chair of the Rules Committee, Howard Smith (D-VA), to kill, in 1961, the most important education bill passed by both chambers since 1862. Rep. Smith thwarted the legislation by refusing to form a conference committee.

[3] Furthermore, the new rules eliminated a few delay tactics used by southern Democrats. For example, under the previous rules, a single member could raise an objection and delay passage until an "engrossed" copy of a pending bill had been prepared. An engrossed copy entailed the preparation of a complete copy of the bill, printed on special paper, and with special ink; so, as the process took hours to prepare, it usually forced postponement of the vote until the following day.

In all, the new rules significantly strengthened the authority of the Speaker. As observed in the *Washington Post*,

> Liberal democrats pushed through the most sweeping change in congressional rules since 1908.... Speaker John McCormack will have more power than any Speaker in over 50 years. (*Washington Post*, January 6, 1965)

Two years later, at the beginning of the 90th Congress, the twenty-one-day rule was struck down by a coalition of conservative Republicans and southern Democrats. Schickler argues that this change undermined the power of the majority party, as it made it more difficult to bypass the Rules Committee.

In contrast, I posit that the elimination of the twenty-one-day rule did not redistribute power within the majority party because it was replaced by other rules that gave northern Democrats even greater control over the Rules Committee. First, the committee adopted new rules that required regular weekly meetings that curtailed the new chairman's power to delay clearance of administration bills.[4] This change was significant because Smith's likely replacement was the most senior member of the committee, another conservative southerner, William Colmer (D-MS). As the *New York Times* recognized:

> The jubilation of moderate and liberal forces over the evident defeat of Rep. Howard W. Smith in Virginia's Democratic primary is tempered by one unpalatable by-product: under the seniority system Rep. William M. Colmer will succeed Mr. Smith next January as chairman of the immensely powerful House Rules Committee.... He obviously would use the Rules chairmanship as ruthlessly as Mr. Smith ever did to try to block liberal legislation from reaching the floor. ("The Tyranny of Seniority" 1966)

Northern Democrats supported the election of Colmer as chair of the Rules Committee in exchange for changing the rules of the committee to guarantee regular meetings. The *New York Times* summarizes:

> The 76 years old conservative agreed to amend committee rules to require regular meetings, thus assuring the flow of legislation desired by members. (Herbers 1967)

Furthermore, liberals filled two other vacancies in the Rules Committee with two additional representatives of their own, giving administration forces, the liberal Democrats, nine to six control. Thus, as a result of the new committee scheduling rules, the increased liberal representation on the committee, and a majority favorable to the administration, liberal Democrats were able to keep the committee under their control.

It is within this environment that the repeal of the twenty-one-day rule occurred. Although several administration supporters wanted to keep the

---

4 The previous chair, Howard Smith, had failed to gain nomination for his seat in the Democratic primaries.

rule as an additional safeguard, most liberal Democrats supported the repeal because it meant that Republicans and conservative Democrats would not be able to bring to the floor measures that could water down policies enacted in previous Congresses and that did not receive a favorable rule by the now more liberal Rules Committee. The *Washington Post* recognized this outcome, observing:

> The liberal committee can now play the Smith role – sitting on any conservative bills that the reshuffled committees on the 90th Congress might write. ("House Liberals Tighten Grip on Rules Committee" 1967)

Given the preceding, then, I consider that the repeal of the twenty-one-day rule in the 90th Congress did not have any effect on the distribution of power within the majority party. Although the twenty-one-day rule was eliminated, so that this mechanism to bypass the Rules Committee was no longer available, the Speaker and liberal Democrats adopted other rules that allowed them to keep a tight hold on the Committee.

CENTRALIZATION OF POWER IN THE SPEAKER

Rules on Suspension Motions, 46th Congress (1879–1881)

In 1879, the Democratic majority adopted a new set of rules and procedures that required thirty minutes of debate on the suspension of the rules and previous question, a measure that guaranteed the minority party the opportunity to express its views. At the same time, the new rules significantly reduced the power of the minority to obstruct the legislative process (Bach 1990). First, the new rules established the priority of conference reports over other House business. Second, the rules reinstated the seconding of suspension motions; thus, motions had to be supported by a majority counted by tellers before being submitted to the House. Previously, any minority could alter the order of business by bringing up issues for a vote that were not supported by a majority but that would put some representatives at odds with their constituency.[5] Motions to suspend the rules of the House were generally used to embarrass the majority and to delay business. Bach explains that

> suspension motions had been offered and roll call votes had been demanded on them, merely to delay proceedings or create political embarrassment. The demand for a second ... would enable members to avoid considering a suspension motion and so avoid going on record as being for or against "political conundrums" that did not affect one single item of legislation of the country. (Bach 1990, 53)

---

[5] In 1879 the Speaker was unable to control legislators' use of motions as a mechanism to delay business through his power of recognition. It is only at the end of this Congress that for the first time the Speaker exercised discretionary power of recognition on suspension motions.

Thus, by requiring that a majority supported a suspension motion, this rule significantly reduced the power of any minority to obstruct business in the House.[6]

Schickler (2000) argues that the changes cancel each other out, as the minority gained power to express its views on the floor but the majority expanded its control over floor business. I argue that by taking intraparty groups into account, we see that the new rules had the overall effect of centralizing power in the Speaker, Samuel J. Randall (D-PA). The rules that curtailed the power of any minority to delay business had a substantial effect because they determined the opportunities for the minority to express its views on the floor. In other words, the rule that mandated thirty minutes of debate did not restore in the minority party the power taken away by the other rules. Indeed, the thirty-minute debate was subject to the decision of the majority, as it was only for bills coupled with the suspension motions, which had to be seconded by a majority. That is, the rule allowed the minority to express its views only on those issues that the majority was willing to consider. Bach argues that

> by permitting debate on the motion, the House allowed itself time to discuss any bill it was **willing** to consider in this way. (Bach 1990, 55)

Hence, the debate requirement did not grant the minority party any power to set the agenda or modify the course of action in the House. And thus the rule changes during the 46th Congress did not cancel each other out, but instead concentrated power in the Speaker and his intraparty group.

House Un-American Activities Committee, 79th Congress (1945–1946)

In the 79th Congress, the House Un-American Activities Committee (HUAC) was granted standing committee status. The committee had been first organized in 1938, with the aim of investigating subversive activities by U.S. citizens. Since its organization in 1938, this committee had been a political tool wielded in the hands of southern Democrats. Its chairman until 1945, Representative Martin Dies (D-TX), had focused the committee's investigations on organized labor (e.g., the Congress of Industrial Organizations), a main constituency of northern Democrats.

Schickler (2000) claims that the change in the committee status undermined the power of the majority, the Democratic Party, because the minority, together with southern Democrats, could use the committee as a platform against liberal northern Democrats (Schickler 2000). I argue that the change enhanced the power of southern Democrats and, as a by-product, the power of Republicans. First, the maneuver to make it a standing committee was

---

[6] The majority constrained the use of suspension motions even more by limiting the opportunities in which the motion could be offered. It established that members could offer it only the first and third Mondays of each month and at the end of the session.

plotted by southern Democrat John Rankin (D-MS), "who took his associates by surprise and engineered the resolution providing permanent standing for the panel" ("Hart Will Head Dies Committee; Representative from New Jersey Had PAC Backing in the Last Election" 1945). The coalition that voted to make this committee permanent included 70 Democrats, nearly all of them southerners, and 137 Republicans. As Zelizer argues, "Martin Dies and John Rankin used the panel to hammer away at liberal institutions and political leaders" (2004, 45). Southern Democrats used the committee to further their political objectives by focusing the spotlight of the investigations on communism in Hollywood and on conducting hearings to investigate, for example, the radio programs in the New York Regional Office of the Price Administration (*NYT*, July 1, 1945). The first chair of the committee, Representative Edward Hart (D-NJ), a compromise choice for Democrats, was soon replaced by a conservative, Representative John Wood (D-GA). A close look into intraparty groups reveals that the changed status of the committee clearly enhanced the power of southerners over northern Democrats.

Legislative Reorganization Act of 1970, 91st Congress (1969–1971)

In October of 1970, the Democratic-controlled Congress adopted a Legislative Reorganization Act (LRA), which intended to open the legislative process to greater public scrutiny and to foster the participation of a larger number of House members in key decisions. First, the 1970 LRA ended the House ban on TV and radio coverage, permitting the media to be present at House hearings, unless a committee majority had determined otherwise. It also improved the computing facilities of Congress, implementing electronic voting on the floor. Furthermore, the 1970 LRA enabled both the majority and minority parties to increase their staffing among more committees.

Second, the LRA removed power from committee chairs (most of them southerners) by constraining the use of proxy voting in committees that previously had not been regulated by rules. The LRA prohibited the use of proxy voting unless the committee had written rules that specifically allowed it, in which case its use was limited to a specific bill or amendment. It also specified that proxies had to be given in writing and had to designate the person on the committee with the authority to use it. The LRA further required committees to keep transcripts of their meetings and to make public all committee roll-call votes.[7] Zelizer (2004) notes that it was the turning point in the path toward removing power from committee chairs:

> Many of these changes empowered committees to function in the face of unresponsive chairmen. Clearly the reorganization did not overturn the committee

---

[7] Still, the LRA did not encompass an overhaul of the committee system, as it did not directly attack the power bases of senior committee members, most of them southerners, thus leaving the seniority system intact.

system. Nonetheless, as one study noted, the legislation marked "the end of an era when powerful committee chairs and other senior members could forestall structural and procedural changes that appeared to undermine their authority." (Zelizer 2004)

Additionally, it called for recorded votes in the Committee of the Whole.

Schickler argues that the 1970 LRA had both promajority changes (for example, dispensing with reading the *Journal*, unless ordered by a majority) and prominority changes (required debate time and staff funding for the minority party). He claims that the two rules cancelled each other so that in this Congress there was no redistribution of power.

In the context of intraparty groups, I argue, it is clear that the 1970 LRA centralized power in the Speaker group, the liberal Democrats. Apart from dispensing with reading the *Journal*, the rules regarding the use of proxy voting weakened southern committee chairs. The staff funding for the minority consisted in giving the minority one-third of a committee's investigative funds (i.e., for temporary staff), a compromise engineered to expand bipartisan support for its approval. However, this provision was discarded in 1971.[8] Therefore, even though the staff increases can be thought of as enhancing the power of the minority party, in no way did they decrease the power of the majority party to set the agenda. With respect to the support for the act, younger liberal Democrats actively supported it. Opposition arose mostly from southern Democrats, who feared measures that would allow any committee member to overcome the power of a recalcitrant chair. All in all, I argue, the introduced changes enhanced the power of the Speaker group, the liberal Democrats.

DECENTRALIZATION OF POWER

Abolishment of the Reed Rules, 52nd Congress (1891–1893)

In 1891, the newly elected Democratic majority abolished rules that curtailed the power of any minority to obstruct business in the House. The Republicans had adopted those rules during the previous Congress under the leadership of Speaker Thomas Reed (R-ME). One of the most notable components of the abolished rules allowed the Speaker, during quorum calls, to count the members who were present in the floor but who refused to vote. Because a quorum is required for the House to make decisions, House members used the device of the "disappearing quorum" to obstruct votes. Thus, its elimination gave any minority the power to thwart business in the House. At the same time, the new rules also increased the Rules Committee's prerogatives, so that bills supported by the committee could avoid some obstruction tactics, although these bills could not avoid the "disappearing quorum."

---

[8] It was revived again in 1974, and discarded again in 1975.

Schickler posits that the two changes cancel each other out – the repeal of the Reed rules was a prominority change, but the increase in the Rules Committee prerogatives was a promajority change (2000, 284). I argue that the main effect of the new rules was decentralization of power because the significance and impact of the abolishment of the Reed's rules far outweigh the increase in the prerogatives of the Rules Committee (Alexander 1916; Binder 1997). Mostly, a minority in the floor could still stop bills endorsed by the Rules Committee, as they were subject to the disappearing quorum. As Schickler acknowledges in his 2001 book, the new rules regarding the committee "protected bills carrying the Rules Committee's endorsement from many filibuster tactics, but not from the disappearing quorum" (Schickler 2001, 50). Therefore, the new rules in this Congress effectively decentralized power, by giving the power to any minority to obstruct business on the floor.

Power to Appoint Members and Chairs of Committees, Calendar Wednesday, and Holman Rule, 62nd Congress (1911–1913)

When the Democratic Party took over the House in the 62nd Congress (1911–1913), a new set of rules and procedures was adopted. They removed power from the Speaker and redistributed it between the two majority intraparty groups, the reform agrarian Democrats and the conservative Democrats.[9] All the members of the majority party supported the new rules. In this Congress, the Democratic majority removed the unilateral power of the Speaker to appoint committee members and chairs, transferring that power to the Ways and Means Committee.[10] This committee became responsible for the selection of all committee members.[11] Galloway argues that

> the rules of the Sixty-second House dealt the final coup de grace to the traditional powers of the Speaker by depriving him of the right to appoint the standing committees of the House, providing instead that they should be "elected by the House, at the commencement of each Congress." They provided further that committee chairmen should be elected by the House and not be appointed by the Speaker. (Galloway 1969, 55)

The new rules decentralized power even more within the majority by strengthening Calendar Wednesday, giving greater power to committee chairs to call up bills they had reported and that did not yet have a rule from the Rules Committee. Furthermore, the Democratic majority restored the Holman rule,

---

[9] Although the Republican Party had lost its majority in the elections of 1910, it still controlled the Senate majority and the presidency (William H. Taft). Because the newly elected House Democratic majority was facing a Senate and a presidency controlled by the Republican Party, they adopted new rules further decentralizing power within the House.

[10] Recall that during the revolt against Speaker Cannon the year before, in 1910, the House had already removed the Speaker's power to appoint the chair and members of the Rules Committee.

[11] To this day, the Speaker retains the power to select members of conference committees.

which decentralized power by allowing the members of the Appropriations Committee to attach riders to its bills.

Schickler argues that these changes enhanced the power of the major-ity party. However, I posit that the new rules decentralized power within the majority. The new rules removed power from the Speaker and transferred it to the non-Speaker group, the conservative Democrats. For instance, under the new rules, the whole party membership, instead of just the Speaker, could decide on committee and chair assignments. Furthermore, the majority party was able to attach preferred riders in a general appropriations bill, making those riders veto-proof. In all, the new rules enhanced the power of the non-Speaker group.

NO CHANGES IN THE DISTRIBUTION OF POWER

Calendar Wednesday, 60th Congress (1907–1909)

During the lame-duck sessions of the 60th Congress, three days before the end of that Congress, the Republican majority adopted Calendar Wednesday. This procedure guaranteed that every Wednesday, committee chairs had the chance to call up bills of their choice that had been reported out of committees and that had not been granted a rule from the Rules Committee.[12] Essentially, Calendar Wednesday gave power to committee chairs who were in disagree-ment with the Rules Committee's decisions on which measures to bring to the floor.

Schickler posits that the enactment of Calendar Wednesday redistributed power by undermining the power of the majority party to set the agenda. I concur, in that Calendar Wednesday decentralized power by transferring it from the Speaker to progressive Republicans. However, I argue that it can-not be counted as a rule that affected the distribution of power during the 60th Congress because it was adopted during its final days. Indeed, Calendar Wednesday was part of the bargaining between the Republican intraparty groups, the conservative group closer to Speaker Cannon and the non-Speaker group, the Progressives, over the distribution of power for the 61st Congress. The main issue in the adoption of the rule, I argue, was the replacement of progressive Republican Theodore Roosevelt with conservative Republican William H. Taft. Among all the rules I consider in this book, this is the only one adopted after a new president had already been elected and before the beginning of the next Congress. Over the four months after the presidential election, Progressives had gained a better read on the preferences of President Taft. Taft's cabinet selection, a group of staunch conservatives, increased Progressives' worries about the policies Taft would pursue. Thus, Calendar Wednesday was Cannon's institutionalized compromise to grant Progressives

---

[12] Currently, Calendar Wednesday is routinely set aside each week.

a calendar day to influence the House agenda during the 61st Congress. Cox and McCubbins argue that

> by the closing weeks of the 60th Congress, many Progressives sought … to change the House's rules. In order to forestall an even worse outcome, the regular Republicans offered a resolution to institute a Calendar Wednesday. (Cox and McCubbins 2005, 60–1)

I argue that the creation of Calendar Wednesday was part of the negotiations on the rules for the next Congress. Although Calendar Wednesday altered the balance of power between the majority intraparty groups by giving power to the progressive Republicans, this alteration did not materialize during the 60th Congress.

Appendix G

Senate's Ideal Point

To measure the position of the Senate with respect to the majority intraparty groups in the House, I surveyed the literature that explores Senate intraparty groups and noted senators' partisan affiliations. I then determined the Senate's overall ideal point. Although the Constitution requires a majority of the Senate to pass a bill, Senate rules on debate mean that bills effectively need supermajorities to pass. Once a senator receives recognition on the floor, that Senator may address the chamber for as long as he or she wishes, and a simple majority of the Senate is insufficient to end the debate. Therefore, I identified the position of the Senate with respect to that of the pivotal senator needed to invoke cloture and end a filibuster. In the contemporary Congress, Rule XXII requires that to invoke the "cloture rule" to end a filibuster three-fifths of the Senate vote is needed. Three-fifths of the Senate membership has been the requirement since 1975. When the cloture rule was adopted for the first time, in 1917, the required majority was two-thirds, so that the filibuster pivots were the 33rd and 67th percentile senators (Wawro and Schickler 2006).[1] To pinpoint the pivot between 1880 and 1917, when there was no written rule about the numbers required to overcome a filibuster, I followed Wawro and Schickler (2006), who identified the pivot with the strict majority, so the exact filibuster pivot changed depending on the incorporation of new states to the Union. Additionally, Wawro and Schickler claim that the bare majority was still successful in passing bills during the few decades after cloture reform because the costs to obstructionists were still too high (2006, 95). To be conservative, I coded the filibuster pivot for the next five Congresses (from the 65th until the 69th Congress, 1917–1927) as the strict majority and estimated the pivot

---

[1] Until the 85th Congress the total membership of the Senate was ninety-six senators so the filibuster pivot was at the 64th percentile from the most liberal senator if the House majority was Democratic and at the 33rd percentile from the most liberal senator if the House majority was Republican.

for each Congress at the time when the new House rules were enacted. For the cases when new rules were adopted more than once in a single Congress, I calculated the filibuster pivot for each. However, even with my conservative approach, differences in the pivot within the same Congress never led to a change in the alignment between the Senate and the House intraparty groups. After calculating the distance between the Senate pivot and the medians of House intraparty groups with Common Space DW-NOMINATE scores, I coded whether the Senate filibuster pivot was closer to the Speaker faction, the non-Speaker faction, or the minority party.

Bibliography

Aldrich, John H. 1989. "Power and Order: The Bases of Institutional Structure and Its Change in the U.S. House of Representatives." In *Home Style and Washington Work.*, edited by Morris P. Fiorina and David W. Rohde. Ann Arbor: University of Michigan Press.

———. 1994. "A Model of a Legislature with Two Parties and a Committee System." *Legislative Studies Quarterly* 19 (3) (August 1): 313–339. DOI:10.2307/440135.

———. 1995. *Why Parties? The Origin and Transformation of Political Parties in America.* 1st ed. Chicago: University of Chicago Press.

Aldrich, John H., Jeffrey D. Grynaviski, and David W. Rohde. 1999. "Three Models of a Legislature with Two Parties." Paper presented at the Conference on Congress and Political Parties. MIT, Cambridge, MA.

Aldrich, John H., and David W. Rohde. 1997. "Balance of Power: Republican Party Leadership and the Committee System in the 104th House." Paper presented at the annual meeting of the Midwest Political Science Association, April 10–13, 1997, Chicago, IL.

———. 1998. "Measuring Conditional Party Government." Paper presented at the annual meeting of the Midwest Political Science Association, April 23–25, Chicago, IL.

———. 2000. "The Consequences of Party Organization in the House: The Role of the Majority and Minority Parties in Conditional Party Government." In *Polarized Politics: Congress and the President in a Partisan Era.*, edited by Jon Bond and Richard Fleisher. Washington, DC: CQ Press.

———. 2000. "The Republican Revolution and the House Appropriations Committee," *Journal of Politics* 62 (1) (February): 1–33.

———. 2001. "The Logic of Conditional Party Government." In *Congress Reconsidered*, edited by Lawrence C. Dodd and Bruce I. Oppenheimer. 7th ed. Washington, DC: CQ Press.

Aldrich, John H., David W. Rohde, and M. M. Berger. 2002. "The Historical Variability in Conditional Party Government, 1877–1994." In *Party, Process, and Political Change in Congress*, edited by Mathew D. McCubbins and David W. Brady. Vol. 2. Stanford, CA: Stanford University Press.

Alexander, De Alva Stanwood. 1916. *History and Procedure of the House of Representatives*. Houghton Mifflin.

Bach, Stanley. 1990. "Suspension of the Rules, the Order of Business, and the Development of Congressional Procedure." *Legislative Studies Quarterly* 15 (1) (February 1): 49–63. DOI:10.2307/440001.

2001. "Resolving Legislative Differences in Congress: Conference Committees and Amendments Between the Houses – Open CRS". Washington, DC: CRS Report for Congress. https://opencrs.com/document/98-696/.

Baer, Kenneth S. 2000. *Reinventing Democrats*. Lawrence: University Press of Kansas.

Barfield, Claude E. 1965. *The Democratic Party in Congress, 1909–1913*. Evanston, IL: Northwestern University.

1970. "'Our Share of the Booty': The Democratic Party Cannonism, and the Payne-Aldrich Tariff." *The Journal of American History* 57 (2) (September 1): 308–323. DOI:10.2307/1918151.

Belsley, David A, and Edwin, Welsch, Roy E Kuh. 2004. *Regression Diagnostics*. Hoboken, NJ: Wiley-Interscience.

Bensel, Richard Franklin. 1984. *Sectionalism and American Political Development, 1880–1980*. Madison: University of Wisconsin Press.

Berdahl, Clarence A. 1949. "Some Notes on Party Membership in Congress, II." *American Political Science Review* pp. 309–320.

Berdahl, Clarence Arthur. 1951. *Our Two-Party System*. Jackson: Bureau of Public Administration, University of Mississippi.

Berry, Jeffrey M. 1999. *New Liberalism: The Rising Power of Citizen Groups*. 1st ed. Washington, DC: Brookings Institution Press.

Beth, Richard S., and James Saturno. 2001. *Speakers of the House: Elections, 1913–2001*. Washington, DC: CRS Report for Congress.

Bibby, John F., and Roger H. Davidson. 1972. *On Capitol Hill: Studies in the Legislative Process*. New York: Holt, Rinehart & Winston.

Binder, Sarah A. 1996. "The Partisan Basis of Procedural Choice: Allocating Parliamentary Rights in the House, 1789–1990." *The American Political Science Review* 90 (1) (March 1): 8–20. DOI:10.2307/2082794.

1997. *Minority Rights, Majority Rule: Partisanship and the Development of Congress*. New York: Cambridge University Press.

Binkley, Wilfred E. 1962. *President and Congress*. 3rd ed. New York: Vintage.

Black, Earl, and Merle Black. 2002. *The Rise of Southern Republicans*. Cambridge, MA: Belknap Press of Harvard University Press.

Blumenthal, Sidney. 1986. *The Rise of the Counter-Establishment: The Conservative Ascent to Political Power*. New York: Times Books.

Bolling, Richard Walker. 1964. *House out of Order*. New York: Dutton.

1968. *Power in the House: A History of the Leadership of the House of Representatives*. New York: Dutton.

Bornet, Vaughn Davis. 1983. *The Presidency of Lyndon B. Johnson*. Lawrence: University Press of Kansas.

Brady, David W., and Charles S. Bullock, III. 1980. "Is There a Conservative Coalition in the House?" *The Journal of Politics* 42 (02): 549–559. DOI:10.2307/2130473.

Brennan, Mary C. 1995. *Turning Right in the Sixties: The Conservative Capture of the GOP*. Chapel Hill: The University of North Carolina Press.

Brodsky, Alyn. 2000. *Grover Cleveland: A Study in Character.* 1st ed. New York: St. Martin's Press.

Broesamle, John J. 1973. *William Gibbs McAdoo: A Passion for Change, 1863–1917.* 1st ed. Port Washington, NY: Kennikat Press.

Burns, James MacGregor. 1963. *The Deadlock of Democracy: Four-Party Politics in America.* 1st. ed., first printing. Englewood Cliffs, NJ: Prentice-Hall.

Canes Wrone, Brandice. 2005. *Who Leads Whom? Presidents, Policy, and the Public.* Chicago, IL: Chicago University Press.

Carey, Mary Agnes. 1999. "Hastert's Choice of Conferees Diminishes Prospects for Survival Of House's Managed Care Bill." *CQ Weekly,* November 6.

Carpenter, Daniel. 2001. *The Forging of Bureaucratic Autonomy: Reputations, Networks, and Policy Innovation in Executive Agencies, 1862–1928.* Princeton, NJ: Princeton University Press.

Carroll, Royce, Jeffrey B. Lewis, James Lo, Keith T. Poole, and Howard Rosenthal. 2009. "Measuring Bias and Uncertainty in DW-NOMINATE Ideal Point Estimates via the Parametric Bootstrap." *Political Analysis* 17 (3) (June 20): 261–275. DOI:10.1093/pan/mpp005.

Carson, Jamie, and Ryan Vander Wielen. 2002. "Legislative Politics in a Bicameral System: Strategic Conferee Appointments in the U.S. Congress." Paper presented at the Annual Meeting of the Northeastern Political Science Association, Providence, Rhode Island.

Ceaser, James W. 1979. *Presidential Selection.* Princeton, NJ: Princeton University Press.

Chamberlain, Lawrence H. 1946. "The President, Congress, and Legislation." *Political Science Quarterly* 61 (1) (March 1): 42–60. DOI:10.2307/2144733.

Champagne, Anthony. 2009. *The Austin-Boston Connection: Five Decades of House Democratic Leadership, 1937–1989.* College Station: Texas A&M University Press.

Cherny, Robert W. 1985. *A Righteous Cause: The Life of William Jennings Bryan.* Boston: Little, Brown.

Chiu, Chang-Wei. 1928. *The Speaker of the House of Representatives Since 1896.* New York: Columbia University Press.

Clancy, Herbert John. 1958. *The Presidential Election of 1880.* Chicago: Loyola University Press.

Clanton, O. Gene. 1998. *Congressional Populism and the Crisis of the 1890s.* Lawrence: University Press of Kansas.

Clements, Kendrick A. 1992. *The Presidency of Woodrow Wilson.* Lawrence: University Press of Kansas.

Clinton, Joshua D., Molly C. Jackman, and Saul P. Jackman. 2013. "Characterizing Chief Executives: Comparing Presidential and Congressional Preferences and Their Effect on Lawmaking, Agency Budgeting, and Unilateral Executive Action, 1874–2010." https://my.vanderbilt.edu/joshclinton/files/2013/06/CJJ_LSQ_nonblind.pdf.

Clinton, Joshua D., and John S. Lapinski. 2006. "Measuring Legislative Accomplishment, 1877–1994." *American Journal of Political Science* 50 (1) (January 1): 232–249. DOI:10.2307/3694268.

Cohen, Marty, David Karol, Hans Noel, and John Zaller. 2008. *The Party Decides: Presidential Nominations before and after Reform.* Chicago: University of Chicago Press.

Coletta, Paolo E. 1973. *The Presidency of William Howard Taft.* 1st ed. Lawrence: University Press of Kansas.

Cooper, Joseph. 1988. *The Origins of the Standing Committees and the Development of the Modern House.* Houston, TX: William Marsh Rice University. http://hdl.handle.net/1911/63017.

Cox, Gary W., Chris Den Hartog, and Mathew D. McCubbins. 2006. "The Motion to Recommit in the U.S. House of Representatives." In *Party, Process, and Political Change in Congress,* Vol. 2: *Further New Perspectives on the History of Congress (Social Science History),* edited by David W. Brady and Mathew D. McCubbins. Stanford, CA: Stanford University Press.

Cox, Gary W., and Mathew D. McCubbins. 1993. *Legislative Leviathan: Party Government in the House.* 1st ed. Berkeley: University of California Press.

——— 2005. *Setting the Agenda: Responsible Party Government in the U.S. House of Representatives.* New York: Cambridge University Press.

CQ Press. 1950. *CQ Almanac 1949.* Washington, D.C.: CQ Press. http://library.cqpress.com/cqalmanac/.

Damon, Richard E. 1971. "*The Standing Rules of the U.S. House of Representatives.*" New York: Columbia University.

Davidson, Roger H., Susan Hammond, and Raymond Smock, eds. 1998. *Masters of the House: Congressional Leadership over Two Centuries.* Boulder, CO: Westview Press.

Deering, Christopher J., and Steven S. Smith. 1984. *Committees in Congress.* 3 Sub. Washington, DC: CQ Press.

"Democratic Study Group: A Winner on House Reforms." 1973. *CQ Weekly,* June 2.

"Democrats Strip Two Southerners of House Ranking; Williams and Watson Lose Seniority for Supporting Goldwater in Election." 1965. *The New York Times,* January 3.

Dennis, Brady, Alec MacGillis, and Lori Montgomery. 2011. "Origins of the Debt Showdown." *Washington Post.* August 6. http://articles.washingtonpost.com/2011-08-06/business/35270282_1_debt-showdown-debt-limit-gop-house.

Dion, George Douglas. 1997. *Turning the Legislative Thumbscrew: Minority Rights and Procedural Change in Legislative Politics.* Ann Arbor: University of Michigan Press.

DiSalvo, Daniel. 2012. *Engines of Change: Party Factions in American Politics, 1868–2010.* New York: Oxford University Press.

Dobson, John. 1972. *Politics in the Gilded Age: A New Perspective on Reform.* 1st ed. Westport, CT: Praeger.

Doenecke, Justus D. 1981. *The Presidencies of James A. Garfield and Chester A. Arthur.* Lawrence: University Press of Kansas.

Ekirch, Arthur Alphonse. 1974. *Progressivism in America: A Study of the Era from Theodore Roosevelt to Woodrow Wilson.* New York: New Viewpoints.

Eldersveld, Samuel. 1964. *Political Parties: A Behavioral Analysis.* 1st ed. New York: Rand McNally.

Eldersveld, Samuel James. 1982. *Political Parties in American Society.* New York: Basic Books.

Epstein, David, and Sharyn O'Halloran. 1999. *Delegating Powers: A Transaction Cost Politics Approach to Policy Making under Separate Powers.* 1st ed. New York: Cambridge University Press.

Evans, C. Lawrence, and Walter J. Oleszek. 1997. *Congress under Fire: Reform Politics and the Republican Majority.* Boston: Houghton Mifflin.

Fausold, Martin L. 1985. *The Presidency of Herbert C. Hoover.* Lawrence: University Press of Kansas.

Fenno, Jr., Richard F. 1966. *The Power of the Purse: Appropriations Politics in Congress.* 1st ed. Little, Brown.

Fenno, Richard F. 1973. *Congressmen in Committees.* Boston: Little, Brown.

Ferejohn, John. 1975. "Who Wins in Conference Committee?" *The Journal of Politics* 37 (4) (November 1): 1033–1046. DOI:10.2307/2129188.

Ferrell, Robert H. 1998. *The Presidency of Calvin Coolidge.* Lawrence: University Press of Kansas.

Feulner, Edwin J. 1983. *Conservatives Stalk the House: The Republican Study Committee, 1970–1982.* Ottawa, IL: Green Hill.

Fleisher, Richard, and John R. Bond. 2004. "The Shrinking Middle in the US Congress." *British Journal of Political Science* 34 (3) (July 1): 429–451. DOI:10.2307/4092328.

Foley, Michael. 1980. *The New Senate: Liberal influence on a conservative institution, 1959–1972.* New Haven, CT: Yale University Press.

Foner, Eric. 1988. *Reconstruction: America's Unfinished Revolution, 1863–1877.* Trade paperback ed. New York: Harper & Row.

Galloway, George Barnes. 1969. *History of the House of Representatives.* 5th ed. New York: T.Y. Crowell.

Gerring, John. 1998. *Party Ideologies in America, 1828–1996.* New York: Cambridge University Press.

Giglio, James N. 2006. *The Presidency of John F. Kennedy.* Lawrence: University Press of Kansas.

Gilligan, Thomas W., and Keith Krehbiel. 1989. "Asymmetric Information and Legislative Rules with a Heterogeneous Committee." *American Journal of Political Science* 33 (2) (May 1): 459–490. DOI:10.2307/2111156.

    1990. "Organization of Informative Committees by a Rational Legislature." *American Journal of Political Science* 34 (2) (May 1): 531–564. DOI:10.2307/2111460.

Gillon, Steven M. 1987. *Politics and Vision: The ADA and American Liberalism, 1947–1985.* New York: Oxford University Press.

Goldman, Ralph M. 1966. *The Democratic Party in American Politics.* New York: Macmillan.

    1979. *Search for Consensus: The Story of the Democratic Party.* 1st ed. Philadelphia: Temple University Press.

    1990. *The National Party Chairmen and Committees: Factionalism at the Top.* Armonk, NY: M. E. Sharpe.

Goodwin, George. 1959. "The Seniority System in Congress." *The American Political Science Review* 53 (2) (June 1): 412–436. DOI:10.2307/1952154.

Goodwyn, Lawrence. 1978. *The Populist Moment: A Short History of the Agrarian Revolt in America.* Abridged. New York: Oxford University Press.

Gould, Lewis L. 1974. *The Progressive Era.* Syracuse, NY: Syracuse University Press.

    1978. *Reform and Regulation: American Politics, 1900–1916.* John Wiley & Sons.

    1991. *The Presidency of Theodore Roosevelt.* Lawrence: University Press of Kansas.

    2001. *America in the Progressive Era, 1890–1914.* 1st ed. Harlow, England: Longman.

2003. *Grand Old Party: A History of the Republicans*. 1st ed. New York: Random House.

2009. *The William Howard Taft Presidency*. Lawrence: University Press of Kansas.

Graff, Henry F. 2002. *Grover Cleveland*. 1st ed. New York: Times Books.

Grantham, Dewey W. 1983. *Southern Progressivism: The Reconciliation of Progress and Tradition*. 1st ed. Knoxville: University of Tennessee Press.

Green, Matthew N. 2010. *The Speaker of the House: A Study of Leadership*. New Haven, CT: Yale University Press.

Greene, John Robert. 1995. *The Presidency of Gerald R. Ford*. Lawrence: University Press of Kansas.

2000. *The Presidency of George Bush*. Lawrence: University Press of Kansas.

Greenstein, Fred I., ed. 2003. *The George W. Bush Presidency: An Early Assessment*. 1st ed. Baltimore: The Johns Hopkins University Press.

Groseclose, Tim, and Charles Stewart III. 1998. "The Value of Committee Seats in the House, 1947–91." *American Journal of Political Science* 42 (2) (April 1): 453–474. DOI:10.2307/2991766.

Gwinn, William Rea. 1957. *Uncle Joe Cannon, Archfoe of Insurgency: A History of the Rise and Fall of Cannonism*. New York: Bookman Associates.

Hale, Jon F. 1995. "The Making of the New Democrats." *Political Science Quarterly* 110 (2) (July 1): 207–232. DOI:10.2307/2152360.

Harbaugh, William. 1973. "Lawyer's Lawyer; the Life of John W. Davis." In *History of U.S. Political Parties, Volume 3 1910–1945*, edited by Arthur M. Schlesinger, Jr., (p. 2086). New York: Chelsea House.

Harris, Carl V. 1976. "Right Fork or Left Fork? The Section-Party Alignments of Southern Democrats in Congress, 1873–1897." *The Journal of Southern History* 42 (4) (November 1): 471–506. DOI:10.2307/2208003.

Harrison, Robert. 2004. *Congress, Progressive Reform, and the New American State*. New York: Cambridge University Press.

"Hart Will Head Dies Committee; Representative From New Jersey Had PAC Backing in the Last Election." 1945. *The New York Times*, January 13.

Hasbrouck, Paul DeWitt. 1927. *Party Government in the House of Representatives*. New York: Macmillan: Johnson Reprint.

Hechler, Kenneth William. 1940. *Insurgency: Personalities and Politics of the Taft Era*. New York: Russell and Russel.

Herbers, John. 1967. "Congress Convenes Today Amid an Air of Uncertainty; Congress Opens Session Today in Air of Conflict and Change." *The New York Times*, January 10.

Herrera, Richard. 1993. "Cohesion at the Party Conventions: 1980–1988." *Polity* 26 (1) (October 1): 75–89. DOI:10.2307/3234996.

Himmelstein, Jerome L. 1990. *To the Right: The Transformation of American Conservatism*. Berkeley: University of California Press.

Hirsch, Mark D. 1973. "Election of 1884." In *History of American Presidential Elections, 1789–2008*, edited by Arthur Meier Schlesinger, Jr., Gil Troy, Fred L. Israel, and Arthur Meier Schlesinger. New York: Chatham House.

Hodgson, Godfrey. 1996. *The World Turned Right Side Up: A History of the Conservative Ascendancy in America*. New York: Houghton Mifflin.

Hofstadter, Richard. 1955. *The Age of Reform*. New York: Vintage.

1963. *The Progressive Movement, 1900–1915*. Englewood Cliffs, NJ: Prentice-Hall.

Hollingsworth, Joseph Rogers. 1963. *The Whirligig of Politics: The Democracy of Cleveland and Bryan.* 2nd printing. Chicago: University of Chicago Press.

Holt, James. 1967. *Congressional Insurgents and the Party System, 1909–1916.* 1st ed. Cambridge, MA: Harvard University Press.

Hoogenboom, Ari Arthur. 1988. *The Presidency of Rutherford B. Hayes.* Lawrence: University Press of Kansas.

"House Liberals Tighten Grip on Rules Committee." 1967. *Washington Post*, January 14.

"Iowa Declares Taft Must Drop Aldrich." 1909. *The New York Times*, October 19.

James, Scott C. 2000. *Presidents, Parties, and the State: A Party System Perspective on Democratic Regulatory Choice, 1884–1936.* 1st ed. New York: Cambridge University Press.

Jenkins, Jeffery A., and Charles Stewart. 2012. *Fighting for the Speakership: The House and the Rise of Party Government.* Princeton, NJ: Princeton University Press.

Jones, Charles O. 1968. "Joseph G. Cannon and Howard W. Smith: An Essay on the Limits of Leadership in the House of Representatives." *The Journal of Politics* 30 (3) (August 1): 617–646. DOI:10.2307/2128798.

――― 1970. *The Minority Party in Congress.* Boston: Little, Brown.

Jones, Stanley. 1993. *The Presidential Election of 1896.* Madison: University of Wisconsin Press.

Jordan, David M. 1971. *Roscoe Conkling of New York – Voice in the Senate.* Ithaca, NY: Cornell University Press.

Josephy, Alvin M. 1980. *On the Hill: A History of the American Congress.* New York: Simon & Schuster.

Katznelson, Ira, Kim Geiger, and Daniel Kryder. 1993. "Limiting Liberalism: The Southern Veto in Congress, 1933–1950." *Political Science Quarterly* 108 (2) (July 1): 283–306. DOI:10.2307/2152013.

Kaufman, Burton Ira, and Scott Kaufman. 2006. *The Presidency of James Earl Carter, Jr.* Lawrence: University Press of Kansas.

Kazin, Michael. 2006. *A Godly Hero: The Life of William Jennings Bryan.* Reprint. New York: Knopf.

Kedar, Orit. 2005. "When Moderate Voters Prefer Extreme Parties: Policy Balancing in Parliamentary Elections." *American Political Science Review* 99 (02): 185–199. DOI:10.1017/S0003055405051592.

Kent, Frank Richardson. 1928. *The Democratic Party: A History.* The Century Company.

Key, Valdimer O. 1949. *Southern Politics in State and Nation.* New York: A. A. Knopf.

――― 1964. *Politics, Parties, and Pressure Groups.* New York: T.Y. Crowell.

Kiewiet, D. Roderick, and Mathew D. McCubbins. 1991. *The Logic of Delegation: Congressional Parties and the Appropriations Process.* 1st ed. Chicago: University of Chicago Press.

Koger, Gregory. 2010. *Filibustering: A Political History of Obstruction in the House and Senate.* Chicago: University of Chicago Press.

Kolkey, Jonathan Martin. 1983. *The New Right, 1960–1968: With Epilogue, 1969–1980.* New York: University Press of America.

Kornacki, John J. 1990. *Leading Congress: New Styles, New Strategies.* Washington, DC: Congressional Quarterly.

Krehbiel, Keith. 1991. *Information and Legislative Organization.* Ann Arbor: University of Michigan Press.

Krehbiel, Keith, and Adam Meirowitz. 2002. "Minority Rights and Majority Power: Theoretical Consequences of the Motion to Recommit." *Legislative Studies Quarterly* 27 (2) (May 1): 191–217. DOI:10.2307/3598528.

Krehbiel, Keith, and Alan Wiseman. 2001. "Joseph G. Cannon: Majoritarian from Illinois." *Legislative Studies Quarterly* 26 (3) (August 1): 357–389. DOI:10.2307/440328.

Krehbiel, Keith, and Alan E. Wiseman. 2005. "Joe Cannon and the Minority Party: Tyranny or Bipartisanship?" *Legislative Studies Quarterly* 30 (4) (November 1): 479–505. DOI:10.2307/3598547.

Krugman, Paul. 2010. "When Zombies Win." *The New York Times*, December 19, sec. Opinion.

Landy, Marc Karnis, and Martin A. Levin, eds. 1995. *The New Politics of Public Policy*. Baltimore: Johns Hopkins University Press.

Lawrence, Eric D., Forrest Maltzman, and Paul J. Wahlbeck. 2001. "The Politics of Speaker Cannon's Committee Assignments." *American Journal of Political Science* 45 (3) (July 1): 551–562. DOI:10.2307/2669238.

Layman, Geoffrey. 2001. *The Great Divide: Religious and Cultural Conflict in American Party Politics*. New York: Columbia University Press.

Lazarus, Jeffrey, and Nathan W. Monroe. 2007. "The Speaker's Discretion Conference Committee Appointments in the 97th through 106th Congresses." *Political Research Quarterly* 60 (4): 593–606. DOI:10.1177/1065912907304498.

Lee, Frances E. 2009. *Beyond Ideology: Politics, Principles, and Partisanship in the U. S. Senate*. Chicago: University of Chicago Press.

Lieberman, Robert C. 1998. *Shifting the Color Line: Race and the American Welfare State*. Cambridge, MA: Harvard University Press.

Link, Arthur S. 1954. *Woodrow Wilson and the Progressive Era*. 1st ed. New York: Harper & Row.

———. 1956. *Wilson: The New Freedom*. Princeton, NJ: Princeton University Press.

Longley, Lawrence D., and Walter J. Oleszek. 1989. *Bicameral Politics: Conference Committees in Congress*. New Haven, CT: Yale University Press.

Lupia, Arthur, and Mathew D. McCubbins. 1998. *The Democratic Dilemma: Can Citizens Learn What They Need to Know?* Cambridge University Press.

Malone, Preston St. Clair. 1962. "The Political Career of Charles Frederick Crisp." Athens: University of Georgia.

Manley, John F. 1973. "The Conservative Coalition in Congress." *American Behavioral Scientist* 17 (2) (November 1): 223–247. DOI:10.1177/000276427301700205.

Mann, Thomas E., and Norman J. Ornstein. 2012. *It's Even Worse Than It Looks: How the American Constitutional System Collided with the New Politics of Extremism*. New York: Basic Books.

Martin, S. Walter. 1954. "Charles F. Crisp, Speaker of the House." *The Georgia Review* 8 (2) (July 1): 167–177. DOI:10.2307/41398021.

Mayer, George H. 1967. *The Republican Party, 1854–1966*. 2nd ed. New York: Oxford University Press.

McCarty, Nolan M., Keith T. Poole, and Howard Rosenthal. 2006. *Polarized America: The Dance of Ideology and Unequal Riches*. Cambridge, MA: MIT Press.

McCoy, Donald R. 1984. *Presidency of Harry S. Truman (American Presidency)*. Lawrence: University Press of Kansas.

McJimsey, George. *The Presidency of Franklin Delano Roosevelt (American Presidency)*. 1st ed. Lawrence: University Press of Kansas.

McKelvey, Richard D. 1976. "Intransitivities in Multidimensional Voting Models and Some Implications for Agenda Control." *Journal of Economic Theory* 12 (3): 472–482.

McMahon, Kevin J. 2004. *Reconsidering Roosevelt on Race: How the Presidency Paved the Road to Brown.* 1st ed. Chicago: University of Chicago Press.

Milkis, Sidney M. 1993. *The President and the Parties: The Transformation of the American Party System since the New Deal.* New York: Oxford University Press.

1999. *Political Parties and Constitutional Government: Remaking American Democracy.* Baltimore: The Johns Hopkins University Press.

Milkis, Sidney M., and Michael Nelson. 1998. *The American Presidency: Origins and Development, 1776–1998.* 3rd ed. Washington, DC: CQ Press.

Mooney, Booth. 1964. *Mr Speaker Profiles of 4 Political Giant.* River Grove, IL: Follett.

Moore, John Robert. 1967. "The Conservative Coalition in the United States Senate, 1942–1945." *The Journal of Southern History* 33 (3) (August 1): 368–376. DOI:10.2307/2204865.

Morgan, Howard Wayne. 1969. *From Hayes to McKinley: National Party Politics, 1877–1896.* Syracuse, NY: Syracuse University Press.

1973. *Unity and Culture: The United States, 1877–1900.* A. Lane, the Penguin Press.

Mowry, George E. 1958. *Era of Theodore Roosevelt: 1900–1912.* New York: Harper.

Nagourney, Adam. 2013. "Democrats Seek New Messenger and a Message – New York Times." *New York Times.* Accessed May 30. http://www.nytimes.com/2002/11/17/us/democrats-seek-new-messenger-and-a-message.html?pagewanted=all&src=pm.

Nash, John F. 1950. "The Bargaining Problem." *Econometrica* 18 (2) (April 1): 155–162. DOI:10.2307/1907266.

Neal, Steve. 1984. *Dark Horse: A Biography of Wendell Willkie.* Garden City, NY: Doubleday.

Nye, Russel Blaine. 1951. *Midwestern Progressive Politics: A Historical Study of Its Origins and Development 1870–1950.* East Lansing: Michigan State College Press.

Offenberg, Richard S. 1963. "The Political Career of Thomas Brackett Reed." Unpublished Dissertation, New York University.

Oleszek, Walter J. 2001. *Congressional Procedures and the Policy Process.* 7th ed. Washington, DC: CQ Press.

Ornstein, Norman J., ed. 1975. "Causes and Consequences of Congressional Change: Subcommittee Reforms in the House of Representatives." In *Congress in Change: Evolution and Reform.* New York: Praeger.

Ornstein, Norman J., Thomas E. Mann, and Michael J. Malbin. 1999. *Vital Statistics on Congress.* Washington, DC: American Enterprise Institute Press.

Oulahan, Richard V. 1923. "Party Chaos Left by Loss of Harding as Chosen Leader; Coolidge's New Prestige Disconcerts the Plans of the Republican Chiefs." *The New York Times*, August 4.

Pach, Chester J, Elmo Richardson, and Elmo Richardson. 1991. *The Presidency of Dwight D. Eisenhower.* Lawrence: University Press of Kansas.

Parmet, Herbert S. 1976. *The Democrats: The Years after FDR.* New York: Macmillan.

Patterson, James T. 1966. "A Conservative Coalition Forms in Congress, 1933–1939."
    The Journal of American History 52 (4) (March 1): 757–772.
    1967. *Congressional Conservatism and the New Deal: The Growth of the Conservative
    Coalition in Congress, 1933–1939.* Lexington: University Press of Kentucky.
Peabody, Robert L. 1963. "The Enlarged Rules Committee." In *New Perspectives on
    the House of Representatives*, edited by Robert L. Peabody and Nelson W. Polsby.
    Chicago: Rand McNally College.
    1976. *Leadership in Congress: Stability, Succession, and Change.* Boston: Little,
    Brown.
Peskin, Allan. 1984. "Who Were the Stalwarts? Who Were Their Rivals? Republican
    Factions in the Gilded Age." *Political Science Quarterly* 99 (4) (December 1): 703–
    716. DOI:10.2307/2150708.
Peters, Ronald M, and Cindy Simon Rosenthal. 2010. *Speaker Nancy Pelosi and the
    New American Politics.* New York: Oxford University Press.
Peters, Ronald M. 1990. *The American Speakership: The Office in Historical Perspective.*
    Baltimore: The Johns Hopkins University Press.
Phillips, Kate. 2009. "New Voices in Congress Will Change the Tone of the Democratic
    Majority." *The New York Times*, January 6, sec. U.S./Politics.
Polsby, N. W. 1981. "Coalition and Faction in American Politics: An Institutional View."
    In *Party Coalitions in the 1980s*, edited by Seymour Martin Lipset. San Francisco:
    Transaction.
Polsby, Nelson W. 2004. *How Congress Evolves: Social Bases of Institutional Change.*
    New York: Oxford University Press.
Polsby, Nelson W., Miriam Gallaher, and Barry Spencer Rundquist. 1969. "The Growth
    of the Seniority System in the U. S. House of Representatives." *The American
    Political Science Review* 63 (3) (September 1): 787–807. DOI:10.2307/1954429.
Polsby, Nelson W., and Aaron Wildavsky. 1976. *Presidential Elections: Strategies and
    Structures of American Politics.* New York: Scribner.
Poole, Keith T., and Howard Rosenthal. 1997. *Congress: A Political-Economic History
    of Roll Call Voting.* New York: Oxford University Press.
Poole, Keith T., and Howard L. Rosenthal. 2011. *Ideology and Congress.* New
    Brunswick, NJ: Transaction.
Rae, Nicol C. 1989. *The Decline and Fall of the Liberal Republicans: From 1952 to the
    Present.* Revised. New York: Oxford University Press.
    1994. *Southern Democrats.* 1st ed. New York: Oxford University Press.
    1998. *Conservative Reformers: The Republican Freshmen and the Lessons of the
    104th Congress.* Armonk, NY: M.E. Sharpe.
Rager, S. 1998. "Uncle Joe Cannon: The Brakeman of the House of Representatives,
    1903–1911." In *Masters of The House: Congressional Leadership over Two
    Centuries*, edited by Roger H. Davidson, Susan Hammond, and Raymond Smock.
    Boulder, CO: Westview Press.
Reichard, Gary W. 1975. *The Reaffirmation of Republicanism: Eisenhower and the
    Eighty-Third Congress.* Knoxville: University of Tennessee Press.
Reinhard, David W. 1983. *The Republican Right since 1945.* Lexington: University
    Press of Kentucky.
Reiter, Howard L. 1996. "Why Did the Whigs Die (and Why Didn't the Democrats)?
    Evidence from National Nominating Conventions." *Studies in American Political
    Development* 10 (02): 185–222. DOI:10.1017/S0898588X00001486.

1980. "Party Factionalism National Conventions in the New Era." *American Politics Research* 8 (3) (July 1): 303–318. DOI:10.1177/1532673X8000800303.

1998. "The Bases of Progressivism within the Major Parties: Evidence from the National Conventions." *Social Science History* 22 (1) (April 1): 83–116. DOI:10.2307/1171565.

2001. "The Building of a Bifactional Structure: The Democrats in the 1940s." *Political Science Quarterly* 116 (1) (April 1): 107–129. DOI:10.2307/2657822.

2004. "Factional Persistence within Parties in the United States." *Party Politics* 10 (3) (May 1): 251–271. DOI:10.1177/1354068804042458.

Riddick, Floyd Millard. 1949. *The United States Congress: Organization and Procedure.* National Capitol.

Ripley, R. B. 1967. *Party Leaders in the House of Representatives.* Washington, DC: Brookings Institution.

Roberts, Jason M. 2005. "Minority Rights and Majority Power: Conditional Party Government and the Motion to Recommit in the House." *Legislative Studies Quarterly* 30 (2): 219–234. DOI:10.3162/036298005X201527.

Robinson, William A. 1930. *Thomas B. Reed: Parliamentarian.* New York: Dodd, Mead.

Rohde, David W. 1974. "Committee Reform in the House of Representatives and the Subcommittee Bill of Rights." *Annals of the American Academy of Political and Social Science* 411 (January 1): 39–47. DOI:10.2307/1040999.

1991. *Parties and Leaders in the Postreform House.* 1st ed. Chicago: University of Chicago Press.

Romer, Thomas, and Howard Rosenthal. 1978. "Political Resource Allocation, Controlled Agendas, and the Status Quo." *Public Choice* 33 (4) (January 1): 27–43. DOI:10.2307/30023066.

Ross, Earle D. 1910. *Liberal Republican Movement.* Seattle: University of Washington Press.

"Rules Unit Powers Restored by House; Members of Eighty-Second Congress Being Sworn In." 1951. *The New York Times*, January 4.

Sanders, Elizabeth. 1999. *Roots of Reform: Farmers, Workers, and the American State, 1877–1917.* 1st ed. Chicago: University of Chicago Press.

Sarasohn, David. 1989. *The Party of Reform: Democrats in the Progressive Era.* 1st ed. Jackson: University Press of Mississippi.

Sartori, Giovanni. 1976. *Parties and Party Systems.* Cambridge: Cambridge University Press.

Schickler, Eric. 2000. "Institutional Change in the House of Representatives, 1867–1998: A Test of Partisan and Ideological Power Balance Models." *The American Political Science Review* 94 (2) (June 1): 269–288. DOI:10.2307/2586012.

2001. *Disjointed Pluralism: Institutional Innovation and the Development of the U.S. Congress.* Princeton, NJ: Princeton University Press.

Schickler, Eric, and Kathryn Pearson. 2009. "Agenda Control, Majority Party Power, and the House Committee on Rules, 1937–52." *Legislative Studies Quarterly* 34 (4): 455–491. DOI:10.3162/036298009789869718.

Schousen, Matthew. 1994. "Who's in Charge? A Study of Coalitions and Power in the US House of Representatives." Durham, NC: Duke University.

Scott, Anne Firor. 1963. "A Progressive Wind from the South, 1906–1913." *The Journal of Southern History* 29 (1) (February 1): 53–70. DOI:10.2307/2205101.

Shafer, Byron E. 1988. *Bifurcated Politics: Evolution and Reform in the National Party Convention*. Cambridge, MA: Harvard University Press.

———. 2000. "The Partisan Legacy: Are There Any New Democrats?" In *The Clinton Legacy*, edited by Colin Campbell and Bert A. Rockman, pp. 1–32. New York: Chatham House.

———. 2003. *The Two Majorities and the Puzzle of Modern American Politics*. Lawrence: University Press of Kansas.

Shelley, Mack. 1977. "The Conservative Coalition in the US Congress, 1933–1976: Time Series Analysis of a Legislative Policy Coalition." University of Wisconsin.

Sheppard, Burton D. 1985. *Rethinking Congressional Reform: The Reform Roots of the Special Interest Congress*. Rochester, VT: Schenkman Books.

Shepsle, Kenneth A. 1978. *The Giant Jigsaw Puzzle: Democratic Committee Assignments in the Modern House*. Chicago: University of Chicago Press.

———. 1979. "Institutional Arrangements and Equilibrium in Multidimensional Voting Models." *American Journal of Political Science* 23 (1) (February 1): 27–59. DOI:10.2307/2110770.

Shepsle, Kenneth A., and Barry R. Weingast. 1987. "The Institutional Foundations of Committee Power." *The American Political Science Review* 81 (1) (March 1): 85–104. DOI:10.2307/1960780.

Shlaes, Amity. 2013. *Coolidge*. New York: Harper.

Sin, Gisela. 2007. *"Separation of Power and Legislative Institutions: A Constitutional Theory of Legislative Organization."* Ann Arbor: University of Michigan.

Sin, Gisela, and Arthur Lupia. 2012. "How the Senate and the President Affect the Timing of Power-Sharing Rule Changes in the US House." *Journal of Law, Economics, and Organization* (November 21). DOI:10.1093/jleo/ews039. http://jleo.oxfordjournals.org/content/early/2012/11/20/jleo.ews039.

Sinclair, Barbara. 1982. *Congressional Realignment, 1925–78*. 1st ed. Austin: University of Texas Press.

———. 1995. *Legislators, Leaders, and Lawmaking: The U.S. House of Representatives in the Postreform Era*. Baltimore: The Johns Hopkins University Press.

Skocpol, Theda. 1996. *Boomerang: Clinton's Health Security Effort and the Turn Against Government in U.S. Politics*. 1st ed. New York: W. W. Norton.

Skowronek, Stephen. 1982. *Building a New American State: The Expansion of National Administrative Capacities, 1877–1920*. New York: Cambridge University Press.

———. 1993. *The Politics Presidents Make: Leadership from John Adams to Bill Clinton*. Cambridge, MA: Belknap Press of Harvard University Press.

Small, Melvin. 1999. *The Presidency of Richard Nixon*. Lawrence: University Press of Kansas.

Smith, Steven S. 1989. *Call to Order: Floor Politics in the House and Senate (Washington, Brookings Institution, 1989)*. Rieselbach, *Congressional Reform*: 41–67. Washington, DC: Brokings Institution.

Socolofsky, Homer Edward, and Allan B Spetter. 1987. *The Presidency of Benjamin Harrison*. Lawrence: University Press of Kansas.

Soule, John W., and James W. Clarke. 1970. "Amateurs and Professionals: A Study of Delegates to the 1968 Democratic National Convention." *The American Political Science Review* 64 (3) (September 1): 888–898. DOI:10.2307/1953470.

Spielman, William Carl. 1954. *William McKinley, Stalwart Republican;: A Biographical Study*. 1st ed. Hicksville, NY: Exposition Press.

Stang, Alan. 1974. "The Right: Conservatives in Congress." *American Opinion* 17: 31–48.

Steiner, Gilbert Y. 1951. *The Congressional Conference Committee: Seventieth to Eightieth Congresses*. Urbana: University of Illinois Press.

Stephenson, Nathaniel Wright. 1930. *Nelson W. Aldrich: A Leader in American Politics*. New edition. New York: C. Scribner.

Stewart, Charles H. 1989. *Budget Reform Politics: The Design of the Appropriations Process in the House of Representatives, 1865–1921*. New York: Cambridge University Press.

Stradling, David. 2013. *Conservation in the Progressive Era: Classic Texts*. Seattle: University of Washington Press.

Strom, Gerald S., and Barry S. Rundquist. 1977. "A Revised Theory of Winning in House-Senate Conferences." *The American Political Science Review* 71 (2) (June 1): 448–453. DOI:10.2307/1978340.

Sundquist, James Lloyd. 1968. *Politics and Policy: The Eisenhower, Kennedy, and Johnson Years*. Washington, DC: Brookings Institution Press.

Swenson, Peter. 1982. "The Influence of Recruitment on the Structure of Power in the U. S. House, 1870–1940." *Legislative Studies Quarterly* 7 (1) (February 1): 7–36. DOI:10.2307/439689.

"The Month in America." 1910. *Success Magazine*, March.

"The Tyranny of Seniority." 1966. *The New York Times*, July 15.

Trani, Eugene P., and David L. Wilson. 1977. *Presidency of Warren G. Harding (American Presidency)*. Lawrence: University Press of Kansas.

Truman, David Bicknell. 1959. *The Congressional Party, a Case Study*. New York: Wiley.

"Urging Coolidge to Lead Tax Fight; Republicans Want the President to Take Charge of Revision Movement." 1923. *The New York Times*, November 17.

Valelly, Richard M. 2009. "The Reed Rules and Republican Party Building: A New Look." *Studies in American Political Development* 23 (02): 115–142. DOI:10.1017/S0898588X09990022.

Vogler, David J. 1970. "Patterns of One House Dominance in Congressional Conference Committees." *Midwest Journal of Political Science* 14 (2) (May 1): 303–320. DOI:10.2307/2110197.

Wang, Xi. 1997. *The Trial of Democracy: Black Suffrage and Northern Republicans, 1860–1910*. Athens: University of Georgia Press.

Wawro, Gregory J., and Eric Schickler. 2006. *Filibuster: Obstruction and Lawmaking in the U.S. Senate*. Princeton, NJ: Princeton University Press.

Weaver, R. Kent. 2000. *Ending Welfare as We Know It*. Washington, DC: Brookings Institution Press.

Weed, Clyde P. 1994. *The Nemesis of Reform: the Republican Party during the New Deal*. New York: Columbia University Press.

Weingast, Barry R., and William J. Marshall. 1988. "The Industrial Organization of Congress; Or, Why Legislatures, Like Firms, Are Not Organized as Markets." *Journal of Political Economy* 96 (1) (February 1): 132–163.

Welch, Richard E. Jr. 1988. *The Presidencies of Grover Cleveland*. 1st ed. Lawrence: University Press of Kansas.

Wilensky, Norman M. 1965. *Conservatives in the Progressive Era – the Taft Republicans of 1912*. University of Florida Monographs, Social Sciences, No. 25, Winter 1965. Gainesville: University of Florida Press.

Wiseman, John B. 1988. *The Dilemmas of a Party Out of Power: The Democrats, 1904–1912*. New York: Garland.

Woodward, C. Vann. 1951. *Reunion and Reaction: The Compromise of 1877 and the End of Reconstruction*. Boston.

Zelizer, Julian E. 2004. *On Capitol Hill: The Struggle to Reform Congress and Its Consequences, 1948–2000*. 1st ed. New York: Cambridge University Press.

ed. 2010. *The Presidency of George W. Bush: A First Historical Assessment*. Princeton, NJ: Princeton University Press.

Index